International Law in the Long Nineteenth Century (1776–1914)

Legal History Library

VOLUME 28

Studies in the History of International Law

VOLUME 11

The titles published in this series are listed at *brill.com/shil*

International Law in the Long Nineteenth Century (1776–1914)

From the Public Law of Europe to Global International Law?

Edited by

Inge Van Hulle
Randall Lesaffer

BRILL
NIJHOFF

LEIDEN | BOSTON

Cover illustration: Congrès de Vienne : [estampe], Nurnberg bei F. Campe, 1815. Bibliothèque nationale de France, public domain.

Library of Congress Cataloging-in-Publication Data

Names: Hulle, Inge Van, editor. | Lesaffer, Randall, editor.
Title: International law in the long nineteenth century (1776–1914) : from the public law of Europe to global international law? / Inge Van Hulle, Randall C. Lesaffer.
Description: Leiden ; Boston : Brill | Nijhoff, 2019. | Series: Legal history library; 28.
Identifiers: LCCN 2019025225 (print) | LCCN 2019025226 (ebook) | ISBN 9789004391147 (hardback) | ISBN 9789004412088 (ebook)
Subjects: LCSH: International law--History. | Public law--Europe--History.
Classification: LCC KZ1242 .I59 2019 (print) | LCC KZ1242 (ebook) | DDC 341.09/034--dc23
LC record available at https://lccn.loc.gov/2019025225
LC ebook record available at https://lccn.loc.gov/2019025226

Typeface for the Latin, Greek, and Cyrillic scripts: "Brill". See and download: brill.com/brill-typeface.

ISSN 1874-1793
ISBN 978-90-04-39114-7 (hardback)
ISBN 978-90-04-41208-8 (e-book)

This book is printed on acid-free paper and produced in a sustainable manner.

Contents

PART 3
The Rise of Modern International Law

Introduction

Randall Lesaffer and Inge Van Hulle

In 1996, at the inception of the 'turn to history' in international law, David Kennedy wrote that 'when international lawyers now speak of the nineteenth century, they really mean its final decades, from roughly 1870 (…) to 1914'.[1] Although few centuries have benefited as much from the boom in scholarly interest in the history of international law as the nineteenth century, Kennedy's implication that the four to five decades preceding the First World War generated most attention still rings true. This can easily been explained. Firstly, as Martti Koskenniemi powerfully argued in *The Gentle Civilizer of Nations*, the work that more than any other spurred the 'turn to history', that international law only emerged as an organised discipline in the 1860s and 1870s.[2] Secondly, both the postcolonial drive, which inspires many historians of international law, and aspirations to overcome the Euro-centrist approach and globalise the historiography of international law trim the lens on the role of international law in European imperialism. The heyday of the imperialist endeavour, the Age of Empire, coincides with the decades of the birth of modern international law.

In most recent years, an increasing number of scholarly studies started to proliferate into the earlier decades of the nineteenth century exploring subjects and questions outside the confines of the leading debate on international law and empire. This book collects ten studies, which offer a small sample of the ever-growing variety of themes and approaches that scholars from different fields – international law, legal and diplomatic history, history of political thought – bring to the historiography of international law during the nineteenth century.

In international history, the 'nineteenth century' is traditionally bracketed between 1815 – the end of the Congress Vienna after the demise of Napoleon (1769–1821) – and 1914 or 1919. The choice of 1815 is a manifestation of winner's history. It implies that not the French Revolution, but the restoration that was wrought by the conservatives monarchies of Eastern Europe and by Great

1 David Kennedy, 'International law in the nineteenth century: history of an illusion', *Nordic Journal of International Law* 65 (1996), 385–420, 391.

2 Martti Koskenniemi, *The Gentle Civilizer of Nations: The Rise and Fall of International Law 1870–1960* (Cambridge: Cambridge University Press, 2002), esp. 11–97.

Britain, set the pace of a new epoch in the development of international order and law, at least in Europe.[3]

The studies collected in this volume stretch the nineteenth century backwards to include the period of the American and French Revolutions, taking the year of the Declaration of Independence of the United States as its starting point.[4] Following in the footsteps of historians of international relations, the editors consider the contribution of the revolutionary period crucial to understanding the dynamics of international order and law in the nineteenth century.[5] The Congress of Vienna attempted to suppress many of the disruptive ideas of the French Revolution and designed an order for Europe to restore the old, pre-revolutionary system as much as possible. Nevertheless, some of the major achievements of the revolutions – popular sovereignty and the secularisation of politics and law – re-emerged and were to have a profound impact on international relations and law during the nineteenth century, both within and without Europe.[6]

This book falls into three parts. Part 1, 'International Law and Revolutions', collects three studies that cover the revolutionary period or deal with the impact of revolution on international law. James Crawford analyses the legal status of the former Emperor Napoleon after his surrender into British hands in 1815. In Chapter 2, Camilla Boisen considers the anti-revolutionary writer Edmund Burke as a crucial linchpin between early modern and later positivist writers with relation to the theories of law enforcement and punishment in the international community of states. Viktorija Jakjimovska investigates great power reactions to the Greek Revolt and the formative role of this event for use of force law and the law of neutrality.

Part 2 turns to the more familiar theme of 'law and empire'. Three of the four papers, however, discuss the decades before 1870. Andrew Fitzmaurice offers a fascinating survey of the British lawyer Travers Twiss's long-term engagement with matters of international law in the context of empire and analyses his understanding of the 'civilising mission'. Inge Van Hulle explores the role of human sacrifice as an argument for imperialist interventions, next to abolition

3 Wilhelm Grewe expressly related the choice of 1815 to the beginning of the ascendancy of Great Britain and names the nineteenth century the 'British age', Wilhelm G. Grewe, *Epochs of International Law* (Berlin: Walter de Gruyter, 2000), 429.

4 David Armitage, 'The Declaration of Independence and international law', *William and Mary Quarterly* 3rd series, 59 (2002) 39–64.

5 E.g. Paul W. Schroeder, *The Transformation of European Politics 1763–1848* (Oxford: Clarendon Press, 1994).

6 Edward James Kolla, *Sovereignty, International Law, and the French Revolution* (Cambridge: Cambridge University Press, 2017).

of the slave trade, by the British in West Africa since the early nineteenth century. Raphaël Cahen exemplifies the Ben Ayad case of the 1850s involving France and Tunisia as an instance of the role of arbitration in imperialist policies. The final chapter in Part 2, by Stefan Kroll, offers a detailed analysis of the intricate workings of extraterritorial jurisdiction in the Shanghai International Settlement between 1863 and 1941.

The three studies in the Part 3, 'The Rise of Modern International Law', cover some less familiar aspects of the formation of modern international law as a self-standing discipline. Frederik Dhondt's narration of the evolution of Belgium's status of permanent neutrality between 1830 and 1870 offers an interesting case study of international law in action, as a fluid and flexible instrument of state policy where legal doctrine and diplomatic opportunism worked together to form and reform legal institutions according to the needs at hand. Ana Delic's chapter explores the deeper roots of modern private international law, which rose together with – public – international law at the end of the nineteenth century, in both the civil and common law traditions, and the role of comparative law therein. Finally, Vincent Genin relates the vicissitudes of the *Institut de Droit International* in its early years, in particular against the backdrop of rising nationalism and the fall-out of the Franco-Prussian War.

PART 1

International Law and Revolution

CHAPTER 1

Napoleon 1814–1815: A Small Issue of Status

James Crawford

1 Introduction

Popular accounts of the last stage of the Napoleonic Wars in 1814–15 tend to overlook a small issue of status. There is no doubt that the Alliance (Great Britain, Prussia, Russia, Austria and associated powers) ultimately defeated the Emperor Napoleon I of France following his brief return to France from Elba in March 1815. But in doing so, who (legally) did they defeat? Perhaps France did not after all lose the Battle of Waterloo?

This chapter considers the basis on which France participated in the Congress of Vienna, the status of Napoleon during the Hundred Days and the legal basis for French responsibility for war damages resulting from the Hundred Days. France participated in the Congress of Vienna on the basis of the recognition of the restored Bourbon government in 1814. This position continued throughout the Hundred Days. During this period, Napoleon was viewed, in the words of the British Prime Minister Liverpool, 'as an outlaw and an outcast; *hostis humani generis*'.[1] This logic did not, however, extend to the terms of the Peace of 1815. A large war indemnity was exacted following the Hundred Days, although French responsibility seems to have had a more equitable than a legal basis. The Allies relied on this and on their concern for general European security to justify these measures, which were considerably more severe than had been agreed with Talleyrand in 1814.[2]

1 Horace Twiss (ed.), *The Public and Private Life of Lord Chancellor Eldon with Selection from His Correspondence* (London: John Murray, 1844), vol. 1, 413.

2 See generally Charles K. Webster, *The Congress of Vienna 1814–1815* (2nd edn., London: Thames & Hudson, 1963); Charles K. Webster (ed.), *British Diplomacy 1813–1815: Select Documents Dealing with the Reconstruction of Europe* (London: G Bell & Sons, 1921); Duc de Broglie (ed.), *Memoirs of the Prince de Talleyrand* (Grolier Society; London and Sydney: Griffith, Farran, Okeden and Welsh, 1891) [hereinafter Talleyrand]; M.G. Pallain (ed.), *Correspondance inédite du Prince de Talleyrand et du Roi Louis XVIII pendant le Congrès de Vienne* (Paris: E Plon et Cie, 1881) [hereinafter Talleyrand & Louis]; Rihzard Metternich, *Memoirs of Prince Metternich 1773–1815* (Mrs Alexander Napier, transl., New York: Scribner, 1880) [hereinafter Metternich].

 | DOI:10.1163/9789004412088_002

2 The Status of the Bourbon Government-in-Exile

Until 1813, Napoleon was recognised by the dynastic powers on the continent of Europe as the French head of state. This despite the fact that he had come to power by usurping the Bourbon monarchy, and at a time when the prevailing conception of sovereign authority was monarchic legitimism.[3] Under this conception, the right to rule was seen as divine and hereditary, a birth right passing from father to son or the nearest male blood relative.[4] This right to rule could not be extinguished by force of political revolution: 'A dynasty enjoyed historic rights to rule a state, and, thus, the prince continued to be sovereign even if in fact displaced from his throne'.[5]

Ironically reflecting this conception of sovereign authority, Napoleon transformed the first French Republic into an Empire. In 1802, he was named consul for life, which office became hereditary at the initiative of a subservient Senate. On 2 December 1804, in the presence of Pope Pius VII, General Bonaparte crowned himself assuming the title of Napoleon I, emperor of the French.[6] When forced to abdicate on 4 April 1814, he wrote that he was 'ready to descend from the throne'.[7]

Napoleon's period of personal rule – whether as first consul or emperor – did not deter legitimist claims to France. Throughout this period, the Bourbon court was maintained in exile in Rhineland, Italy, Brunswick, Courland,

3 The term 'legitimité' only entered French political discourse during the period of the Revolution. De Maistre used it in 1810 in reference to hereditary kingship: Joseph de Maistre, *Essai sur le principe générateur des constitutions politiques et des autres institutions humaines* (Lyon: J.B. Pelagaud et cie, 1846), 10, 54. De Stael and Thiers both attributed the usage to Talleyrand: Anne-Louise-Germaine de Stael, *Considérations sur la révolution française* (1818, Paris : Charpentier, 1861), vol 2, 185; Adolphe Thiers, *Histoire du consulat et de l'empire* (21 vols., Paris, 1845–74), vol. 18, 445.

4 Laurence B. Packard, *The Age of Louis XIV* (New York: Holt, 1929), 7; Herbert H. Rowen, 'L'état c'est moi. Louis XIV and the State', *French Historical Studies* 2 (1961) 83–98, 83.

5 Thomas D. Grant, *The Recognition of States: Law and Practice in Debate and Evolution* (Westport, CT: Greenwood Press, 1999), 8–9. Contemporary legal writers rejecting legitimism are discussed in Charles H. Alexandrowicz, 'The Theory of Recognition in fieri', *British Yearbook of International Law* 34 (1958) 176–198, 197. See Johann Heinrich Gottlob von Justi, *Historical and Legal Writings* (1760); J Steck, *Examination of Different Matters of Political and Legal Knowledge* (1783); Georg Friedrich von Martens, *A Compendium of the Law of Nations Founded on the Treaties and Customs of the Modern Nations of Europe* (Cobbett trans., London: Cobbett and Morgan, 1802); Johann Ludwig Klüber, *Modern International Law in Europe* (1831).

6 Carlton Hayes, *A Political and Social History of Modern Europe* (New York: Macmillan, 1929), 533.

7 Alphonse de Lamartine, *The History of the Restoration of the Monarchy in France* (New York: Harper, 1851), 175.

Prussia, Poland, and finally England.[8] Following the execution of Louis XVI, Louis XVIII had proclaimed himself as regent and, upon the death of the dauphin in 1795, as king. He never abandoned his claim, though his efforts 'to regain his throne between 1795 and 1812 had been singularly fruitless'.[9] But from 1812, the royalist movement in France and support for it among the Allies began to gather force.[10]

In Frankfurt in November 1813, a decision was taken, in Metternich's words, '[t]o carry the war beyond the Rhine into the interior of France' and thereby 'to strike a blow at the very existence of the Emperor Napoleon which might be decisive in its consequences'.[11] Thereupon, the efforts of the Allies turned towards convincing the French to abandon Napoleon.[12] Later in his memoirs, Metternich clarified his sense that keeping France within its original borders was necessary to European stability, that Napoleon would never have agreed to this and therefore that regime change was necessary.[13] This is reflected in the declaration of the tsar upon the occupation of Paris, in which he proclaimed (unilaterally) that the Allied sovereigns 'ne traiteront plus avec Napoléon Bonaparte, ni avec aucun de sa famille'.[14]

Negotiations among the Allies as to the future regime of France progressed at Langres in early 1814. Metternich reported that Austria preferred a Bourbon restoration, Russia the accession of Napoleon's son and Sweden a new, third choice.[15] But he noted the tsar's impression that a Bourbon restoration would enflame revolutionary tendencies among the French nation:

> 'It is against the Bourbons', said the Emperor to me; 'and to bring these back to a throne which they had not known how to keep would be to expose France, and eventually all Europe, to another Revolution, of which no one can foretell the consequences. To choose a new ruler is a very difficult undertaking for a foreigner. My resolution, therefore,

8 E.J. Knapton, 'Some Aspects of the Bourbon Restoration of 1814', *Journal of Modern History* 6 (1934) 405–424, 407; Philip Mansel, 'From Exile to the Throne: The Europeanization of Louis XVIII', in P. Mansel and T. Riotte (eds.), *Monarchy and Exile. The Politics of Legitimacy from Marie de Médicis to Wilhelm II* (Basingstoke: Palgrave Macmillan, 2011), 181–213, 182; Hayes, *Political and Social History*, 567.

9 Knapton, 'Some Aspects', 407.

10 Ibid, 408–409.

11 1 Metternich 213.

12 1 Metternich 214.

13 1 Metternich 224–225.

14 Déclaration de l'Empereur de Russie, Paris, 31 Mars, 1814, in *British and Foreign State Papers* (170 vols., London : H.M.S.O., 1841–1977), vol. 1-1, 131 ([hereinafter BFSP].

15 1 Metternich 225.

> is taken … we must summon the original assemblies, and demand that a proper number of deputies should be sent to Paris to decide both these points in the name of the nation'.[16]

Metternich replied with the Austrian view, that the Bourbon family had 'undying rights', that France would recognise this and that to propose a new leader could lead to confusion and prolong conflict.[17] Metternich reported that in the face of an uncompromising negotiating position, the tsar conceded his point: 'I do not insist on my idea against the wish of my allies: I have spoken according to my conscience; time will do the rest; it will also teach us who was right'.[18]

Consequently, after the first defeat of Napoleon, the Allied ministers negotiated a treaty with the Bourbon government.[19] In terms of the resulting First Treaty of Paris, the French throne was, in the name of 'legitimacy', restored to Louis XVIII. It was further agreed that France should regain the limits of its territory as it had been prior to the revolution, and should pay no indemnity. Similar monarchical restorations were carried out elsewhere in Europe. The Bourbon Ferdinand VII was restored to the Spanish throne and Piedmont and Savoy's Victor Emmanuel I was restored as king of Sardinia. To settle all outstanding matters in the reconstruction of Europe, a congress was convened in Vienna, commencing in September 1814. Talleyrand joined the assembly to represent France.

Peace was short-lived, however. In March 1815 Napoleon again marched on Paris, and Louis XVIII fled for Belgium. Napoleon swiftly set up a 'temporary Government', which ruled from 20 March 1815 until Louis XVIII was restored to power for a second time (on 8 July 1815), a period dubbed 'the Hundred Days', although by my calculations actually consisting of 103 days.

During his time in exile in Ghent, Louis XVIII had continued to issue proclamations '*du Roi de France*'.[20] He wrote:

> Notre premier soin, comme notre premier devoir, ont été de faire reconnoitre une distinction juste et nécessaire entre le Pertubateur de la paix et la Nation Française opprimée. Fidèles aux principes qui les ont toujours guidés, les Souverains, nos Alliés, ont déclaré vouloir respecter l'indépendance de la France, et garantir l'intégrité de son Territoire. Ils

16 1 Metternich 226–227.
17 Ibid. 228.
18 Ibid. 229.
19 Webster, *Congress of Vienna*, 59.
20 E.g., Proclamation du Roi de France, Gand, 2 May 1815, 2 BSFP 1026.

> nous ont donné les assurances les plus solennelles de ne point s'immiscer dans son Gouvernement intérieur: c'est à ces conditions que nous sommes décidés à accepter leurs secours généreux.[21]

The Bourbon Government was party to the declaration of the Congress of Vienna responding to the escape from Elba.[22] The correspondence of Talleyrand and Louis XVIII reflects that, during this period, Talleyrand remained engaged in diplomacy and military planning with the Allies in Vienna.[23] Further, France was invited to[24] and did join the Treaty of Alliance of 25 March 1815 against Napoleon.[25] The Final Act of the Congress of Vienna of 9 June 1815 was also signed on behalf of France by a representative of Louis XVIII.[26]

The possibility of replacing Louis XVIII and Napoleon with a third option appears not to have been considered seriously at this stage. Of such a possibility, Liverpool wrote to Castlereagh:

> As this alternative, however, is not likely under present circumstances to occur, it does not appear to be necessary to say more upon it. The principle [of Bourbon restoration] as above laid down cannot possibly be disputed; the expediency of acting upon it to a certain degree will hardly be denied ...[27]

Instead, the focus of the Allies' negotiations was the consequences for France of the Hundred Days. In these negotiations, the French delegates took the position that there had been no breach of the peace between France and the Allied powers during the Hundred Days. They argued:

> Les Puissances Alliées n'ont pas un instant cessé de reconnoitre Sa Majesté Très Chrétienne comme Roi de France, et conséquemment les droits qui lui appartiennent en cette qualité. Elles n'ont pas un instant cessé

21 Proclamation du Roi de France, Gand, 2 May 1815, 2 BSFP 1026, 1027.

22 See Declaration des Plénipotentiaires des 8 Puissances, sur l'évasion de Napoléon Bonaparte, Vienna, 13 March 1815, 2 BFSP 655.

23 See generally Talleyrand & Louis, 349ff.

24 Treaty of Alliance against Bonaparte, between Great Britain and Austria, Prussia and Russia, Vienna, 25 March 1815, Art. 8, 2 BFSP 448.

25 Le Plénipotentiare Français aux Plénipotentiaires des 4 Cours, Vienna, 27 March 1815, 2 BFSP 678–679.

26 2 BFSP 7; and see Stephan Talmon, *Recognition of Governments in International Law* (Oxford: Clarendon Press, 2001), 117.

27 Liverpool to Castlereagh. Memorandum, 30 June 1815, Webster, *Congress of Vienna*, 340.

> d'être avec lui dans des relations de paix et d'amitié … Elles ont pris cet engagement d'une manière formelle, bien qu'implicite, dans leurs Déclarations du 13e. Mars et dans le Traité du 25e. Elles l'ont rendu plus étroit, en fesant entrer le Roi, par son Accession à ce Traité, dans leurs Alliance contre l'Ennemi commun …[28]

This position the Allied plenipotentiaries maintained throughout.[29] There was nevertheless some confusion as to whether or not the Allies had been at war with France. The Duke of Wellington, commander of the Allied troops at Waterloo and then-commander of the Allied forces in occupied France, reflected this uncertainty in a letter to Castlereagh on the question of ownership of looted art held by France: 'It is not now necessary to discuss the question, whether the allies were or were not at war with France; there is no doubt whatever that their Armies entered Paris under a Military Convention …'[30]

Lord Chancellor Eldon provided a legal opinion to Prime Minister Liverpool addressing the question whether Napoleon should be considered 'as a French Subject & *France at War with us*, or a French Rebel & *France at peace with us*'.[31] A biographer remarks that Eldon's 'plea for the detention of Bonaparte in 1815, that he had neither king nor country, but had constituted himself an independent belligerent, and was thus at the mercy of his captors, was perhaps more subtle than sound'.[32] But that was in effect the basis on which the Allies proceeded.

3 The Status of Napoleon during the Hundred Days

The terms of Napoleon's abdication in 1814 were governed by the Treaty of Fontainebleau.[33] Under it, Napoleon was obliged to renounce all individual and familial claims to the throne not only of France but of other countries.

28 Les Plénipotentiares de France aux Plénipotentiares des 4 Cours Alliées, sur les Arrangement Définitifs, Paris, 21 September 1815, 3 BSFP 221, 223.

29 Les Plénipotentiares des 4 Cours Alliées aux Plénipotentiares de France, sur les Arrangement Définitifs, Paris, 22 September 1815, 3 BSFP 225.

30 Duke of Wellington to Viscount Castlereagh, 23 September 1815, 3 BFSP 207, 210.

31 Legal Opinion of the Lord Chancellor of Great Britain to the Prime Minister, 1815 (exact date unknown), reproduced for the first time in John Hall Stewart, 'The Imprisonment of Napoleon: A Legal Opinion by Lord Eldon', *American Journal of International Law* 45 (1951) 571–577, 573–574 (emphasis added).

32 J.M. Rigg, 'Scott, John (1751–1838)', 51 *Dictionary of National Bibliography* 49, 52.

33 Traité entre l'Autriche, la Russie et la Prusse, et Napoléon Buonaparte, Paris, 11 April 1814, 1-1 BFSP 134.

Article 1 read: 'L'Empereur Napoléon renonce, pour lui, et ses Successeurs et Descendans, ainsi que pour chacun des Membres de sa Famille, à tout droit de Souverainté et de Domination, tant sur l'Empereur François et le Royaume d'Italie, que sur tout autre Pays'.[34]

In the Treaty, Elba was made a principality for the duration of Napoleon's life, giving him a special status. Article 3 provided: 'L'Ile d'Elbe, adoptée par Sa Majesté l'Empereur Napoléon pour le lieu de son séjour, formera, sa vie durant, une Principauté séparée, qui sera possédée par lui en toute Souveraineté et propriété'.[35] On 26 February 1815, Napoleon escaped from Elba to land at Fréjus in the Provence on 1 March 1815.[36] By an *Ordonnance du Roi* on 6 March 1815, Louis XVIII declared Napoleon a 'traitre et rebelle' and called for his arrest and trial before a Conseil de Guerre.[37] On 11 March 1815, in a *Proclamation du Roi de France au Peuple Francais,* the King referred to him as 'l'Ennemi ... qui veut y renouveler la Guerre Civile'.[38] Unabated, Napoleon proceeded swiftly to Paris. On 19 March 1815 Louis XVIII fled for Belgium, leaving Napoleon to set up a government.

The status of Napoleon during this time was determined by agreement between the Allies. The immediate response of the Committee of Eight[39] took the form of the Declaration of 13 March 1815, which read in relevant part:

> En violant ainsi la Convention qui l'a établi dans l'Ile d'Elbe, Bonaparte détruit le seul titre légal dont son existence dépendoit. En reparoissant en France, avec des projets de confusion et de désordre, il s'est mis hors de la protection de la Loi, et il manifeste à l'Univers, qu'il ne peut y avoir ni paix ni trêve avec lui. Les Puissances déclarent, en conséquence, que Napoléon Bonaparte s'est exclu des relations civiles et sociales, et que, comme Ennemi et Perturbateur du Monde, il a encouru la vindique publique.[40]

34 Ibid, Art. 1.
35 Ibid, Art. 3.
36 Ibid, 155.
37 Ordonnance du Roi, Paris, 6 March 1815, 2 BSFP 1014, art I.
38 Proclamation du Roi de France aux Peuple Français. Au Chateau des Tuileries, 11 March 1815, 2 BSFP 1021. Note also reference to Napoleon as 'L'Ennemie de la Patrie' in Proclamation du Roi de France aux Peuple Français. Au Chateau des Tuileries, 12 March 1815, 2 BSFP 1022.
39 Austria, Spain, France, Great Britain, Portugal, Prussia, Russia and Sweden.
40 Déclaration des Plénipotentiaires des 8 Puissances, sur l'évasion de Napoléon Bonaparte, Vienna, 13 March 1815, 2 BFSP 655. See also Webster, *Congress of Vienna,* 95–96.

The loss of legal protections proclaimed in the Declaration is reflected in a change of style. Before the escape from Elba, Napoleon is referred to as 'Napoleon', reflecting provisions in the 1814 Agreement that he could keep his title. In the declaration and afterwards, he is styled 'Bonaparte'. The British prime minister described Napoleon as a 'captain of freebooters or banditti and consequently out of the pale of protection of nations [that] headed his expedition as an outlaw and an outcast; *hostis humani generis*'.[41]

In a letter to Louis XVIII of 17 March 1815, Talleyrand recounted that, in light of the quick progress of Napoleon northwards, the Five Powers[42] had considered what to do if Napoleon successfully re-established himself in Paris? The powers' decision was made in the Declaration of 13 March 1815: 'C'est à cela [the decision to treat Napoleon as an outlaw] que l'on s'en tiendra'.[43] In his next letter, dated 19 March 1815, Talleyrand explained further that the Allies 'ne traiteraient jamais' with Napoleon and expressed their sense that, given Napoleon's status as an outlaw, Switzerland might participate in his suppression without prejudice to its neutrality: 'Il sera aussi fait une démarche vis-à-vis de la Suisse. La question actuelle est hors de la neutralité, l'homme qui force l'Europe à s'armer n'étant qu'un brigand'.[44]

Correspondence of Joseph de Maistre, ambassador in St Petersburg on behalf of the Kingdom of Sardinia, dated 13 July 1815, confirms that: 'Ainsi les alliés déclarent solennement qu'ils ne font la guerre *qu'à sa personne*; et lorsqu'enfin sa personne est tombé sous leurs mains, ils n'en parlent plus!'[45] On 25 March 1815, Austria, Great Britain, Prussia and Russia signed a treaty[46] to which France acceded,[47] according to which, 'having taken into consideration the consequences which the Invasion of France by Napoleon Bonaparte, and the actual situation of that Kingdom', the parties agreed:

> to direct in common, and with one accord, should the case require it, all their efforts against [Napoleon], and against all those who should already have joined his faction, or shall hereafter join it, in order to force him to desist from his Projects, and render him unable to disturb in future the tranquillity of Europe and the General Peace.

---

41 Twiss, *Public and Private Life of Lord Chancellor Eldon*, vol. 1, 413.
42 Austria, France, Great Britain, Prussia and Russia.
43 Talleyrand to Louis XVIII, Vienna, 17 March 1815, Talleyrand & Louis, 351.
44 Talleyrand to Louis XVIII, Vienna, 19 March 1815, Talleyrand & Louis, 352–353.
45 Albert Blanc, ed., *Correspondance diplomatique de Joseph de Maistre 1811–1817* (Paris: Michel Lévy, 1860), 87.
46 Treaty of Alliance, 25 March 1815, 2 BFSP 443.
47 Accession of France, 27 March 1815, 2 BFSP 674.

True to their word, the Allies did indeed refuse any diplomatic engagement with Napoleon following his return to power. On 4 April 1815, Napoleon wrote to the British Prince Regent.[48] In response Viscount Castlereagh stated that the Prince Regent 'has declined receiving the Letter addressed to him' and instructed that it be transmitted unopened to the Allies in Vienna.[49] On 6 May, the Earl of Clancarty wrote from Vienna to inform Castlereagh of its contents.[50] Napoleon had vowed that he would 'continue at peace, to observe the stipulations of the Treaty of Paris':

> After reading these papers, it was considered whether any, and what answer should be made thereto, when the general opinion appeared to be, that none should be returned, and no notice whatever taken of the proposal. Upon this, as indeed upon all other occasions subsequent to the resumption of authority by Buonaparte, wherein the present state of the Continental Powers, with regard to France, has come under discussion, but one opinion has appeared to direct the Councils of the several Sovereigns. They adhere, and from the commencement have never ceased to adhere, to their Declaration of the 13th of March, with respect to [Napoleon]. They are in a state of hostility with him and his Adherents…[51]

Following his defeat at Waterloo, Napoleon's second abdication was announced to the French people by the *Commission de Gouvernement* on 24 June 1815. Agreement was quickly reached to end the war, in the form of a convention between the Commissioners of the Prussian and English armies, and those of the French army. As its preamble reflected, this took the form of an agreement between the armies themselves rather than between states:

> Cejourd'hui 3 Juillet, 1815, les Commissaires nommés par les Commandans en Chef des Armées respectives, savoir:
>
> M. le Baron Bignon, chargé du Portfeuille des Affaires Etrangères ; M. le Comte Guilleminot, Chef de l'Etat Major de l'Armée Française; et M. le Comte de Bondy, Préfet du Département de la Seine;–munis des Pleinspouvoirs de Son Excellence le Maréchal Prince d'Eckmühl, Commandant en Chef de l'Armée Française, d'une part;

48 Viscount Castlereagh to General Caulaincourt, Downing Street, 8 April 1815, 2 BFSP 1031.

49 Ibid.

50 The Earl of Clancarty to Viscount Castlereagh. Vienna, 6 May 1815, 2 BFSP 1031.

51 Ibid, 1032.

> Et M. le Général Major Baron de Muffling, muni des Pleinspouvoirs de Son Altesse M. le Maréchal Prince Blücher, Commandant en Chef de l'Armée Prussienne;–et M. le Colonel Hervey, muni des Pleinspouvoirs de Son Excellence le Duc de Wellington, Commandant en Chef de l'Armée Anglaise; de l'autre, – sont convenus des Articles suivans:[52]

This form was confirmed by the ratification of the agreement by the Prince of Eckmühl later that day.[53] Louis XVIII was restored to power for a second time on 8 July 1815.

Despite these indications that Napoleon was never recognised as having any *de iure* authority to govern during the Hundred Days, it appears that there was some confusion as to his status. After Napoleon's confinement on Saint Helena, the Prime Minister Lord Liverpool requested an opinion from Lord Chancellor Eldon as to their prisoner's legal status. As we have seen, Eldon's response suggested that he was unsure as to whether Napoleon should be considered 'as a French Subject & France at War with us, or a French Rebel & France at peace with us'.[54] On this question he was (characteristically) indecisive, though he did suggest that there were grounds for attributing to Napoleon the status of 'a distinct, substantive Enemy, independent of any relation to the Sovereign of France, with whom we might be at Peace, or in Alliance'. Under either possibility, existing law did not allow for his perpetual imprisonment by Great Britain unless it be justified as an exception based on necessity. He suggested that Great Britain might 'steer clear' of the difficulty of determining Napoleon's status by according him a status apart:

> If, before the Emperor of Elba entered France, to regain the throne he was not a French Subject, does his Attempt to regain that Throne again make him a French subject, or a French subject in rebellion – If, upon Grounds resulting out of the various situations & characters, in which [he] has been placed, & with which he has been clothed, you can consider him as, in no way, in the relation of Subject, or subject in rebellion ag[ainst] France, then may not the War be considered as a War against him, ag[ainst] him as our Enemy, without reference to any Character, that he may be alledged to have, bound up in the national Character of

52 Convention entre les Commissaires des Armées Prussienne et Anglaise, et ceux de l'Armée Française, pour la suspension des Hostilités entre l'Armée Française et les Armées Alliées, 3 July 1815, 3 BFSP 193.

53 3 BFSP 193, 195.

54 Legal Opinion 1815 (exact date unknown), reproduced in Stewart, 'Imprisonment', 573–574.

> France – against him & his adherents making, as an Enemy against us, an hostile Attempt to break down the System of Government, which existed in France, thereby introducing a System of Gov[ernment] in direct subversion of a Treaty with our allies, founded upon their & our insecurity under any such Government as he would introduce into France? If we can make this out, (& does there not seem to be ground for saying that we can?) then might we not steer clear of the difficulty, that belongs to excluding from Peace with France or French Subject or a French Rebel? [H]e would then be a distinct, substantive Enemy, independent of any relation to the Sovereign of France, with whom we might be at Peace, or in Alliance? [A] conquered Enemy indeed, with whom, according to the Law of Nations, we should deal as mercifully as our Security would admit after he was conquered. But then we should only have to determine, as between ourselves & him, whether we did so treat, and the rules of the Law of Nations would be to be applied in the decision of that Question of fact, without reference to any Rule of that Law to him as a Subject of any Sovereign?[55]

4 Responsibility for the Hundred Days and the Terms of Peace

The terms of the First Treaty of Paris were generous. France's borders were set at their 1792 limits, thereby conceding some of the Revolution's territorial gains along the Belgian, German and Italian borders. The Allied troops were withdrawn within three days of the treaty. Most significantly, all Allied claims to war damages were waived.

Following the Hundred Days, the Allies' mood was markedly less conciliatory. Negotiations concerned three major points: territorial adjustments (including the demolition of certain French border fortifications), the payment of an indemnity and the provisional occupation of France. The indemnity appears to have been justified on the basis of equity or comity. The adjustments and occupation were justified as necessary to secure peace.

Shortly after the second Bourbon restoration, France took a strategic negotiating position to concede some monetary indemnity in order to preserve its territorial integrity. Castlereagh wrote to Liverpool that 'Talleyrand has hinted that whilst they are prepared for pecuniary sacrifices with certain bounds, neither the King nor his ministers will ever consent to sacrifice the smallest

---

55 Ibid.

portion of French territory'.[56] Castlereagh reports that upon hearing of this from Russia, his reply emphasised the security aims of the Allies rather than their financial interests.[57]

Internal negotiations among the Allies reflected conflicting policy goals. A letter from Castlereagh to Liverpool dated 17 August 1815 reflected the positions of the various Allies.[58] Throughout the discussions, it seems not to have been questioned that they had a right as against the French state to indemnification for expenses relating to the Hundred Days. Debate instead focused on the measures to be taken for prospective European security. The primary interest of Britain and Russia was the quick settlement of the conflict and the minimisation of expenses. The interests of Prussia and Austria seemed more attuned to territorial gains and gaining subsidies for their armies occupying France.

The logic behind the occupation measure ultimately chosen was described in a memorandum by Wellington to Castlereagh. The memorandum first described disagreements between Allies as to the extent of military measures desired against France.[59] Wellington continued, describing the justifications of occupation:

> All persons appear to agree that the maintenance of the authority of the King is essential to the interests of the other Powers of Europe; and, notwithstanding the difference of opinion regarding the extent of the force which ought to be maintained for a time in France, and regarding the difficulties of executing this measure, and after all that has been said of its inefficiency in affording security to the allies in general, it appears to be generally admitted that it is necessary to adopt it. It is necessary to adopt it with different objects in view; first, to give security to the Government of the King, and to afford him time to form a force of his own with which he can carry on his government, and take his fair share in the concerns of Europe; secondly, to give the allies some security against a second revolutionary convulsion and reaction; and, thirdly, to enable the allies to enforce the payment of those contributions which they deem

56 Castlereagh to Liverpool (No 16), Paris, 24 July 1815, in Webster, *Congress of Vienna*, 351.

57 Ibid.

58 Castlereagh to Liverpool, Paris, 17 August 1815, in Webster, *Congress of Vienna*, 362–367.

59 Wellington to Castelreagh. Memorandum on the Temporary Occupation of Part of France. Paris, 31 August 1815, in Webster, *Congress of Vienna*, 374. These disagreements, which were not directly relevant to the questions dealt with here, are detailed in contemporary British correspondence collected in Webster.

> it just toward their own subjects to lay of France in payment of the expenses of the war.[60]

According to Talleyrand's Memoirs, France was first included in this discussion in September 1815.[61] A Draft Treaty of 20 September 1815 provided for certain payments by France to the Allies. The preamble of the draft treaty first noted:

> Leurs Majestées Impériales et Royales ont proposé à Sa Majesté le Roi de France et de Navarre, les Bases d'un Arrangement propre à leur assurer de justes indemnités pour le passé ainsi que des garanties solides pour l'avenir, – seules conditions auxquelles il soit possible d'atteindre à une pacification prompte et durable; et Sa Majesté Très Chrétienne ayant accédé aux dites propositions, il a été convenue de les consigner dans un Traité Définitif.[62]

This reflected two motivations for obligations on France following the Hundred Days: indemnification for Allied costs and the restoration of European public order.

With respect to indemnification, Article 4 of the draft treaty provided:

> Le devoir des Souverains Alliés envers les Peuples qu'ils gouvernent les ayant portés à demander une Compensation des sacrifices pécuniaires que le denier armement général a fait imposer à des Pays, déjà fortement épuisés par cette longue suite de guerres soutenues contre les Pouvoirs Révolutionnaires de la France, et Sa Majesté Très Chrétienne n'ayant pas pi se refuser à admettre le principe sur lequel cette Réclamation se fonde, la somme de 600,000,000 francs sera fournie par la France aux Puissances Alliées à titre d'indemnité.[63]

The draft treaty also proposed that France contribute 200,000,000 francs toward the refurbishment of its neighbours' (namely the Netherlands, Germany and Piedmont) defensive fortifications[64] and pay the expenses of an army of occupation for up to seven years.[65]

---

60 Webster, *Congress of Vienna*, 375.

61 3 Talleyrand 188–189.

62 *Projet de Traité avec la France*, Preamble, 3 BFSP 217.

63 *Projet de Traité avec la France*, Art. 2, 3 BFSP 219.

64 Ibid. Art. 5, 3 BFSP 219–220.

65 Ibid. Art. 6, 3 BFSP 220; and Eugene White, 'Making the French Pay: The Costs and Consequences of the Napoleonic Reparations, *European Review of Economic History* 5 (2001) 337–365, 339.

The reply of the French plenipotentiaries dated 21 September 1815, as noted above, objected to territorial changes, but France, through Talleyrand, acquiesced in the idea of payments:

> Elle ne peut pas davantage avoir pour motif les dépenses faites par les Puissances Alliées, car il est juste que les sacrifices aux quels elles ont été forcées par une guerre entreprise pour l'utilité commune, mais pour l'utilité plus spéciale de la France, ne restent pas à leur charge; il est également juste qu'elles se contentent d'un dédommagement de même nature que le sacrifice. Or, les Puissances Alliées n'ont point sacrifié de Territoire.[66]

The French logic appears to link the payment more to equity or comity than legal obligation. Talleyrand continues '[Sa Majesté Très Chrétienne] consentira pareillement au payement d'une Indemnité, mais qui laisse les moyens de suffire aux besoins de l'Administration Intérieure du Royaume...'[67]

Allied thought continued to link the measures to indemnity and security. As Castlereagh wrote to Liverpool on 25 September 1815 of an audience he had had with Louis XVIII, the Allies 'founded their claims in no degree upon the right of conquest, but upon the two principles of indemnity and security'.[68] Talleyrand ceased to be prime minister of France on 26 September 1815, but correspondence between France and the Allies continued. In a conference on 2 October 1815, the Allies and France agreed to consolidate the pecuniary contributions in a single indemnity of 700,000,000 francs.[69] The treaty as adopted provided for this indemnity without mention of the refurbishment of fortifications:

> La partie pécuniaire de l'Indemnité à fournir par la France aux Puissances Alliées, est fixée à la somme de 700,000,000 de Francs. Le mode, les termes et les garanties du payement de cette somme, seront réglés par une Convention Particulière, qui aura la même force et valeur que si elle était textuellement insérée au présent Traité.[70]

66 Les Plénipotentiaires de France aux Plénipotentiaires des 4 Cours Alliées, sur les Arrangements Définitifs, Paris, 21 September 1815, 3 BFSP 221, 223.

67 Ibid, 224.

68 Castlereagh to Liverpool, 25 September 1815, in Webster, *Congress of Vienna*, 380.

69 Procès Verbal de la Conférence des Plénipotentiaires des 4 Cours Alliées, avec le Duc de Richelieu, sur les Bases des Rapports avec la France, 3 BFSP 228. Further: White, 'Costs and Consequences', 337.

70 Treaty between Austria, Great Britain, Prussia and Russia, and France, Paris, 20 November 1815, Art. 4, 3 BFSP 280, 288.

The refurbishment of fortifications, however, was included in this sum as reflected in the Allies' agreement on the distribution of the indemnity.[71]

The 1815 terms of peace between France and the Allied powers are particularly significant insofar as they related to looted art treasures.[72] Throughout the period of the Revolution, the Consulate and the First Empire, France amassed a vast collection of artworks from the territories it annexed or controlled. In the peace settlement of 1814, the Allies did not raise the issue of the looted art. By virtue of the treaty's silence on the matter, it was presumed that ownership over it would remain with France as the legitimate spoils of war. Indeed, it has been said that during the Napoleonic era plunder was 'generally recognized as legitimate means of acquisition of artistic objects'.[73] It was also justified under the various peace treaties or armistice agreements that France had negotiated to include specific contracts for artworks.[74]

The attitude of the majority of the Allies in negotiating for peace following the Hundred Days was significantly changed. Correspondence from the Duke of Wellington, commander of the Allied army in occupation of France at the time, to Viscount Castlereagh in September of 1815 describes the change in attitude that followed the Hundred Days:

> The conduct of the allies, regarding the Museum [where the looted art was held], at the period of the Treaty of Paris, might be fairly attributed to their desire to conciliate the French Army, and to consolidate the reconciliation with Europe, which the Army at that period manifested a disposition to effect; but the circumstances are now entirely different. The Army disappointed the reasonable expectations of the World, and seized the earliest opportunity of rebelling against their Sovereign, and of giving their services to the Common Enemy of mankind, with a view to the

---

71 Protocole de la Conférence entre les Plénipotentiaires des 4 Cours Alliées, sur la Distribution de l'Indemnité Pécuniaire ; et qui tiendra lieu d'une Convention Particulière sur cet objet, Paris, 6 November 1815, 3 BFSP 242.

72 Wayne Sandholtz, *Prohibiting Plunder: How Norms Change* (Oxford: Oxford University Press, 2007), 71.

73 Andrzei Jakubowski, *State Succession in Cultural Property* (Oxford: Oxford University Press, 2015), 35 (citing Hugo Grotius, *The Rights of War and Peace, Including the Law of Nature and of Nations. Translation of De Jure Belli Ac Pacis* (1680, transl. 1901) 3.4-6.323-344; Sandholtz, *Prohibiting Plunder*, 53–55.

74 Jakubowski, *State Succession in Cultural Property*, 38. See e.g. Traité de paix entre la République Française et la Saint-Siege, Tollentino, 19 February 1797, in Georg-Friedrich von Martens (ed.), *Recueil des Traités ...*, (2nd series, Göttingen: Dieterich, 1817–1835), vol. 2, 130, by which the Pope agreed to hand over many works of significant value from the Vatican collections in order to secure a peace deal with France.

> revival of the disastrous period which had passed, and of the scenes of plunder which the World has made such gigantic efforts to get rid of. This Army having been defeated by the Armies of Europe, they have been disbanded by the united counsel of the Sovereigns; and no reason can exist why the Powers of Europe should do injustice to their own Subjects, with a view to conciliate them again.[75]

Castlereagh supported this position and communicated it to the Allied plenipotentiaries participating in the peace negotiations.[76] He wrote that:

> If we are really to return to peace and ancient maxims, it cannot be wise to preserve just so much of the abuses of the past; nor can the king desire, out of the wrecks of the Revolution, of which his family has been one of the chief victims, to perpetuate in his house this odious monopoly of the arts.[77]

His position was supported by Prussia and Austria. Nevertheless, France maintained that the art was acquired by them according the laws of war.[78] Its position was supported by Russia.[79] Unable to achieve consensus, an obligation to restore plundered art was not included in the Second Treaty of Paris.

Nevertheless, widespread restoration of the looted art did take place. In the end, it was forced upon the French by the Allied forces present in Paris. The restitution of plundered art in 1815 marked a change in attitude and laid the foundations for the development of international cultural heritage law.[80] When the Congress of Vienna reopened on 20 September 1815, the *Gazette de la Cour* contained the following summary:

> The courts of Austria, England and Prussia are united on the principle that masterpieces of art and science that had become, in all of Europe, the spoils of revolutionary wars, should be returned to their owners ... As a result of this principle, the masterpieces taken in Italy, in Germany,

---

75 Duke of Wellington to Viscount Castlereagh, 23 September 1815, 3 BFSP 207, 210.

76 Viscount Castlereagh to the Plenipotentiaries of Austria, Prussia and Russia, September 1815, 3 BSFP 203.

77 Ibid., 206–207.

78 Sandholtz, *Prohibiting Plunder*, 67–68.

79 Sandholtz, *Prohibiting Plunder*, 67–88.

80 Jakubowski, *State Succession in Cultural Property*, 37.

> in Spain and in the Low Countries will be removed from the Museum of Paris and from other sites where they may be found.[81]

But these works were returned, as so many had been taken, under military auspices and without further legitimation.

5 Conclusions – Absence of Theory or a Theory of Absence?

The Bourbon dynasty was considered legitimate in accordance with the monarchic theory of sovereign power prevailing at the outset of the nineteenth century. Following Louis XVIII's restoration, the monarchy's claim to rule France was collectively recognised by the European heads of state. This acknowledgment of that monarchy's authority to negotiate on behalf of France at the Congress of Vienna was never withdrawn, and numerous treaties were concluded with the Allies.

Explaining Napoleon's status during the Hundred Days presents a greater challenge, as reflected by Lord Chancellor Eldon's questions. It is easier to describe his status in the negative: he was *not* considered a head of state. That his temporary government was not recognised is clear from the substantive terms of the treaties concluded between the Allies and France, and the contemporaneous diplomatic commentary.

But if Napoleon and his government of the Hundred Days did not represent the French state, on what basis were reparations for damages incurred by France during this period? In a December 1815 address to the Chamber of Deputies, the French finance minister's description reflects a theory of responsibility, or perhaps attribution, by adoption:

> Si l'on considère que ce Déficit représente à-peu-près ce qui reste dû pour le service des 100 jours de désastres, on trouvera que la justice du Roi est bien libérale, en daignant l'adopter comme Dette de l'Etat.[82]

Acknowledgements

The author, member of the International Court of Justice, thanks his University Trainee, Douglas Pivnichny and his Research Associate, Rosalind Elphick for their assistance with this paper.

81 Text reproduced in Sandholtz, *Prohibiting Plunder*, 68.

82 2 BFSP 184, 190.

CHAPTER 2

The Law of Nations and the Common Law of Europe: The Case of Edmund Burke

Camilla Boisen

1 Introduction[1]

In contemporary international law discourse, a good many sceptics question the efficacy of international law in the absence of formal institutions and any effective enforcement mechanisms. However, as most legal philosophers point out, such scepticism is unhelpful for understanding how international law works, even without the institutional framework normally associated with a legal system. We need to 'train our imagination', as the French novelist and diplomat Jean Giraudoux phrased it, to move beyond the simple definitions of law. For too long, these have been conceived on a domestic model and have been presented as the standard for how law ought to operate in advanced democracies; it is this model which underlies the deficiencies of international law.[2]

'Training' their imaginations in relation to international law was indeed what the early modern jurists did. They reshaped their jurisprudence to address endemic religious and cultural disputes in a new global world by undertaking a more systematic theorising of the law of nations, and its relation to the law of nature. The inherent ambiguity of the terms 'nature' and 'law', evident from the time of the Greeks and Stoics, exacerbated the problem of analysing the relation between the two systems of law. This relationship perplexed even the most adept natural jurists. Thinkers such as Francisco Suárez and Hugo Grotius played on its ambiguity and ambivalence and never entirely reconciled it in their works. For instance, obligations arising from natural law norms and how these were effected in the law of nations remained elusive. The natural law jurists, or naturalists, for the most part, did acknowledge a positive law of nations, which stood in an ambiguous relation to natural law, from which the primary law of nations was derived – for some the necessary law of nations.

1 This paper revisits and revises arguments first proposed in 'Subjecting International Relations to The Law of Nature: a neglected aspect of the early modern jurists and Edmund Burke', *Theoria – Journal of Social and Political Theory*, Vol. 60, issue 134, March, (2013), pp. 69–90.

2 Gerhard Von Glahn and James L. Taulbee, *Law Among Nations – An Introduction to Public International Law*, 8th edn. (New York: Pearson Longman, 2007), 6.

 | DOI:10.1163/9789004412088_003

The secondary law of nations, discovered by *a posteriori* methods, was recognised to be the product of more civilised countries. Despite the problematic position of natural law within the emergence of positivism, natural law was still part of nineteenth-century international law.[3]

In this chapter, I want to show how the problem of enforcement was addressed by the early modern jurists and particularly by Edmund Burke. To do so, I will begin by broadly exploring the ideas of Vitoria, Gentili and Suárez to draw out Grotius' unique perspective on international punishment *qua* Pufendorf's denial of a separate law of nations, and the latter's unbending insistence that punishment required a supreme ruler and was therefore technically only applicable in civil war. Central to their discussions was whether or not the law of nature could be enforced, how it corresponded with individual or communal obligations, and how it was possible to retain a system of rights and duties for states and peoples that ensured that violations of natural law would be punished. Using Grotius as an exemplar, who to a large extent equated 'international law' with punishment, I demonstrate that while the early modern jurists emphasised states' right to intervention, they were in agreement that the law of nature could not prescribe who should do the punishing.

For Edmund Burke, the moral law of the Commonwealth of Europe could. On the issue of third-state retaliatory measures, which had preoccupied his early modern predecessors, Burke provided a solution by envisioning a way of how international community issues could be protected and enforced in the law of nations. This aspect of enforcement in Burke's political thought has been neglected and under-recognised in existing Burkean scholarship, which primarily focuses on Burke as a critic of empire and the natural rights tradition, but generally fails to situate Burke's international writings in a broader history of international law.[4] By resituating Burke's scholarship in this way, I argue that his conceptualisation of the law of nations and his thoughts on the universality and authority of enforcement were quite distinct from anything

3 Casper Sylvest, 'The Foundations of Victorian International Law', in Duncan Bell (ed.), *Victorian Visions of Global Order: Empire and International Relations in Nineteenth-Century Political Thought* (Cambridge: Heinemann, 2007), 47–66, 59.

4 There are of course exceptions. See for instance Jennifer M. Welsh, *Edmund Burke and International Relations. The Commonwealth of Europe and the Crusade against the French Revolution* (London: Macmillian Press, 1995); David Boucher, *Political Theories of International Relations. From Thucydides to the Present* (Oxford: Oxford University Press, 1998); Richard Bourke, 'Edmund Burke and International Conflict', in Ian Hall and Lisa Hill (eds.), *British International Thinkers from Hobbes to Namier* (New York: Palgrave Macmillan, 2009), 91–116; David Armitage, *Foundations of Modern International Thought* (Cambridge: Cambridge University Press, 2012) considers Burke's 'reason of state' idea in the history of international thought Also, Camilla Boisen, 'Triumphing over Evil; Edmund Burke, and the Idea of Humanitarian Intervention', *Journal of International Political Theory*, 2016, Vol. 12(3), pp. 276–298.

previously proposed, insofar as we get the foundational argument for customs as the source of 'the common law of Europe' – an aspect distinctly lacking in contemporary understandings of international law. Burke's jurisprudence binds the legal and the moral in international law, correlates the right to the obligation, and ensures that violations of the norms and rules of the international community would carry with it enforcement to punish the offenders and restore order. Seen from this perspective, Burke deserves as much scholarly fame as his predecessor Vattel, for being one of the eighteenth century's great minds of international law.

I will conclude by briefly reflecting on the implications of Burke's position for contemporary disputes about humanitarian international law, suggesting that Burke provides a modern audience with a unique approach to thinking about international justice.

2 The Law of Nature and Nations: Vitoria, Gentili and Suárez

The discovery of the Americas was to destroy all orthodox convictions about the world, prompting a vigorous score of political and religious debates about how this paradigm-changing discovery would fit into Christian theology. Intellectual debates about the capabilities and rationale of non-Europeans, the emergence of state sovereignty in the wake of religious resistance, natural rights, property and the enforceability of international morality as understood to be natural law took new heights when confronted with such religious and cultural diversity. What duties and rights, if any, could the Europeans have towards or claim against non-Europeans as afforded or commanded by the law of nature? The law of nature was of course universal, but to what extent did it regulate relations among individuals as well as states? For the early modern jurists, the problem had been to determine the extent to which international law was derived from the universal *ius naturale* and, correspondingly, from the states' variously prescriptive *ius gentium*. Most assumed that the universal and ethical norm of natural law applied equally and concurrently to inter-national and intra-national relations. The one great exception to this view was Hobbes, who defined natural law as self-preservation.[5]

Derived from natural law, the 'law of nations' emerged as a common law for civilised societies. It was understood as those principles that civilised societies recognised as universally valid and binding. The common law for civilised states, as James Schall points out, came to be identified with international law.

5 Peter Stanlis, 'Edmund Burke and the Law of Nations', *The American Journal of International Law* 47 (1953), 397–413, 397.

The possibility of the law of nations as having the legal authority to arbitrate wars presupposed that it was widely recognised. The legitimacy of such recognition somehow had to be based on reason. Through practical and general reasoning, this law was considered to account for the common things found at the basic structures of all civilised societies.[6] The idea of universality requires a short detour in clarifying a well-known issue in natural law scholarship: the question of what creates moral obligation. For most of the early natural law theorists and jurists, such as Grotius, Suárez and Gentili, obligations conformed to the precepts of natural law in the firm belief that God was its author.[7] While Grotius implied that the source of obligation was human nature and that our natures have been endowed by God,[8] Gentili asserted that people who did not worship God stood outside natural law and could not enjoy its protection.[9] For Suárez, reason was the instrument by which one discovered or derived the precepts from natural law. Reason is the foundation of natural law, he argues, and it provides the criterion of objective right and wrong. However, it is not itself law. Reason does not give the obligation, it reveals it, and ultimately it is God's law that makes natural law obligatory. Why is this important to highlight? The jurist Samuel Rachel (1628–1691), in trying to discern the two systems of law, alluded to what he saw as 'the problem of [these] old jurists [who] say that knowledge of the Law of Nature is obtained by Reason, and the knowledge of

6 James V. Schall, 'Natural Law and the Law of Nations: Some Theoretical Considerations', *Fordham International Law Journal* 15 (1991), 997–1030, 1005, 1017.

7 David Boucher, *The Limits of Ethics in International Relations: Natural Law, Natural Rights and Human Rights in Transition* (Oxford: Oxford University Press, 2009), 112.

8 For Grotius, natural law's obligatory character rested on the dual foundation of right reason and God, with each independently of the other able to carry the weight. The dual foundation in Grotius' natural law theory, and his intentionally ambiguous account of God's role in it, has given rise to much speculation about whether his political thought contributed to the secularisation of natural law. This is the now infamous 'impious hypothesis' controversy. Richard Tuck has endorsed Grotius as the instigator of a modern secular natural law, seeing his anti-scepticism as paving the way for modern natural rights theories. See Richard Tuck, 'The "Modern" Theory of Natural Law', in Anthony Pagden (ed.), *The Languages of Political Theory in Early-Modern Europe* (Cambridge: Cambridge University Press, 1987), 99–119; Richard Tuck, *The Rights of War and Peace: Political Thought and the International Order from Grotius to Kant* (Oxford: Oxford University Press, 1999). See also Knud Haakonssen, 'Hugo Grotius and the History of Political Thought', *Political Theory* 13 (1985), 239–265. For criticism, see especially Brian Tierney, *The Idea of Natural Rights. Studies on Natural Rights, Natural Law and Church Law 1150–1625* (Cambridge: Wm. B. Eerdmans Publishing Company, 2001). See also Camilla Boisen, 'Hugo Grotius', in David Boucher and Paul Kelly (eds.), *Political Thinkers. From Socrates to the Present* (Oxford: Oxford University Press, 2017), 196–213; Boucher, *Limits of Ethics*.

9 Alberico Gentili, *Three Books on the Law of War* (1612), tr. J.C. Rolfe (Oxford: Clarendon Press, 1933), 1.9.65.

the Law of Nations by Reasoning'.[10] If we are to take Rachel's statement to be accurate, what are the implications for enforcement? As we shall see, conceptualising the law of nations as a secondary law of nature meant that a *right* was furnished for intervening and punishing crimes pertaining to the law of nature, but not an *obligation per se*. This is particularly evident in Grotius' writings, who took his cue from his Spanish scholastic predecessors.

Francisco de Vitoria (1492–1546), took seriously the jurisprudential challenge that the discovery of the new world presented for conventional international jurisprudence. He sought to establish the rights and obligations of political communities,[11] not in any real 'communitarian' sense as we might understand today, that is, that these political communities could somehow override the common rights and duties of mankind. What Vitoria did was to anchor the *ius gentium* on solid Thomist ground, where the unity of states was framed, not in a contractual way, but instead as 'organic communities' informed by natural law.[12] Vitoria's arguments rested upon his idea that universal rights took priority over those specific communities, and that the violation of those rights justified the legitimate intervention of a foreign state to restore them and, if necessary, punish the wrongdoers.[13] Here, one of the problems Vitoria sought to address was that of authority, that is, of the *ius gentium* having the force of law. Vitoria's message was clear: our rights and obligations go beyond the community we live in. There are certain mutual obligations attached, but more than that, in this universal moral community of rights, the rulers of states had a duty to intervene as representatives of the whole international community. Such duties were sanctioned by the *ius gentium*. Vitoria noted that 'enemies remain subject to the ruler as to their own proper *judge*',[14] and asserted that:

> the prince has the authority not only over his own people but also over foreigners to force them to abstain from harming others; this is his right by the law of nations and the authority of the whole world. Indeed, it seems he has this right by natural law: the world could not exist unless

10 Samuel Rachel, *Dissertations on the Law of Nature and of Nations* (1676), tr. J.P. Bate (Washington, DC: Carnegie Institution, 1916), Chapter 25, 180.

11 Beate Jahn, *The Cultural Construction of International Relations. The Invention of the State of Nature* (New York: Palgrave, 2000), 67.

12 Schall, 'Natural Law and the Law of Nations', 1006, footnote 20.

13 Boucher, *Limits of Ethics*, 167.

14 Jose Manuel de Aguilar, 'The Law of Nations and the Salamanca School of Theology'. *Thomist – A Speculative Quarterly Review* 9 (1946), 186–221.

> some men had the power and authority to deter the wicked by force from doing harm to the good and the innocent.[15]

Not only did Vitoria emphasise that there was a duty to intervene, but also that natural law provided the jurisdiction and the moral foundation for such interventions. Although there was a strong moral basis for such obligations under natural law, which extended to the *ius gentium*, or was sanctioned by it, it were nevertheless, as Suárez was to make more explicit, imperfect obligations that came under the concessive or permissive natural law.

For the Italian jurist Alberico Gentili (1552–1608), the law of nations comprised those rules or standards which all, or the majority, of (civilised) nations employed with regard to regulating their relations. The laws derived from natural reason, which dictated what was just and right and was therefore not accidental. As unwritten law it resembled a custom and was established in the same way. Gentili wanted to say that such customary unanimity could not fail to be recognised in the same way that all races of men were agreed to the existence of God.[16] Gentili's methodological approach was to subject the law of nations to the test of natural law. However, save a few instances, he did not elaborate on its content. Instead, he was at pains to disassociate it from *a priori* methods, and sought to secure the law of nations in common sense and justice and harmony of humankind. Even though the law of nations had its basis in natural reason and natural law, it had an element of positive law as well, because of the emphasis put on its establishment by custom and general agreement. Here, Gentili related the law of nations to the universal community of humankind. Nations comprised of something he termed *societas gentium*, a community of states. The law of nations was to regulate and embody the rights and obligations that existed among nations. This meant that both non-Catholic as well as non-Christian nations were included in the *societas gentium*, meaning that infidels were afforded the common courtesies under the law of nations such as diplomatic immunity and treaty-making powers.[17]

The implications of Gentili's conceptualisation of the law of nations were far-reaching. Let me illustrate this with an example: by relating the obligation to acquire 'waste lands' to the universal community of mankind, instead of the later common practice of exclusively to nations, Gentili could use this idea of a world community to justify colonial conquest of the New World, the suggestion

15 Francisco de Vitoria, *Political Writings*, Anthony Pagden and Jeremy Lawrence (eds.) (Cambridge: Cambridge University Press, 1991), 305.

16 Gentili, *Three Books on the Law of War*, 1.1.11.

17 Boucher, *Limits of Ethics*, 201.

being that there was a natural right conferred to the Europeans to occupy land by means of possession.[18] The obligations which this 'world community' conferred on people came from the law of nature, which gave them their moral basis, but was in turn regulated by the law of nations. Nevertheless, these obligations remained imperfect: saving the innocents from unnecessary violence or making reparations towards the broken bond of humanity was something we should do, but only if it did not cause unnecessary injury towards ourselves.

Francisco Suárez (1548–1617), the Spanish Jesuit theologian, took it upon himself to present a detailed study of the law of nature and the law of nations for the purpose of proving a clear distinction between the two systems of law.[19] He was only mildly successful in his endeavours.[20] However, his work on the justice of war is quite enlightening. War, for Suárez, was not a moral necessity. If a precept was said to be morally necessary, it needed to be prescribed by natural law, a criterion war failed to meet. War could, however, be deemed as a righteous act. In this way, war fell under the requirements of the law of nations because Suárez understood it as encompassing the actual exercise of the law of nature's concessive principle. From the concessional law of nature, some natural laws came into play only as a consequence of certain human acts. The obvious example that Suárez gave was that the precepts of natural law that forbade theft only came into play on the presupposition that private property had been instituted by human acts. Another was that we have a moral right to action on the basis of the precepts of natural law; however, the exercise of such a right has its basis in human agreement – enacted by human will.

What Suárez presented was a natural law that furnished the opportunity for rational agents to choose a right action freely. Natural law was both indicative of what was in itself good, and of that which was in itself evil. But it was also 'preceptive' in the sense that it created obligations in human beings to do good and avoid evil. As Knud Haakonssen notes, Suárez's natural law 'reflects the two inseparable sides of God's nature, namely his rational judgement of good and evil and his will prescribing the appropriate behaviour'.[21] This duality deserves further explication.

---

18 Gentili, *Three Books on the Law of War*, 1.1.11.

19 Francisco Suárez, *Selections from Three Works*, tr. Gwladys L. Williams, A. Brown and J. Waldron (Oxford: Clarendon Press, 1944), 2.17.8.

20 For an excellent account of Suárez's conception of the law of nations see John Doyle, 'Francisco Suárez and The Law of Nations', in Mark W. Janis and Carolyn Evans (eds.), *Religion and International Law* (Leiden and Boston: Martinus Nijhoff, 1999), 103–120.

21 Knud Haakonssen, *Natural Law and Moral Philosophy. From Grotius to the Scottish Enlightenment* (Cambridge: Cambridge University Press, 1996), 22. For further discussion on this, see Haakonssen's section on Suárez in this work. He also addresses the paradox usually

Suárez understood the law of nations as encompassing the actual exercise of the concessive principles of the law of nature. These concessive principles were imperfect obligations under natural law, but, when acted upon, they were rights exercised through the customs of all civilised nations. What Suárez was seeking to emphasise was the necessary connection between concessive and prohibitive – 'preceptive' – law. This point becomes obvious in the case of war. The existence of a precept prohibiting aggressive warfare must be a presupposition of the existence of the right to make war itself. In this context, the right of defence not only results in the permission to make war, but it is also an obligation to make use of that permission. As Suárez states 'One might say that the permission or concession [...] falls under the *jus gentium*; while, on the other hand, the precepts attendant [there upon] are part of preceptive natural law'.[22] Thus, just war grounded in self-defence pertains to natural law.

Suárez pointed out that war has its foundation 'in some kind of human agreement'. There was an obligation arising from that agreement that demanded good faith and justice as stipulated by natural law. Suárez concluded that the actual use of such powers was not in fact law but rather the effect of law: 'for the law under discussion does not spring from such use; on the contrary, the use has its source in that law'.[23] The law Suárez was referring to was law as a moral right (*ius reale*). In this way, the *ius gentium* was the moral right of peoples. In affirmation of this distinction, he contended that 'the *jus gentium* is not so much indicative of what is [inherently] evil, as it is constitutive of evil. Thus, it does not forbid evil acts on the grounds that they are evil, but renders [certain] acts evil by prohibiting them'.[24]

Having elucidated Suárez' conception of the law of nations, let us turn to how Suárez envisaged states' moral obligations of enforcing violations of natural law. It is clear that his understanding of just war depended not upon absolute moral conclusions; if this were so, then all wars would pertain to natural law. Suárez argued that war belonged to those concessions of the law of nature that conditions the common good of men, but were, nevertheless, not absolutely necessary for the welfare of societies. Just war was not a moral necessity, but belonged in the realm of moral expediency. Warfare in general depended

ascribed to Voluntarism: 'If natural law were simply a matter of God's will without need for reasons, then it would in principle be possible that God could allow humanity to hate him' (21). However, to think that God is the object of hatred must surely be a contradiction in terms? For this, see especially footnote 10.

22 Suárez, *Selections from Three Works*, 2.17.6.

23 *Ibid.*, 7.

24 *Ibid.*, 2.19.2.

on the imposition of a free will and, in this way, it was a moral right adjudicated by the law of nations.

What does this mean for the case of just wars and military intervention? We have an obligation to prevent the suffering of innocents and the violations of natural law, but those obligations are imperfect under natural law. In effect, Suárez grounded the law of nations on the principle that law could be permissive as well as preceptive. Suárez advanced a natural law that did not consist only of restraints on power, commands and prohibitions. It also defined an area of permissiveness where agents were free to choose the right action. For example, ships from the various nations of the world were free to seek shelter in any port, but they might not wish to avail themselves of the right to do so. Grotius would later draw on Suárez's distinction between concessive and prescriptive natural law principles.

For all the conceptual confusion in early modern jurisprudence in attempting to differentiate the law of nature and the law of nations, what gradually became defined was a set of legal principles for punitive actions in case gross violations of natural law were taking place. Correlative with this right was the imperfect obligation to prevent such violations. However, prescribing who should undertake such actions proved challenging, and moreover, most of the natural jurists stipulated the success of such interventions as a necessary condition. For Vitoria, the amount of good to be attained had to be weighed against the potential harm caused by punitive or 'humanitarian' interventions. Intervention to save the innocents, or punish violators of natural law afforded a right to do so; and a choice not to. Grotius, as we will see next, was more explicit than his predecessors in insisting that individuals and states have a natural right to punish perpetrators who contravened the law of nature.

3 International Punishment? Grotius and Pufendorf

Punitive wars were a common feature in just war theory, and had been since the medieval period. Gentili recognised states' right to punish as a measure of self-preservation. The right to punish became especially utilised in the juridical writings of Hugo Grotius (1583–1645), who ultimately saw war as an instrument of right.[25] It 'is undertaken for the Sake of Peace […]',[26] where just *wars*

25 Edward Dumbauld, *The Life and Legal Writings of Hugo Grotius* (Oklahoma: University of Oklahoma Press, 1969), 73.

26 Hugo Grotius, *The Rights of War and Peace* (Indianapolis: Liberty Fund, 2005), 1.1.1.

'are usually defined to be those, whereby Injuries are revenged'.[27] His primary aim was to formulate a set of universal rights and duties that would secure peace by constraining states in their internal and external relations. Essential for Grotius to upholding international order and peace was the right of punishment, which was a central tenet for his just war theory.[28]

The power of punishment was derived from natural law, which furnished states' natural rights to punish violations against nature, including a variety of offences such as cannibalism and oppression of innocents. Grotius' assertion that states had a right and an obligation to punish transgressions of natural law was derived from his understanding of the law of nature and how it was prosecuted and enforced in the state of nature.[29] The correlation was the individual's right to self-defence and self-preservation, which necessitated the right to punish after transferring those rights to states. On the universal jurisdiction to punish, Grotius remarked that 'it is so much more honourable, to revenge other People's Injuries rather than their own, by as much as it is more to be feared, lest out of a Sense of their own Sufferings, they either exceed the just Measure of Punishment, or, at least, prosecute their Revenge with Malice'.[30] Nevertheless, proportionality always featured as an essential part of Grotius' just war theory. Grotius harboured the idea that all states had a right and a duty to punish other states for violations committed against the law of nature. In fact, war ought not to be undertaken unless it was for the enforcement of rights.[31]

It is important to distinguish what category of rights Grotius was conceptualising. Grotius had a conception of a right, or *ius*, as something we possess, a moral quality or power. Grotius wrote '[i]n which Sense Right is a moral quality annexed to the Person, enabling him to have, or to do, something justly'.[32] This kind of right was a subjective right. Subjective rights belonged intrinsically to the individual and they were a power or a force that enabled him to seek out

27 *Ibid.*, 2.20.8 [Grotius' italics].

28 Pärtel Piirimäe, 'Alberico Gentili's Doctrine of Defensive War and its Impact on Seventeenth-Century Normative Views', in Benedict Kingsbury and Benjamin Straumann (eds.), *The Roman Foundations of the Law of Nations: Alberico Gentili and the Justice of Empire* (Oxford: Oxford University Press, 2010), 187–209, 202. I have explored some of the following points of Grotius' theory of punishment elsewhere: see Camilla Boisen and David Boucher, 'The Medieval and Early Modern Legacy of Rights: The Rights to Punish and to Property', in William Bain (ed.), *Medieval Foundations of International Relations* (New York: Routledge, 2016), 148–165.

29 Alexis Blane and Benedict Kingsbury, 'Punishment and the *ius post bellum*', in Kingsbury and Straumann, *Roman Foundations of the Law of Nations*, 241–265, 247.

30 Grotius, *The Rights of War and Peace*, 2.20.40.

31 *Ibid.*, *Prolegomena*, 25.

32 *Ibid.*, 1.1.4.

justice for himself, or for the collective. Objective rights, on the other hand, were granted by law, whether civil or divine. The distinction between objective and subjective rights and how it pertained to the secularisation of natural law has been subject of much debate. Grotius has been the victim of scholarly efforts to place him as the secularising turning point of the tradition.[33] This notwithstanding, it might be problematic, as Knud Haakonssen has suggested, to perceive the right to punish wrongdoers as a moral quality in the sense that it cannot be regarded as a moral power in the same way in which man holds other rights such as the right to self-defence and the right to property.[34]

Grotius attempted to remedy this problem. He focused on the powers or entitlements that arose from subjective rights and their corresponding obligations. As such, he distinguished between questions of entitlement (rights) and questions of worthiness (aptitudes). 'This moral quality when perfect', Grotius noted, 'is called by us a Faculty; when imperfect, an Aptitude'.[35] Rights for Grotius were a matter of what he termed expletive justice and conformed to the basic requirements of the social order by upholding the rights of others. Moral claims, or aptitudes, fell into the domain of what he called attributive justice, and flowed from all 'those Virtues that are beneficial to others, as Liberality, Mercy, and prudent Administration of Government'.[36] Expletive justice required to follow the law, whereas attributive justice afforded a space where one may exercise one's higher virtues.[37] The central point underlying this distinction was Grotius' denial that juridical rights and duties were derived directly from the requirement of the common good. The political and legal obligations stopped short of securing individuals the ability to be virtuous and did not require enforcing what virtuous behaviour required.[38] Rights for Grotius, then, were in the domain of liberty, where one might pursue one's self-interest. They were not to be seen as directly related to the requirements of the common good, because these requirements might change over time by convention.[39]

33 See supra, footnote 7.

34 Haakonssen, 'Hugo Grotius and the History of Political Thought', 242.

35 Grotius, *Rights of War and Peace,* 1.1.4.

36 *Ibid.*, 1.1.8.

37 Jeremy S. Geddert, 'Beyond Strict Justice: Hugo Grotius on Punishment and Natural Right(s)', *The Review of Politics* 76 (2014), 559–588, 581. See also Mark Somos excellent account of Grotius's theory of virtue as an indicator of the intricate relationship between religion and law in 'Virtue' *Cambridge Companion to Hugo Grotius*, eds. Edited by Randall Lesaffer and Janne Nijman (Cambridge: Cambridge University Press, 2019 forthcoming).

38 Camilla Boisen and Matthew C. Murray, 'Dignity, Sociability and Capability Exploring Nussbaum's Interpretation of Grotius' in Boisen and Murray (eds.), *Distributive Justice Debates in Political and Social Thought* (London: Routledge, 2016), 88.

39 Grotius, *Rights of War and Peace*, 1.1.4-9. See also Nigel E. Simmonds, 'Grotius and Pufendorf', in Steven Nadler (ed.), *A Companion to Early Modern Philosophy* (Oxford: Blackwell Publishing, 2002), 210–224, 215.

The essence of punishment took into account a notion of aptitude, which by way of definition 'doth not contain in it a Right strictly so called, but gives Occasion to it'.[40]

The moral requirements that arose from human natural sociability could not furnish states with absolute obligations to intervene when natural law was grossly violated precisely because such obligations were not 'thick' enough. Nature could not determine to whom punishment was directly appropriated, which remained at the core of Grotius' idea of enforcement. While the law of nature dictated that those free of crimes might exact punishment,[41] it did not determine to whom punishment was directly due. For Grotius, then, all states had a right and an imperfect duty, meaning that they might or might not act upon the obligation to punish other states for violations committed against the law of nature. Having a right did not necessarily imply that it should be exercised in all given situations. Grotius erred on the side of caution and warned of the dangers of using wars of punishments as mere pretexts, such as those under the guise of civilising barbarous peoples.[42]

Since the permissive right to punish violations of natural law took centre stage in Grotius' understanding of international justice, Grotius' underlying assertion was that punishment needed to have a deterrent effect. This was where a Grotian conception of punishment as a moral power might be considered. Citing Plato, Grotius said:

> No wise Man punishes an Offender, because he hath offended, but that he may not offend again. For what is once done cannot be recalled, but what is to come may be prevented. Therefore all Punishments have regard to the future, and he that punisheth should not be angry, but provident.[43]

To deter someone from consorting with animals, for example, would be to prevent him or her from committing a mortal sin. It was, as Grotius said, that 'when one Man punisheth another man equal to him in Nature he ought to propose some End to himself'. We do not punish 'for the Sake of Punishment, but of some Good'.[44] For Grotius, then, punishment was exacted as precautionary, rather than as retaliatory or vengeful. And while it could be said that the permissive right to punish was subjective, a possession, or a power, the

40 Grotius, *Rights of War and Peace*, 2.20.2.

41 *Ibid*, 2.20.3.

42 *Ibid*, 2.20.41.

43 *Ibid.*, 2.20.4.

44 *Ibid.*, 2.20.4 (Grotius's italics).

command, and indeed the whole rationale, nevertheless stemmed from natural law and ultimately from God.

Samuel von Pufendorf (1632–1694) outright denied the existence of a positive *ius gentium* distinct from the law of nature. States were universally subject to the law of nature only. There were of course rights based upon treaties and also on costums but they were only valid between the states that had concluded these treaties and customs. States might at any time renounce them: this would be an immoral act, but only insofar as they violated the law of nature that governed agreements between sovereigns. It would not be possible for a custom gradually to assume the force of law. Pufendorf presumed that all law had an author, and, in order to qualify properly as law, it also needed to be enforceable. This was the Hobbessian element that many have attributed to Pufendorf, at least as far as human positive law was concerned. Law required a sovereign to enact and enforce it and entailed the 'binding of a superior'.[45] For Pufendorf – going beyond Hobbes –, both natural law and human positive law satisfied this criterion; the law of nations did not; and contrary to Grotius he denied that international punishment could have any validity. Punishment would require a supreme sovereign and was therefore only applicable in civil law. Because the force inflicting 'punishment' in the international context did not emanate from an authoritative superior, states could not have the right to punish, but they might have a just cause for war. Only God, the author of natural law, had the right to punish transgressions of natural law at the international level. Because God worked in mysterious ways, and not according to set timetables, it was almost impossible to correlate God's punishment with the crime. It might, for example, be administered many years after the crime.[46]

Pufendorf was especially wary of the sort of arguments for war that justified reforming the cultural practices of the American Indians. As he contended:

> [b]y having said that punishment is imposed 'by the authority of the state', we separate it from those evils to which men are exposed involuntary in war, or a fight, and from the stubbornness or open injury of another [...]. The power to exact penalties is a part of sovereignty, and so no one can impose upon another a penalty, properly speaking, unless he has sovereignty over him.[47]

45 Samuel von Pufendorf, *Of the Law of Nature and Nations, Eight Books* (1672), tr. C.H. Oldfather and W.A. Oldfather, intro. Walter Simons (Oxford: Clarendon Press, 1934), 1.2.6.

46 *Ibid.*, 2.3.23. See also, Boisen and Boucher, 'Medieval and Early Modern Legacy of Rights'.

47 Pufendorf, *Of the Law of Nature and Nations*, 8.3.4-7.

Yet, Pufendorf's denial of the law of nations does leave us wondering: if the idea is inconceivable that implied agreements between states would somehow entail perfect obligations, what sort of 'enforcement' is he prescribing? States for Pufendorf were in the state of nature because they had no earthly sovereign nor had they agreed to a social contract. Obligations in the state of nature were imperfect because there was no temporal supreme sovereign to enforce them; nevertheless, they were just as morally obligatory as perfect obligations were enforceable in civil law.

Neither was what we might term 'customary international law' enough to demand obligation. Such customs would entail observances due to the mere consent of people and not of the law of nations. They only appeared to be observed by a certain tacit agreement, especially in warfare – which Pufendorf held to be the origins of that sort of 'customary law'. The interest and security of nations did not lie in customs, but in 'the observance of the law of nature, which is much more sacred'.[48] If the law of nature was intact, mankind, Pufendorf stipulated, had no need of the law of nations.

The logic of Pufendorf's argument rests on the notion that irrespective of its presumed authority, a custom's origin was important. If any custom was 'based upon the natural law, without a doubt far more is done to give it dignity than if its origin is based upon the simple agreement of nations'.[49] The ingenious move of Pufendorf was to make states morally subject to the law of nature, thereby cementing the view that there was a universal moral order that demanded commitment from states. Using the framework that Hobbes had laid out for him, natural law had a sovereign capable of enforcing it, enabling Pufendorf to argue that natural law was as morally obligatory as positive law.[50] He, then, in his own distinct way, denied the arbitrariness of morality by contending that it was simply not a matter of convention between states.

Samuel Rachel, a contemporary of Pufendorf, explicitly objected to Pufendorf's contention that not all nations were expected to be bound by the law of nations. This objection, Rachel argued, consisted of stressing that the rules of the law of nations could not be traced back to specific treaties. The mere proposition that a tacit consensus existed was sufficient for something to become accepted and observed as law, regardless of the uncertainty of its origin. Rachel thereby relied upon the force of customs as law on the basis of their authority

48 *Ibid.*, 2.3.23.

49 *Ibid.*

50 Camilla Boisen and David Boucher, 'Hobbes and the Subjection of International Relations to Law and Morality', in Raia Prokhovnik and Gabriella Slomp (eds.), *International Political Theory After Hobbes. Analysis, Interpretation and Orientation* (New York: Palgrave Macmillan, 2011), 81–101, 92–93.

and not their enforcement.[51] This problem of legal authority and enforcement in international law was, as we shall see next, something Edmund Burke tried to overcome.

4 Edmund Burke and International Moral Obligation

Regardless of how it came to be expressed in early modern jurisprudence, natural law remained the moral basis of international justice. Once men had been separated into corporate nations it could never be applied directly and abstractly, but always indirectly through the justice of the various civil laws, customs, conventions, institutions and historical circumstances of each nation. This understanding of natural law and the law of nations became even more evident for eighteenth-century thinkers such as Christian Wolff and Edmund Burke, who took the necessary step to separate the two systems of law. As a more positivistic international law emerged, the Grotian attribution of states' right to punish was gradually inundated.

The Swiss jurist Emer de Vattel (1714–1767) denied states the right to punish other nations for serious breaches of natural law. States were perceived as naturally equal, and it was therefore to be presumed that each side had just cause for believing itself to be wronged. The voluntary law of nations could not make right what was naturally wrong: 'It must never be forgotten', Vattel argues,

> that *this voluntary Law of Nations*, established from the necessity and for the avoidance of greater evils, *does not confer upon him whose cause is unjust any true rights capable of justifying his conduct and appeasing his conscience, but merely makes his conduct legal in the sight of men, and exempts him from punishment.*[52]

Vattel stressed that Grotius' mistake lay in his confusion that the freedom attributed to individuals and sovereign states somehow gave rise to a right to punish crimes against nature. A state's right to punish only existed against those who injured it. Any action beyond this would violate the autonomy of the moral person of the sovereign state. Vattel warned that an unsubstantiated right to punish crimes against nature gave states ruled by ambitious men too

51 Rachel, *Dissertations on the Law of Nature and of Nations*, 85–88.

52 Emer de Vattel, *The Law of Nations, or Principles of the Law of Nature, Applied to the Conduct and Affairs of Nations and Sovereigns*, Béla Kapossy and Richard Whatmore (eds.) (Indianapolis: Liberty Fund, 2008), 3.12.190 [Vattel's italics].

easy a pretext for waging war and 'opens the door to all the passions of zealots and fanatics'.[53]

Edmund Burke (1729–1797) departed from the known discourse on the law of nations explored so far by developing an understanding of the law of nations that was based almost wholly on the common practices among states. Burke vehemently advocated in favour of the defeat of Revolutionary France and the restitution of the *ancien regime*. His anti-revolutionary objectives required intervention in France, the justification for which he found in the common law of Europe, which he presented as 'customary' law of nations of sorts. Instead of basing his case for intervention on traditional foundations such as natural law and its modern derivative natural rights, Burke came to argue that the French Revolution had no precedent in the prescriptions of constitutional law, nor in the law of nations.[54]

Burke envisaged states going beyond their mere geographical entities. They were 'moral essence[s]',[55] incorporating a sense of continuity based on prescription, historical circumstance and divinity. What sustained the order among the members of the European international society was the mutual fundamental social, political and cultural sympathy that extended across sovereign borders.[56] Europe was 'virtually one great state having the same basis of general law, with some diversity of provincial customs and local establishments', but nevertheless 'agreeing in the fundamental parts'.[57] He termed this vision of a European international society the 'Commonwealth of Europe', in

53 *Ibid.*, 2.1.7. In this cursory account of Vattel's law of nations, I am not attempting to link Vattel's treatise with a modern account of positivism. Some excellent recent studies have shown why such a view is problematic: see Emmanuel Jouannet, *Vattel and the Emergence of Classic International Law*, tr. G. Bellande, R. Howse (Oxford: Hart, 2009); Vincent Chetail and Peter Haggenmacher (eds.), *Vattel's International Law from a XXIst Century Perspective* (Leiden: Brill, 2011).

54 It is almost impossible to understate the centrality that historians such as Paul Lucas, but above all J.G.A. Pocock, have had in presenting Burke as a common law theorist and recovering his reliance on the common law tradition of Coke, Hale and Blackstone. See Paul Lucas, 'On Edmund Burke's Doctrine of Prescription; or, An Appeal from the New to the Old Lawyers', *Historical Journal* 11 (1968), 35–63 and John G.A. Pocock, 'Burke and the Ancient Constitution: A Problem in the History of Ideas', *Historical Journal* 3 (1960), 125–143; John G.A. Pocock, *The Ancient Constitution and the Feudal Law. A Study of English Historical Thought in the Seventeenth Century.* (Cambridge: Cambridge University Press, 1987).

55 Edmund Burke, 'Letters on a Regicide Peace I', in Edmund Burke (ed.), *Works* (London: Henry Frowde for Oxford University Press, 1907), 163.

56 Ibid., 86.

57 Ibid., 156.

which these thoughts on diversity and unity came together.[58] Shared within the Commonwealth were common customs, legal heritage and 'manners', and Burke could accentuate these cultural similitudes throughout Europe as forming part of the long-standing tradition of the Christian European civilisation which its shareholders should dedicate themselves to preserving.

In Burke's view, manners were all-encompassing, and were ultimately more important than laws. It was the deep bond of affection between the European states, arising from their similitude, which led to this deep-rooted unity among them. To this he famously stated:

> Men are not tied together to one another by papers and seals. They are led to associate by resemblances, by conformities, by sympathies [...] Nothing is too strong a tie of amity between nation and nation as correspondence in laws, customs, manners, and habits of life. They have more than the force of treaties in themselves. They are obligations written in the heart ... The secret, but irrefragable bond of habitual intercourse, holds them [men] together, even when their perverse and litigious nature sets them to equivocate, scuffle, and fight about the terms of their written obligations.[59]

War was still a reality, but the potential for animosity between states was ameliorated by these common sympathies and shared sentiments, bringing about certain equanimity.[60] As such, Burke premised the European international order on conformity with the standards of European civilisation.[61]

Burke's conceptualisation of the law of nations applied distinctively to the Commonwealth of Europe. It was from his idea of 'similitude' that his common law theory was articulated. The 'publick law of Europe' was derived from the common practices of the European states as 'ancient conventions' and was constituted as customary law. It had a 'kind of connexion in virtue of ancient relations'.[62] He followed the legal tradition of William Blackstone, who held that the common law of England regarding life, liberty, and property was inevitably more binding than any statute of King or Parliament.[63] Common law theory was given a distinctively historical force not embedded in universal rational

---

58 David P. Fidler and Jennifer M. Welsh. *Empire and Community. Edmund Burke's Writings and Speeches on International Relations* (Boulder: Westview Press, 1999), 48–49.

59 Burke, 'Letters on a Regicide Peace I', 155–156.

60 Boucher, *Political Theories of International Relations*, 320.

61 Welsh, *Edmund Burke and International Relations*, 74, 80–81.

62 Burke, 'Letters on a Regicide Peace III', 260.

63 Edmund Burke, 'Reflections on the Revolution in France' in Burke (ed.), *Works*, 168.

principles but rather in national custom. Using prescription as his model of thought, 'international customary law', as Burke understood the law of nations to be, or the 'Public Law of Europe' as he termed it, was produced according to the same sort of process as common law. Common law was common and immemorial and handed down through generations by use and experience. Common law's authority stemmed from its perpetual usage and in its practice, public participation and acceptance lay its validity. Thus, its 'goodness' referred to its validity, legality and authoritative status as well as the wisdom, justice and the reasonableness of the custom.[64]

Burke understood the European law of nations as conforming to the English common law. For instance, in writing on the balance of power, which formed a key aspect of his understanding of the law of nations, he noted that it 'had been ever assumed as the known common law of Europe at all times, and by all powers'.[65] Burke regarded common law as holding a foundational status for the customary law of the Commonwealth of Europe, in that it confirmed, affirmed and maintained social unity, but did not create it. The critical notion here, as the seventeenth-century jurist Matthew Hale articulated, was not one of legitimacy being sought in the origins and ends of customs, but in the continuous and present usage and the acceptance and practice of rules, making common law an important form of social solidarity.[66] The legitimacy of customs was something that resonated with Burke, and he particularly appealed to this spirit of social solidarity in his crusade against revolutionary France. Burke's understanding of common law was consistent with his insistence on the diverse autonomy of states; as such autonomy was not based on any particular conception of the good but rather acted as a means of coordination. Hence, it was based on collective experience and not on fiat.

In the traditions of common law theory, Burke regarded the English constitution – and the relationships of state power defined by it – as ancient custom by arguing that 'our constitution is a prescriptive constitution [...] it is a constitution whose sole authority is, that it has existed time out of mind [...]. Prescription is the most solid of all titles, not only to property, but, which is to secure that property, to government'.[67] Burke used prescription both in a

64 Gerald J. Postema, *Bentham and the Common Law Tradition* (Oxford: Clarendon Press, 1986), 3–7.

65 Burke, 'Letters on a Regicide Peace III', 259.

66 Matthew Hale, *The History of the Common Law of England* (Chicago: University of Chicago Press, 1971), 40–44.

67 Edmund Burke, 'Speech on Reform of Representation in the House of Commons (June 1784)', in Edmund Burke (ed.), *The Speeches of the Right Honourable Edmund Burke* (Dublin: James Duffy, 1853), 407–408.

juridical and a moral sense. It was through presumption that people obeyed political authority.[68] Burke spoke to the fortitude of common law, saying, '[t]here is a sort of presumption against novelty, drawn out of a deep consideration of human nature and human affairs [....]', alluding to the unnaturalness of the revolutionary dogma.[69] Burke's notion of 'humanity' assumed people's mutual exchanges were to be regulated by just precepts. Human beings for Burke were made to exist as communities and the authoritative task of the common law was to ensure the corporate pursuit of common goods.

What then resonated in Burke's thought was the idea that custom was the primary source of law. The authority to order according to the common good rested with the people as a collective whole and expressed the common reason of the community.[70] For Burke, this idea of common reason *was* the objective rational normative order embedded in the customs and rules of society. He thereby opposed Hobbes and Pufendorf, who had argued that customs and precedents had no particular authority unless so accorded by the sovereign. They believed that customs could only have authoritative status insofar as validated by natural reason, meaning the natural reason of the sovereign.[71] Burke, on the other hand, saw reason as embedded in the precedent of collective custom, rather than in the creative and potentially disruptive power of a single will. Edward Coke's distinction between the ordinary faculty of reason, 'natural reason', and the special reason of law or rather reason *within* law, which he termed 'artificial reason', underlines Burke's understanding of the legitimacy of collective custom. The collective good of society, and the law that is instituted to protect it, is not the result of philosophical reasoning but rather the accumulation and refinement of collective experience. This concept of law is essentially Burkean.

For Pocock it became clear that the foundations of Burke's legal thoughts originated in the common law theory of the late sixteenth century.[72] According to Pocock, Burke's perennial appeal to 'the wisdom of the ages' was conceptually an articulation of the idea of Coke's 'artificial reason'. When Burke

68 Boucher, *Political Theories of International Relations*, 318.

69 Burke, 'Letters on a Regicide Peace I', 160.

70 Postema, *Bentham and the Common Law Tradition* 1986, 45–46.

71 *Ibid.*, 47–48.

72 Pocock, *The Ancient Constitution and the Feudal Law*, 35–36. Pocock notes that common lawyers moved beyond the seeming tension between law as custom and law being in constant change by believing that common law, and with it the constitution, was immemorial. The concept of custom is in fact ambiguous: being in constant adaption it will give rise to ideas that are historical. It is also possible to regard it as that which has been retained throughout; its authority lies in the fact that it has survived unchanged (37).

contended that the law of nations had been established by consent, it was exactly this ancient consent embodied within the law as 'artificial reason' upon which he was expounding; it was in 'our hearts' that the spirit of immemorial law was laid.[73] He reasoned that the constitution and therefore the law of nations had no original principles; it was immemorial and prescriptive, and it was the ancient usage that necessarily legitimated the present state of affairs. Burke, then, appealed to the ancient customs and rules of the Commonwealth of Europe, which was itself legitimised by these customs upholding it. Although the common law theory that Burke presented had a particularly British context, he saw an explicit analogy between the Ancient Constitution and European common law, which was to shape his particular view of the law of nations.

With his underlying belief in the Commonwealth of Europe regulated by customary law, Burke's conception of the law of nations was distinct from the early modern jurists we encountered previously. Although Burke drew on Vattel for authority in his revolutionary writings, his conception of the law of nations and its application was distinct exactly because it was grounded on customs and manners rather than relying on abstract principles of natural law.[74] Vattel had argued that the law of nations was an application of natural law to the moral person of the state in its mutual relations with other states. He had categorised it into the necessary and voluntary law of nations, the latter effectively constituting positive international law.[75] While Burke pursued symmetry between the individual and the nation, unlike Vattel and Grotius, the individual was not used as an abstract analogy to an equally abstract conception of the state. Burke instead emphasised the idea of the civil social man. Man had a common nature, which was substantially adapted by history, religion, manners, habits, institutions and customs.

Considering nations as moral essences required a prescriptive law of nations to uphold the moral order of the Commonwealth of Europe. The law of nations was not a mere pretence of treaties and conventions. Rather, it was in common jurisprudence that the elements and principles of the law of nations were contained, which Burke declared 'the great ligament of mankind'.[76] He could therefore say that the law of nations was derived from constitutional law:

73 Burke, 'Reflections on the Revolution in France', 21.

74 Emphasising the customary foundations of Burke's conception of the law of nations lends further support to the ultimately unpersuasive task of presenting Burke as a natural law theorist. See also Boisen, 'Triumphing over Evil', pp. 283–286.

75 Vattel, *The Law of Nations*, 11.

76 Burke, 'Letters on a Regicide Peace I', 147.

> It has ever been the method of publick jurists, to draw a great part of analogies on which they form the law of nations from the principles of law which prevail in civil community. Civil laws are not all merely positive. Those which are rather conclusions of legal reason, than matters of statutable provision, belong to universal equity and are universally applicable.[77]

This analogy between civil laws and the law of nations was vital for Burke's justification of intervention in Revolutionary France:

> [t]he right of man to act anywhere according to their pleasure, without moral tie, no such right exists. Men are never in a total state of independence from each other [...]. The *situations* in which men relatively stand produce the rules and principles of that responsibility, and afford directions to produce in exacting it'.[78]

Thus, Burke could argue that the French Revolution had no precedent in the prescriptions of constitutional law nor therefore in the law of nations. 'What in civil society is a ground of action', Burke exclaimed, 'in political society is a ground of war'.[79] The exercise of such jurisdiction was for Burke a matter of moral prudence. The law of nations that Burke conceptualised was an integral part of what he termed 'the law of civil vicinity', which corresponded with his idea of a wider moral international social context – the Commonwealth of Europe. The proximity and habitual association of states subsequently entailed certain rights and responsibilities. In civil law, this was the law of neighbourhood, which was the right of a neighbour to protest when he 'sees a *new erection,* in the nature of nuisance, set up at his door'.[80] Burke applied these precepts of civil law to the relations among states:

> Now where there is no constituted judge, as between independent states there is not, the vicinage itself is the natural judge. It is, preventively, the assertor of its own rights; or remedially, their avenger. Neighbours are presumed to take cognisance of each other's acts [...]. This principle ... is as true of nations as of individual men, [and] has bestowed on the grand

77 Ibid., 159.
78 Ibid., 158.
79 Ibid., 160.
80 Ibid., 159.

> vicinage of Europe a duty to know, and a right to prevent, any capital innovation which may amount to the erection of a dangerous nuisance.[81]

Burke's conception of the law of nations was the abridgement of the authority of customs as law and their enforcement. There was a strict correlation between Burke's idea of the law of vicinity and his insistence on not conceiving of state sovereignty as an absolute value and the guiding principle of order.[82] Sovereignty understood as non-intervention was to Burke a 'false principle' that went against historical precedent, custom and the law of nations itself.[83] He further stated: 'the rule of law, therefore, which comes before the evil, is amongst the very best part of equity, and justifies the promptness of the remedy [...]'.[84]

What did this mean for enforcement? The French Revolution posed a threat against the very foundations of all good and orderly society, and Burke extended his theory of common law into a duty to prevent violations of rights. 'It is one of the greatest objects of human wisdom to mitigate those evils, which we are unable to remove', Burke benevolently declared. He stated: 'Distance of a place does not extinguish the duties or the rights of men'.[85] By appealing to the law of vicinity, he recognised that custom established a specific determination and duty in order to react against this evil in the name of 'good faith and public integrity'.[86] States have an unambiguous obligation to intervene to preserve themselves as members of the Commonwealth of Europe when violations against the customs that underpin the very commonwealth threaten to tear it apart.

Although we find that natural law does not provide the foundation for international order in Burke's writings as it did for Grotius and Vattel, there are nevertheless analogies between Burke's understanding of the common law of Europe and how the early modern jurists based their philosophies of international law on natural law. They are, similarly, foundations upon which injunctions may be based. Janis has argued that 'much of what passed in the traditional law of nations as natural law looks rather like what we know nowadays as general principles of law'.[87] David Boucher has recently suggested that

81 Ibid., 160.

82 Fidler and Welsh, *Empire and Community*, 51.

83 Burke, 'Heads for Consideration on the Present State of Affairs', v, 222.

84 Burke, 'Letters on a Regicide Peace I', 159–160.

85 Ibid., 158.

86 Burke, 'Letters on a Regicide Peace III', 237.

87 Mark W. Janis, *An Introduction to International Law* (New York: Aspen Publishers, 2003), 63.

customary international law functions in a similar way to how natural law used to function, and demonstrates the importance of customary international law in articulating the universal obligations of states and holding them accountable for their actions.[88] For the German jurist and president of the Imperial Court of Justice, Walter Simons (1861–1937), it was 'customary law' that instilled in sovereign states responsibility.[89] This, as I have tried to show, is something that Burke could have agreed with.

During the course of the nineteenth century, attempts were made to place international law on more positivist footing, rejecting its previously held natural law and natural rights base. As such, international law became gradually equated with customary law and state practice.[90] In developing his theory of legal positivism, the British legal philosopher John Austin (1790–1859) reiterated some of Pufendorf's early ideas. Here, he did acknowledge a certain effectiveness of international legal rules but characterised them, however, as being a form of mere 'morality', wanting ultimately to liberate positive law 'from the perennial confusions with the precepts of religion and morality [...]' so 'encouraged by Natural Law thinkers [....]', as H.L.A. Hart noted in his commentary on Austin's *The Province of Jurisprudence Determined.*[91] Pufendorf, on the other hand, would have differed from Austin in believing that the two were not equally obligatory. As for Burke, he would have made sure that both could be equally enforced.

Examining the issue of enforcement has afforded us an opportunity to reflect more critically on Burke's place within the history of international law and the inheritance he created for the nineteenth century. Burke's legal philosophy is situated between two strands of international legal thought – between natural law and contemporary international customary law – occupying, so to speak, both sides of the same coin. By emphasising the force of 'customary international law', Burke does not share a close affinity nor is he a precursor to the sort of international legal positivism that characterised the later nineteenth- and early twentieth century, where international law was gradually equated with the codification of customary law. For once, Burke's unconventional

88 David Boucher, 'The Recognition Theory of Rights, Customary International Law and Human Rights', *Political Studies* 59 (2011), 753–771.

89 Walter Simons, *The Evolution of International Public Law in Europe since Grotius* (New York: William S. Hein, 2004), 73.

90 Boucher, *Limits of Ethics*, 86–87.

91 Herbert L.A. Hart, 'Introduction', in John Austin, *The Province of Jurisprudence Determined and The Uses of the Study of Jurisprudence* (London: Weidenfeld and Nicolson, 1954), x.

understanding of the law of nations as the common law of Europe did not require codification for enactment. On the other hand, basing the right to intervene on natural law or on internationally recognised standards assumes that all mankind hold the potential of being a single community and is therefore subject to the same legal standards. Burke denied the possibility of universally applicable international laws, which are based on the construction of an abstract natural human condition whose principles could justify intervention anywhere. By conceptualising the 'Publick Law of Europe' as the law of nations proper, Burke was touching on the fundamental flaw in other theories of international law that justified intervention as the kind of obligation associated with universality and natural law.

5 Conclusion

Although the early modern jurists recognised a need for enforcement mechanisms in instances of gross violations of natural law, they set different criteria, as a result of which such violations could not warrant arbitrary expediency, or automatic intervention. This is because there was no correlative, absolute duty associated with the right to intervene. The right of intervention was justified by an all-encompassing set of arguments based on the relationship between the law of nations and natural law, which interpreted the law of nations as an aspect of permissive natural law. For Grotius, there were correlative obligations that came from natural law, but they were largely imperfect; that is they did not impose an absolute duty to intervene. Dereliction of these obligations gave certain individuals or states the right, and even the permissive duty, to punish transgressors of natural law for corrective and deterrent purposes.

As a far more positivist age emerged with emphasis on the sovereignty of states, invoking natural law as a basis of international law became obsolete. Discussions about the moral basis of the *ius gentium*, which had characterised the work of the great jurists, were far less explicit in the precursors to the treatises on public international law of the nineteenth century. Although Pufendorf had denied that international law was different or separate from natural law, he argued that the system of moral international rules prescribed thereby, if violated, would not be enforced by states but rather by God. (Although, waiting for divine intervention leaves certain immediacy wanting when expediency is required!)

Burke is distinct in prescribing specific common and customary law foundations, binding the legal and the moral in international law as in domestic law and as a result making any enforcement by means of intervention a corollary. As it is, the problem of enforcing duties to prevent severe human rights violations, such as genocide, is still a distinct problem in today's debates about international justice, and very much tips the scales in favour of non-intervention. This is in spite of a customary international law that stipulates universal humanitarian obligations of states to hold them accountable for their actions. Here, however, claims of legitimacy continue to be entrenched by sovereign state recognition (despite recent attempts at redescribing state sovereignty as 'responsibility'). In this context, the absence of a prescribed universal community upon which to anchor customary norms, such as Burke described, is a plausible explanation as to why modern customary international law is still in search of more solid foundations.

CHAPTER 3

Uneasy Neutrality: Britain and the Greek War of Independence (1821–1832)

Viktorija Jakjimovska

1 Introduction

The nineteenth century brought civil wars to the forefront of the international legal agenda.[1] Hostilities within the boundaries of one state were now seen as a domestic matter except if they constituted a direct threat to the interests of third states, or, more generally, to the equilibrium and repose of Europe.[2] Whereas some states remained impartial spectators of internal hostilities, others were more willing to intervene on behalf of one of the parties to the conflict. Though both attitudes operated under different rules, when third states addressed foreign civil war they consequently transformed its nature. For instance, if a third state proclaimed to be neutral, it treated civil strife as a war proper and thus elevated rebels to the status of lawful belligerents. Further, if states succumbed to the temptation to intervene on behalf of the rebels, they internationalised the conflict. The outcome was a mass of state practice, which greatly influenced the development of international law related to civil war.

Although many scholars writing on the law of civil wars in the nineteenth century take as a starting point the American Civil War (1861–1865), the first half of the nineteenth century saw the elaboration of important legal concepts. It is therefore useful to delve into the legal discussions of this period to see how the great powers first developed practices in the so-called 'semi-peripheral'[3]

1 More than one half of the wars in nineteenth century (55%) involved problems of state creation and destruction of empires: Kalevi J. Holsti, *Peace and War: Armed Conflicts and International Order, 1648–1989* (Cambridge: Cambridge University Press, 1991), 143.

2 Ti-Chiang Chen, *The International Law of Recognition: With Special Reference to Practice in Great Britain and United States* (Praeger: New York, 1951), 303.

3 For discussions on the Ottoman Empire as 'semi-periphery' see: Arnulf Becker Lorca, *Mestizo International Law: A Global Intellectual History, 1842–1933* (Cambridge: Cambridge University Press, 2014); Umut Özsu, 'From the Semi-Civilized State to the 'Emerging Market': Remarks on the International Legal History of the Semi-Periphery', in Ugo Mattei and John D. Haskell

 | DOI:10.1163/9789004412088_004

parts of the world, which later became the object of contestation when used amongst themselves. The Greek war of independence offers a specific context in which the legal outcomes of foreign policy became very visible.

In recent years, the Greek war of independence has received a great amount of attention. All too often, however, scholars have limited the level of analysis to theoretical debates[4] or viewed the civil war through the lenses of diplomatic history making only scattered references to legal questions.[5] Moreover, the few attempts to delve in legal history have been limited to the concept of collective intervention.[6] In particular, scholars have downplayed the role of neutrality, which sits at odds with the fact that nineteenth-century neutrality law played a key role in the development of important civil war concepts such as recognition of belligerency.[7]

The contribution of this chapter relates mainly to the identification and analysis of British legal responses in the context of the Greek war of independence by shedding light on the motives that prompted Britain – as a third state – to create, expand or discard certain rules. The chapter falls into four sections. The first part gives a brief overview of the civil war and an outline of the shifting policy of Great Britain: non-interference, neutrality and collective intervention. The second part focuses on the principle of non-intervention as advocated by Britain and the challenges of pursuing such a policy. The third part is

(eds.), *Research Handbook on Political Economy and Law* (Cheltenham: Edgar Elgar, 2015), 246–260. Certain international legal aspects of the Ottoman Empire are sketched in Umut Özsu, 'Ottoman Empire', in Bardo Fassbender and Anne Peters (eds.), *The Oxford Handbook of the History of International Law* (Oxford: Oxford University Press, 2012), 429–448.

4 Alex Heraclides, 'Humanitarian Intervention in International Law 1830–1939: The Debate', *Journal of the History of International Law* 16 (2014), 26–62.

5 See Gary J. Bass, *Freedom's Battle: The Origins of Humanitarian Intervention* (New York: Alfred A Knopf, 2008); John Bew, '"From an Umpire to a Competitor": Castlereagh, Canning and the Issue of Intervention in the Wake of Napoleonic Wars', in Brendan Simms and D.J.B. Trim (eds.), *Humanitarian Intervention: A History* (Cambridge: Cambridge University Press, 2011), 117–138.

6 See Davide Rodogno, *Against Massacre: Humanitarian Interventions in the Ottoman Empire 1815–1914* (Princeton: Princeton University Press, 2012), 88; Davide Rodogno, 'Humanitarian Intervention in the Nineteenth Century', in Alex J Bellamy and Tim Dunne (eds.), *The Oxford Handbook of the Responsibility to Protect* (Oxford: Oxford University Press, 2016), 20–37; Simon Chesterman, *Just War or Just Peace? Humanitarian Intervention and International Law* (Oxford, Oxford University Press, 2001), 29. For a more comprehensive legal approach, see Roscoe R Oglesby, *Internal War and the Search for Normative Order* (The Hague: Martinus Nijhoff, 1971), 18–24; Will Smiley, 'War without War: The Battle of Navarino, the Ottoman Empire, and the Pacific Blockade', *Journal of the History of International Law* 18 (2016), 42–69.

7 See Maartje Abbenhuis, *An Age of Neutrals: Great Power Politics, 1815–1914* (Cambridge: Cambridge University Press, 2014).

comprised of two subsections. The first one discusses how the proximity of the Ionian Islands – a protectorate of Great Britain – to the theatre of the civil war led to its early proclamation of neutrality. The second subsection then moves on to consider the amalgam of circumstances that drove Britain to posit itself as a neutral in the conflict addressing, in particular, the British conception of neutrality under the law of nations and municipal neutrality laws. The final part embarks on Britain's decision to intervene and the justifications put forward. The chapter does not attempt to elaborate every legal concept in detail, but merely maps the legal questions, which Britain had to deal with in relation to the civil war.

2 Great Britain and the Greek War of Independence – General Overview

The Greek War of Independence (1821–1832) was preceded by an invincibly complex history.[8] In a nutshell, a revolutionary organisation *Philiki Etairia* was formed in Odessa to organise a rebellion movement in the Greek provinces of the Ottoman Empire.[9] In 1821, under the leadership of Alexander Ypsilantis – a general from Greek origins in the army of the Russian Tsar Alexander I –, the organisation formally announced the rebellion against Ottoman rule.[10] While the revolt that Ypsilantis initiated in the Danubian Principalities[11] was quickly quashed, parallel resistance movements in the Peloponnese were successful. From the Ottoman perspective, Islamic law (Sharīʿa) prescribed that

8 See generally Matthew S Anderson, *The Eastern Question, 1774–1923: A Study in International Relations* (London: Macmillan, 1966); Douglas Dakin, *The Greek Struggle for Independence, 1821–1833* (Berkeley: University of California Press, 1973); George Finlay, *History of the Greek Revolution* (London: William Blackwood and Sons, 1861); Barbara Jelavich, *Russia's Balkan Entanglements 1806–1914* (Cambridge: Cambridge University Press, 1991); Christopher M. Woodhouse, *The Greek War of Independence: Its Historical Setting* (London: Hutchinson's University Library, 1952).

9 David Brewer, *The Greek War of Independence: The Struggle for Freedom from Ottoman Oppression and the Birth of the Modern Greek Nation* (Woodstock: Overlook Press, 2001), 26–35.

10 Richard Clogg, *The Movement for Greek Independence 1770–1821: A Collection of Documents* (London: Macmillan, 1976), 201–203. On the role of the European Enlightenment ideals in the Greek revolution, see Victor Roudometoff, 'From Rum Millet to Greek Nation: Enlightenment, Secularization and National Identity in Ottoman Balkan Society, 1453–1821', *Journal of Modern Greek Studies* 16 (1998), 11–48.

11 'Danubian principalities' was a common denominator for Wallachia and Moldavia – Ottoman provinces put under the protection of the Russian Empire by the Treaty of Küçük Kaynarca of 1774, 45 CTS 349.

those individuals who raised arms against the Ottoman Porte abrogated the *dhimma* – a pact which regulated the relations between *dhimmi*[12] and the Porte – and were consequently treated as *harbi* (warring non-Muslims) who were liable to appropriate penalties (inter alia, imprisonment, exile and confiscation of property).[13]

Within several months after the start of the revolution, disorder and mayhem prevailed in the Peninsula and caused a surge of attacks on international maritime commerce. The protraction of the conflict left internecine bloodshed on both sides; numerous atrocities were committed against both the Greek[14] and the Muslim[15] populations. In 1822, the Ottoman attack at Chios – which left thousands killed and enslaved – was the most striking in a series of incidents that escalated the uprising into a full-blown civil war.[16] These, and similar episodes, provoked an amount of public debate unlike any other revolutionary struggle within Europe.[17] The Ottoman Porte came under a hail of criticism for its inhumane methods for suppression of the rebellion,[18] but also for being unable to maintain the order in its realm and protect the life and property of foreign subjects.[19]

---

12 Orthodox Christians in the Ottoman Empire were designated as *dhimmi* (protected non-Muslim groups) and were allowed a certain degree of self-governance under the millet system. See further Edmund C Bosworth, 'The Concept of *Dhimma* in Early Islam', in Benjamin Braude and Bernard Lewis (eds.), *Christians and Jews in the Ottoman Empire: The Functioning of a Plural Society* (New York: Holmes & Meier, 1982), 37–51; Benjamin Braude, 'Foundation Myths of the Millet System', in *Ibid.*, 69–90.

13 Hakan Erdem, '"Do not think of the Greeks as agricultural labourers": Ottoman responses to the Greek War of Independence', in Faruk Birtek/Thalia Dragonas (eds.), *Citizenship and Nation-State in Greece and Turkey* (London and New York: Routledge, 2005), 67–84, 68.

14 See Brewer, *Greek War of Independence*, 66; Finlay, *History of the Greek Revolution*, 226–231.

15 Barbara Jelavich, *History of the Balkans: Eighteenth and Nineteenth Centuries* (New York: Cambridge University Press, 1983), 229–239; Finlay, *History of the Greek Revolution*, 172–188; Thomas Gordon, *History of the Greek Revolution, and of the Wars and Campaigns Arising from the Struggle of the Greek Patriots in Emancipating Their Country from the Turkish Yoke* (Edinburgh: William Blackwood, 1844), vol. 1, 311.

16 See Philip P. Argenti (ed.), *The Massacres of Chios Described in Contemporary Diplomatic Reports* (London: John Lane and Bodley Head, 1932). Archival studies, however, show that the Porte was concerned with the excesses of force by the janissaries, and in particular with the problem of killing and enslavement of the innocent *reaya*: see Erdem, 'Ottoman responses', 70–72.

17 See for example Eugène Delacroix' famous painting 'Scène des massacres de Scio' (Musee du Louvre, 1824).

18 For the report of Ottoman atrocities in British newspapers see, for instance, *The Times*, 18 May 1821; *The Times* 6 June 1821; *The Times* 19 June 1821.

19 See for example the Opinion of the Law Officers of the Crown from 19 September 1821 where they advised the British naval officers in Smyrna on the measures of self-defence 'under the most urgent necessity and with greatest caution' to be adopted 'against the

The Greek conflict eventually became a legal quagmire for Great Britain. Initially, Britain was reluctant to interfere; its position was to treat the conflict as a domestic matter and broker smooth relations with the Ottoman Empire. The strengthening of the Greek rebellious movement and the lack of coherent policy soon blew up in the face of the British officials. First, the impediments to international maritime commerce in the eastern Mediterranean increased. Second, the Greek conflict became enmeshed in the Russo-Ottoman tensions, which threatened to destabilise the post-Vienna arrangement.[20] This pushed Britain to adopt a pro-active collective foreign policy that aimed at undermining Russia's influence in the Balkans whilst hoping for a resolution of the Greek conflict. The ongoing Russo-Ottoman hostilities and the pressing Greek crisis demanded a policy of containment against Russia's wish unilaterally to impose its own solution to the Greek question. Britain thus rushed into signing a protocol for action in the Greek affair just before the conclusion of the Ackerman Convention between Russia and the Ottoman Empire.[21] This protocol then grew into the Treaty of London, which the Sublime Porte saw as intervention in the internal affairs of its Empire and a humiliation in the light of the long-standing friendly relations with the great powers of Europe.

In sum, the British attitude towards the Greek War of Independence was changing. Archival records reveal that Britain's legal interest during the crisis centred on three points: policy of non-interference, neutrality and intervention. The last included the threat and eventual use of force by the allied Russo-British-French forces in the Mediterranean. The British government offered justifications for its actions throughout.[22] Although the Greek question started with Britain's concern on how to protect its commercial interests in the Mediterranean that were affected by the civil war, the threat and the eventual use of force against the Ottoman forces in 1827 became the hallmark of the crisis debate. It was this action, in particular, that questioned the British neutral attitude in the conflict.

---

excesses of the Populace, or of the Turkish Government': London, The National Archives [hereinafter TNA], FO 83/2385.

20 See Barbara Jelavich, *Russia and the Formation of the Romanian National State, 1821–1878* (Cambridge: Cambridge University Press, 1984), 27–31.

21 Convention between Russia and the Ottoman Porte explanatory of the Treaty of Bucharest, 25 September 1826, in Clive Parry (ed.), *The Consolidated Treaty Series* (231 vols., Dobbs Ferry: Oceana, 1969–1981), vol. 76, 411 [hereinafter CTS].

22 In the nineteenth century, states usually took the trouble to expressly justify – as a matter of international law – their resort to force: see Agatha Verdebout, 'The Contemporary Discourse on the Use of Force in the Nineteenth Century: A Diachronic and Critical Analysis', *Journal on the Use of Force and International Law* 1 (2015), 223–246; Randall Lesaffer, 'Aggression before Versailles', *European Journal of International Law* 29 (2018), forthcoming.

3 Policy of Non-intervention: Piracy and Insurgency

Since the Congress of Vienna, Britain led a general policy of non-intervention in the internal affairs of third states. The policy was explicitly outlined in the circular letter of the Foreign Secretary, Viscount Castlereagh (1769–1822), to the British ministers at foreign courts as a response to the increased interventionist policy of the European continental powers in the context of the Holy Alliance.[23] Therein Britain considered intervention to be contrary to the sanctity of treaties and the established system of international law. This position indeed corresponded to the early nineteenth-century legal doctrine according to which state interactions were governed by certain fundamental principles, inter alia, the right of external independence and equality.[24]

Initially, the British role in the Greek conflict was one of non-interference. For Castlereagh, Greeks 'formed a branch of that organised spirit of insurrection which is systematically propagating itself throughout Europe'.[25] He, therefore, invoked the same principle of non-intervention that he advocated during the revolutions in Italy and Spain.[26] However, the pattern of hostilities resulted in a significant increase of insurgent cruisers on the high seas that harassed foreign commerce. Given the extent of British shipping activity in the eastern Mediterranean and the proximity of the Ionian Islands – then under the protection of Great Britain – to the hostilities, British legal and policy officials had to reconsider the status of the insurgents at sea. The question was whether those persons, whose attacks against maritime commerce of a state

23 Viscount Castlereagh to the British Ministers at Foreign Courts, 19 January 1821, FO 881/1875. The 'Holy Alliance' was a conservative and anti-revolutionary coalition created in 1815 between Russia, Austria and Prussia: see Holy Alliance between Austria, Prussia and Russia, 11 (26) September 1815, 65 CTS 199.

24 Johan-Ludwig Klüber, *Droit des gens moderne de 'Europe* (Sttutgart: JG Gotta, 1819), 69; Georg Friedrich Von Martens, *Précis de droit des gens moderne de l'Europe* (Gottingue: Dietrich, 1821), 215; See further Lesaffer, 'Aggression before Versailles'; Miloš Vec, 'Intervention/Nichtintervention. Verrechtlichung der Politik und Politisierung des Volkerrechts in 19. Jahrhundert', in Ulrich Lappenhuper and Reiner Marcowicz (eds.), *Macht und Recht. Völkerrecht in den internationalen Beziehungen* (Paderborn: Schoningh, 2010), 135–160. On the relationship between hegemonic and egalitarian tendencies of the nineteenth century see Nico Kirsch, 'International Law in Times of Hegemony: Unequal Power and the Shaping of the International Order', *European Journal of International Law* 16 (2005), 369–408; Gerry Simpson, *Great Powers and Outlaw States: Unequal Sovereigns in the International Legal Order* (Cambridge: Cambridge University Press, 2004), 102–108.

25 Earl of Londonderry to His Imperial Majesty the Emperor of all the Russias, 16 July 1821, in Charles K. Webster (ed.), *The Foreign Policy of Castlereagh, 1815–1822: Britain and the European Alliance* (London: G.Bell and Sons, 1924), 360–361.

26 Ibid., 361.

with which the offender's parent state was at peace, could be assimilated to pirates?

At the beginning of the nineteenth century, maritime incidents of insurgency had sometimes been brought under to the loose label of piracy.[27] Throughout the centuries, the legal term 'pirate' acquired several meanings related to various practices.[28] The English term 'piracy' generally referred to any intrusion on property rights, while the Latin form often used to refer to pirates – hostes humani generis – usually concerned unauthorised action against public order.[29] This meant that acts lacking license from an established sovereign were unlawful and made those who pursued them 'outlaws'.[30] In England, jurists and admiralty judges defined piracy as depredation upon the high seas without a lawful commission of war or reprisals.[31] Thus for the act to qualify as 'piracy' it must have been committed without the colour of belligerent rights.

British naval officers in the East Mediterranean were now faced with the difficulty of qualifying the Greek insurgents at sea who now interfered with British commerce. The Foreign Office asked the King's Advocate, Sir Christopher Robinson, whether such persons could be assimilated to pirates. Robinson delivered the following opinion:

> [I]t would not be proper to consider Persons as Pirates who may be cruizing under a state of alleged Hostilities, whether regular or irregular, provided their intentions were in fact satisfactorily distinguished from the mere predatory character of Piracy as considered in Law – at the same time, as Sir Graham Moore describes the insurgent Greeks to be acting without ... authority of an independent government, and without any established system of civil policy, or public law – I think it would be consistent with the neutrality or forbearance that His Majesty's Government might be disposed to use and practice under existing Circumstances to instruct His Majesty's Cruisers to interpose by all amicable means, to

27 See early nineteenth-century jurisprudence of the US Supreme Court, for example, United States v Klintock, 18 U.S. 144 (1820); United States v Smith, 18 U.S. 5 Wheat. 153 (1820); United States v. Holmes, 18 U.S. 5 Wheat. 412 (1820).

28 Alfred Rubin, *The Law of Piracy* (Newport: Naval War College Press, 1988), 30–31.

29 *Ibid.*, 30.

30 *Ibid.*, 31.

31 William Winne, *The Life of Sir Leoline Jenkins* (London: s.n., 1724), vol. 1, lxxxvi-lxxxiv. See further William Blackstone, *Commentaries on the Laws of England* (Oxford: Clarendon Press, 1769), vol. 4, 67–71 who defined piracy as 'act of robbery and depredation upon the high seas' against which every community has a right to exercise their right of self-defence.

> protect the Ships of His Majesty's Subjects, or of the Ionian Islands under His Majesty's protection, from being treated by such Cruisers as liable to all the restrictions to which Neutral Commerce is required to submit in a state of War, between regular and recognized Governments.-It may be a matter of discretion, on what Occasions and to what extent this interposition should be authorized; But … a reasonable limitation of the arbitrary pretensions of such Cruizers, would be justified, and may perhaps be found to be expedient for the protection of British Commerce in the Mediterranean.[32]

It seems evident that to determine the status of 'unrecognised' insurgents on the high seas, Robinson applied a motive-based approach. The Greek rebels did not possess the intent to seize goods at sea for purely private ends. On the contrary, they were taking public action to overthrow the Ottoman authority; hence, their acts were politically motivated. Here, the decisive point is the 'personality of the actor', rather than the 'quality of the act'.[33] The insurgents were not enemies to mankind and therefore did not elicit universal jurisdiction of all states. Robinson did not delve further into the lawfulness of the license under which Greek corsairs were sailing. Apparently, he could not equate the taking *animo furandi* with a fact-pattern of taking *jure belli*, notwithstanding the lack of license from a recognised authority. The textual reading of the opinion suggests that the distinction between pirates and lawful belligerents was to be found in the divide between private and public motives. The opinion, in fact, followed an established line of reasoning of the Law Officers of the Crown. For example, in 1729, they advised that 'a pirate is a sea thief, who to enrich himself, either by force or surprise, sets upon merchants or others trading upon the high and open seas' for private gain.[34] By strict applicability of the law of nations, vessels lacking proper commission could not lawfully seize vessels. In practice, however, such capture was not to be considered piracy if the seizers took the captured vessel to a prize court.[35]

32 King's Advocate to Foreign Office, 4 October 1821, FO 83/2385.

33 Gerry Simpson, 'Piracy and the Origins of Enmity' in Matthew Craven, Malagosia Fitzmaurice and Maria Vogiatzi (eds.), *Time, History and International Law* (Leiden: Martinus Nijhoff, 2007), 219–230, 228.

34 Quoted in Arnold D. McNair, *International Law Opinions. Selected and annotated by Lord McNair* (Cambridge: Cambridge University Press, 1956), 267.

35 *Ibid.* Opinions given later followed the same reasoning: see, e.g. 28 July 1848, FO 83/2230. Also Wooddeson qualifies the element of a 'sovereign authorization' in cases of the taking of property of others but not of the right to transfer the title: Richard Wooddeson, *A Systematical View of the Laws of England; As Treated of in a Course of Vinerian Lecture, Read*

Robinson refused to consider the insurgents as legitimate belligerents. According to him, notwithstanding their political aims, the Greeks lacked organisation and public law. Political organisation and lawful authority of the rebellious community mattered to the extent that such community could properly license privateers to stop and search British ships for contraband and establish prize courts for *in rem* proceedings. The opinion thus produced an ambiguous line of reasoning. It suggested that the Greek rebels did not fit neatly within the laws of war but neither could they be labelled pirates in an absolute and unqualified sense. This put the rebels in a legal vacuum. They were not lawful belligerents nor were they plunderers. These considerations raised important questions among legal and policy officials: was the law adequate to meet current trends relating to internal conflicts? The distinction pirate-rebel, then, was central to the understanding of the need for the government to device new legal means to deal with such category of persons. The reading of the legal opinion shows why the British government had to consider, in the first place, the issue of recognition of the Greek insurgents.

Apparently, Robinson's legal opinion provided a gateway for the executive branch to decide whether Greek rebels could acquire legal personality by way of recognition.[36] Categorisation of persons as belligerents or civilians raised the question of war or peace, which was solely in the domain of the executive branch. The task of the British government, then, was to 'identify' the pirates as criminals or warriors. Were they subject to a regime of enforcement or to a regime of warfare?[37] Meanwhile, Robinson advocated for a conduct of non-interference where use of force could only be justified in cases of necessary and immediate protection of British and Ionian subjects and property.[38] His

at Oxford, During a Series of Years, Commencing in Michaelmas Term (Dublin: E. Lynch, P. Wogan, P. Byrne, A. Grueber, W. M'Kenzie, J. Moore, J. Jones, W. Jones, R. M'Allister, H. Watts, and J. Rice, 1794), 432.

36 Indeed, many contemporary scholars discuss the current problem of 'unlawful combatants' in the light of the historical debate of 'unrecognised' pirates as persons who remain outside of any legal protection. See Douglas Guilfoyle, 'The Laws of War and the Fight Against Somali Piracy: Combatants or Criminals?', *Melbourne Journal of International Law* 11 (2010), 1–13; Eugene Kontorovich, 'A Guantanamo on the Sea: The Difficulties of Prosecuting Pirates and Terrorists', *California Law Review* 98 (2010), 234–269.

37 Gerry Simpson shows clearly how the status of pirate throughout centuries was fluid and its conduct often lay at the crossroads between legitimate 'war' and illegitimate 'crime': Gerry Simpson, *Law, War, and Crime: War Crimes, Trials and the Reinvention of International Law* (Cambridge: Polity Press, 2007), 160.

38 Chasing rebel vessels as pirates would be interpreted as taking a pro-governmental stance. This reasoning can be seen in several Law Officer's Opinions throughout the nineteenth century with marked consistency. See for e.g. 28 July 1848, FO 82/2400. See also 4 August 1873, FO 83/2385: 'Spanish [rebel] ships are manned by crews whose only alleged

indeterminate opinion could be seen as a plea for conceptualising political piracy. The question thus remained as to how a large community of people pursuing a political project for national liberation by way of armed resistance could be recognised as belligerent and as such become a subject of international law during war?

4 Neutrality

From 1815, Britain's policy was to stay aloof from foreign conflicts and promote peace in Europe and the Americas. Defending this policy in the Parliament, the British Foreign Secretary, George Canning (1770–1827), stated that if Britain was about to be dragged into war, the grounds for it should be clearly British: 'If a war must come, let it come in the shape of satisfaction to be demanded of injuries – of rights to be asserted, of interests to be protected, of treaties to be fulfilled'.[39] Canning admired the American system of neutrality from Washington's days.[40] Indeed, for the United States at the end of the eighteenth century, neutrality had been 'identity, as well as interest'.[41] Great Britain recognised the benefits of such a policy and quickly shifted to defend and expand the rights of neutrals.

The main idea of neutrality was to regulate the relations of the neutrals with belligerents. The law of neutrality, in general, consisted of the duty of abstention and the principle of impartiality. Neutrals had to abstain from anything connected to the theatre of war such as providing contraband articles to the warring parties, trade with blockaded ports or using neutral territory as a base for hostile operations.[42] At the beginning of the nineteenth century, Britain acquired a stricter approach to the duty of abstention by prohibiting hostile

crime or offence is that they are in revolt against the Government at Madrid, and, in our opinion, they cannot properly be visited or detained or seized unless the Government which orders or approves of such visit, detention, or seizure is prepared to support the Government at Madrid against all persons and parties who may be in insurrection against that Government'. On the right to self-defence of property and life of British subjects see: 19 September 1821, FO 83/2385.

39 House of Commons, 16 April 1823, vol. 8, cc 1056.

40 Ibid., cc 1019–58.

41 John Fabian Witt, *Lincoln's Code, The Laws of War in the American History* (New York: Free Press, 2012), 59.

42 See, for example, the Case of Emanuel reported in Christopher Robinson (ed.), *Reports of Cases Argued and Determined in the High Court of Admiralty: Commencing with the Judgments of the Right Hon. Sir William Scott, Michaelmas Term 1789* (London: A. Strahan 4th ed., 1812), 296–302.

expeditions from its country including building and equipping of vessels of war, and recruitment of British subjects for foreign wars in which Britain was neutral. The result was the adoption of more burdensome neutral duties,[43] and abandonment of the so-called imperfect neutrality.[44]

4.1 *Neutrality of the Ionian Islands*

Unlike Great Britain, the Ionian Islands under the guidance of its protector, Great Britain, resorted more decidedly to neutrality and did so at a much earlier time.[45] The Ionian Islands became independent by the Treaty of Paris in 1815, but were placed under the 'immediate and exclusive protection' of Great Britain.[46] Britain appointed a crown official as Lord High Commissioner who was responsible for legislation and general administration (internal sovereignty) but who had also appointed a constituent assembly to make a national constitution. Ionian military forces were put under the orders of the British navy and all ports and harbours placed under the jurisdiction of Britain. British high officials rightly saw such arrangement as that of a mere colony.[47]

After the outbreak of the Greek rebellion, the main task of the Ionian authorities was to deal with the rising number of volunteers enlisting to fight for the Greek cause.[48] This seriously affected the Anglo-Ottoman relations in the Mediterranean when the Lord High Commissioner after warning against

43 Stephen Neff, *The Rights and Duties of Neutrals: A General History* (Manchester: Manchester University Press, 2000), 99.

44 According to Cornelius van Bynkershoek, there are two kinds of neutrality, perfect (absolute) and imperfect (qualified). A state achieved perfect neutrality when it was not bound to the belligerents by previous treaties or alliances: see Cornelius Van Bynkershoek, *Questionum Juris Publici*, (Philadelphia: Fry and Kammerer 1810, transl. Peter Stephen Du Ponceau), vol. 1, 69–70.

45 See The Ionian Ships, 2 Spinks 212 (1855).

46 Treaty between Austria, Prussia and Russia and Great Britain, 5 November 1815, 65 CTS 241. The treaty was also ratified by the Ottoman Porte in 1819, see 'Acte de ratification de la Porte Ottomane, sa Avril relativement à la cession des iles ioniennes à la Grande – Bretagne, et de Parga à la Turquie, du 24 Avril 1819', in Georg Friedrich von Martens (ed.), *Nouveau recueil de traités d'alliance, de paix, de trêve, de neutralité, de commerce, de limites, d'échange etc et de plusieurs autres actes servant à la connoissance des relations étrangères des puissances et Etats de l'Europe ... depuis 1808 jusqu'à present* (Gottingue: Dietrich, 1829), vol. 5, 387.

47 Castlereagh to Liston, 20 November 1815, FO 139/36. See further Maria Paschalidi, *Constructing Ionian Identities: The Ionian Islands in British Official Discourses: 1815–1864* (London: unpublished thesis, 2009), 96.

48 Meyer to Castlereagh, 14 April 1821, FO 78/103; Haneky to Strangford, 10 July 1821, FO 78/99.

civilian participation in the Greek war,[49] and acceptance of the Greek blockade along the coast of Morea,[50] had to officially proclaim neutrality of the Ionian Islands:

> [The Government of the United States of the Ionian Islands] 'fully sensible of the duties it is called upon to fulfil, and mindful of the true interests of the Country, proclaims its Neutrality, and its positive intention not to interfere in any manner during the continuance of the above-mentioned Contest.[51]

The declaration was subsequently enforced by legislative regulations, which provided for the following measures: first, prohibition to participate in hostilities, non-compliance of which would cause loss of British diplomatic protection;[52] second, prohibition of equipping and arming foreign vessels in Ionian ports;[53] third, Ionian vessels were prohibited to engage on behalf of the Greek insurgents;[54] fourth, Ottoman naval fleet and Greek corsairs were prohibited entrance into any Ionian port.[55] The British Colonial Office subsequently approved the 'principle of perfect and invariable neutrality'[56] and instructed the Lord Commissioner 'to adopt the most energetic measures' to achieve this object.

However, the failure of the Ionian authorities and the British navy ships to enforce such measures contributed to serious violations of the Ionian neutral duties.[57] This called for adoption of more serious measures, such as martial

---

49 Proclamation of the Senate, 9 April 1821, *British and Foreign State Papers 1820–1821* (170 vols., London: HMSO, 1841–1977), vol.8, 1282 [hereinafter BFSP]: '[*g*]*uidance* to all subjects…in the event of their taking part in the present disturbances, or joining in any attack or warlike operations which may take place, they will necessarily lose all right or pretension to the interference on their behalf of the Government of these States, or of the British Consuls charged with protecting their rights with whatever foreign country they may reside' (emphasis added).

50 Ibid.

51 Proclamation, 7 June 1821, CO 136/1085.

52 Adam to Strangford, 5 August 1821, CO 136/1103.

53 Adams to Bathurst, 6 June 1821, CO 136/1085.

54 Lane to Hankey, 6 August 1821, CO 136/1148.

55 Adam to Bathurst, 11 June 1821, CO 136/1085.

56 Proclamation of the Lord High Commissioner, 9 October 1821.

57 Maitland to Bathurst, 26 June 1821, CO 136/1085; Travers to Adam, 21 July 1821, CO 136/1308; Travers to Adam, 9 August 1821, CO. 136/1308. For critics of the Lord Commissioner's policy in the Ionian Islands see Hansard, House of Commons, 23 February 1821, 2nd ser. IV; 7 June 1821,2nd ser. V; 14 May 1822, 2nd ser. VII.

law[58] and disarmament[59] of the Ionian subjects. Also, additional legislation was enacted which provided for specific measures to be taken against those Ionian subjects who violated national laws relating to declared neutrality. These included expulsion from the territory of the Ionian Islands, confiscation of property and individual punishment in case of capture.[60]

Ionian neutrality, however, came with two caveats. First, notwithstanding that neutrality was officially proclaimed, the Lord High Commissioner did not consider the Greek insurgents as lawful belligerents. According to him, Greek vessels still lacked commission from a lawful authority without which they could only be treated as pirates.[61] During the years, the heated tensions arising out of their proximity to a fierce civil war, the Ionian authorities were 'forced' to grant certain belligerent rights to the Greeks. For example, although initially the Greek blockade of the Morean coast was not formally acknowledged,[62] for practical reasons Ionian authorities were forced to prohibit Ionian vessels sailing to blockaded ports.[63] Second, the duty of impartiality was not strictly upheld by the Ionian authorities. Officially, domestic neutrality measures were adopted with respect to both contending sides.[64] However, because of personal preferences and in the name of cordial diplomatic connections with the Ottoman Empire, Ionian authorities and the British navy were particularly cautious towards the Ottomans when enforcing neutrality measures.[65] All differences were to be resolved in coordination with the Ottoman fleet, especially with regard to issues arising out of Ottoman closure of ports which were usually settled by local agreements between the British and Ottoman navies.[66]

---

58 Maitland to Bathurst, 15 October 1821, CO 136/1102; Maitland to Bathurst, 21 October 1821, CO 136/1085.

59 Proclamation of 6 November 1821, CO 136/1085; Maitland to Bathurst, 1 March 1828, CO 136/20.

60 Act of the Ionian Parliament respecting the punishment of Ionian subjects for engaging in the War between Turkey and Greece of 2 April 1822, *British and Foreign State Papers* (London: James Ridgway and Sons, 1851), 1005.

61 See Moore to Croker, 14 August 1821, TNA, ADM 1/438; Adam to Theotoky, 16 July 1821, CO 136/1084.

62 Clifford to Moore, 29 May 1822, ADM 1/439.

63 Lane to Residents, 3 June 1823, CO 136/1149.

64 See Adam to Travers, 20 September 1821, CO 136/1270.

65 See Maitland to Adams, 27 June 1821, CO 136/1085; and Bathurst to Maitland, 31 July 1821, CO 136/305.

66 For example, the local agreement concluded on 2 August 1823 with respect to the Ottoman closure of ports of the Morean coast. See Moore and Adam to Captain Bay, 2 August 1823, CO 136/21; Captain Bay to Adam, 2 August 1821, CO 136/21.

4.2 *Neutrality of Great Britain*

Between 1823 and 1826, Britain remained determined to keep the Greek conflict at bay and maintain strict neutrality. It, however, only gradually started treating both parties as belligerents *inter se in justo bello*. The process of assuming neutral duties was taking place on two fronts: international and domestic. On both fronts, Britain struggled to apply traditional inter-state legal principles to its relations with the Greek non-state armed groups.

On the international plane, there was no formal act that proclaimed neutrality: belligerent rights were gradually accorded to the Greeks depending on their normative capacity to exercise the corresponding obligations. One such condition concerned the level of political and civil organisation of their struggle fulfilled by the establishment of the provisional government,[67] and the promulgation of the provisional constitution.[68] The establishment of tribunals and prize courts where captured British ships could vindicate their rights was also of significance in this light.[69] Until 1823, however, there was much confusion on the part of the Foreign Office as to the exact conduct to be adopted in relation to the insurgents. For the period between 1821 and 1823, the correspondence of the British naval forces in the Mediterranean reveals that 'in the absence of positive Instructions' from London they maintained 'the most perfect neutrality'.[70] The term 'neutrality', however, was not used in a technical legal sense but rather as a political principle of non-interference in the conflict.[71] For example, the British commander-in-chief in the Mediterranean reported that his ships did not acknowledge the blockade at Corinth proclaimed by the Greek Provisional Government,[72] and did not allow any visitation or search on British ships.[73] Finally, in 1823, the Foreign Office sent instructions to the naval officers in the East Mediterranean forbidding any British interference in the contest, but also calling for respect of all international rules originating from a strict neutrality, including blockades proclaimed by either of the contending parties.[74] Some documents, however, show that in many instances there was

67 Proclamation d'independence de l'Assemblee Nationale Hellénique, 27 January 1822, 9 BFSP 629–632.

68 Constitution Provisoire de l'Hellénie, 13 January 1822, 9 BFSP 620–629.

69 See especially Part 5 of the Hellenic Constitution, 9 BFSP 627–628.

70 Vice-Admiral Sir Graham Moore to Croker, 23 July 1822, ADM 1/439.

71 On the same conclusion, see Herbert A. Smith, *Great Britain and the Law of Nations, Volume 1: States* (London: PS King and Son, 1932), 286.

72 Declaration of the Provisional Government of Greece, announcing the Blockade of Turkish Ports, 25 March 1822, 9 BFSP 798.

73 Vice-Admiral Sir Graham Moore to Croker, 23 July 1822, ADM 1/439.

74 Croker to Sir Graham Moore, 30 April 1823, ADM 2/1693.

only partial observance of neutrality justified by the limited capacity of the insurgents to implement belligerent measures in accordance with the customary usages of war of the time. For instance, some insurgent blockades were not observed because of the lack of official notice, or the insufficiency of force to maintain them.[75]

On the domestic plane, it was the issue of foreign enlisting on behalf of the Greeks that led Britain to impose neutral duties on itself. The problem of individual (private) interference in foreign internal conflicts was dealt with under the Foreign Enlistment Act of 1819. On 6 June 1823, Britain issued a general proclamation for putting in execution the Foreign Enlistment Act of 1819.[76] This Proclamation, however, was of a general character and did not mention the Greek rebellion. Only in 1825, a proclamation explicitly referring to the Greek conflict was issued to prevent British subjects from taking part in the contest.[77] Interestingly, the drafting of the later proclamation suggests that Britain was still hesitant to name the Greeks as belligerents publicly. Archival documents reveal that on advise of the King's Advocate the words 'belligerents' and 'hostilities' in the first draft were considered to be rather 'harmful' to be directly applied to the Greeks and were thus changed to 'contest' in the final draft.[78]

The act, in fact, was first adopted in relation to the Spanish American rebellions to combat the phenomenon of massive succour of men and arms within the neutral territory of Britain.[79] The systematic engagement of British subjects in belligerent service of the rebels showed the limits of the existing British statutes, which prevented enlisting to serve 'foreign prince, state,

75 Canning to Wellesley, 31 December 1824, reproduced in Smith, *Great Britain and the Law of Nations*, 294–296.

76 British Proclamation, for putting in execution the Law made to prevent the enlisting or engagement of His Majesty's Subjects in Foreign Service, and the fitting-out or equipping, in His Majesty's Dominions, Vessels for warlike purposes, without His Majesty's Licence, 6 June 1823, 10 BFSP 648–653.

77 Proclamation of the King of Great Britain, prohibiting British Subjects from taking part in the Contest between The Ottoman Porte and the Greeks, or between other Belligerents, 30 September 1825, 13 BFSP & 525–530. See also Charles Zorgbibe, 'Sources of the recognition of belligerent status', *International Review of the Red Cross* 129 (1977), 111–127, 119.

78 Robinson to Canning, 30 September 1825, FO 83/2385.

79 For a detailed account on the adoption of the Foreign Enlistment Act see David Waddell, 'British Neutrality and Spanish-American Independence: The Problem of Foreign Enlistment', *Journal of Latin American Studies* 19 (1987), 1–18. See further Nir Arielli, Gabriela A Frei and Inge Van Hulle, 'The Foreign Enlistment Act, International Law, and British Politics, 1819–2014', *International History Review* 38 (2016), 636–656, 637–642.

or potentate' but did not comprehend a belligerent community.[80] Moreover, as the law stood, if prosecution for such persons was instituted, courts would have to treat them as pirates, unlike those who were fighting with the parent state.[81] In order to uphold its neutral duty, Britain was left with two choices: to either recognise the colonies as states or close the loophole in the law.[82] In 1819, Parliament adopted the Foreign Enlistment Act which now criminalised the acts of equipping or fitting out armed vessels or enlisting in the service of 'foreign prince, state, potentate' but also 'colony, province or part of any province or people, or of any person or persons exercising or assuming to exercise the powers of government in or over any foreign country'.[83]

The act in itself was not meant as an instrument to accord belligerent rights to insurgents. However, it did introduce an element of impartiality in that it implicitly put the two warring sides in the conflict on the same footing.[84] The motive for the drafting of such an act, according to Canning, was to produce equality between two sides of an internal conflict.[85] Robinson opined that the utility of the act was to show the world that Britain respected the law of nations and the duties of strict neutrality.[86] According to Castlereagh 'it was manifestly against the law of nations to allow, that troops should be raised for one belligerent party, and not for another'.[87] In this way, Britain expanded its obligations of impartiality in the context of foreign internal conflicts under domestic law. This consisted of using all reasonable means to prevent large-scale commissioning of fighters. The trend of adopting domestic neutrality laws at the time was embryonic, and in certain aspects, was in confluence with the principle of non-intervention.[88]

80 9 Geo. 2 c.30 (1736) and 29 Geo. 2 c.17 (1756). For the history of foreign enlistment in England see James F. Stephen, *A History of the Criminal Law of England* (London: Macmillan and Co, 1883), vol. 3, 257–262. For a parallel development with the US neutrality laws see Gerald J. Wheeler, *Foreign Enlistment Act, 1870, 33 and 34 Vict. c.90., With Notes of the Leading Cases on This and the American Act* (London: Eyre & Spottiswoode, 1896).

81 25 August 1817, FO 83/2385.

82 2 February 1819, FO 83/2385.

83 59 Geo. 3, c.69, Bill to prevent the Enlisting or Engagement of His Majesty's Subjects to serve in Foreign Service, and the fitting out or equipping, in his Majesty's Dominions, Vessels for warlike purposes without His Majesty's Licence, 6 BFSP 130–139.

84 Also Chen, *The International Law of Recognition*, 390. But see Hersch Lauterpacht, *Recognition in International Law* (Cambridge: Cambridge University Press, 2012), 178.

85 Hansard, House of Commons, 16 April 1823, vol 8 cc 1052–1053.

86 *Ibid.*, 3 June 1819, vol 40 cc 899, 900.

87 *Ibid.*, cc 867–910.

88 It is not certain whether a proclamation of the Foreign Enlistment Act in a context of foreign civil war meant *ipso facto* a proclamation of neutrality. See for instance Robert

In practice, the Foreign Enlistment Act rendered British vessels conveying British subjects from British ports to engage in foreign service liable to detention and to penalties as specified. Despite the more stringent domestic laws, the British government was still receiving complaints of civilian volunteers sailing under the British flag along with the Greek fleet. The Law Officers advised that in such cases, the Act did not authorise British ships to chase and seize these vessels at sea unless it could be proved that they were equipped in British ports for military operations, or were to be employed as a transport- or store-ship as provided in the 7th clause of the Foreign Enlistment Act.[89]

Another related, yet much contested issue concerned enlistment of financial succour to the Greek insurgents. When hostilities gained larger proportions, insurgents could not solely rely on local resources and voluntary contributions but turned to acquire international loans. This raised two concerns. First, there was the question whether foreign loans were permissible in cases of declared British neutrality. In a general opinion on this issue, the Law Officers stated that a loan given in way of business would not per se constitute an infringement of neutrality.[90] Second, there was the question whether loans could be raised by insurgents who fought against a legitimate government. While in principle the Law Officers did not discriminate between the warring parties on the issue of raising loans, English courts did. For the Law Officers, the purpose of the loan did not matter as long as there was interest exacted on the capital. By contrast, for the judges the purpose mattered; individuals could not raise loans for supporting war efforts against a foreign government.[91]

Granting belligerent rights to rebels carried political and legal implications. From a political perspective, such actions were interpreted as giving legitimacy to the cause of the Greek rebellion and by that as recognition of the right of the Greek people to revolt against the Ottoman Empire. From a legal perspective, the neutrality law gave normative equality to the warring parties vis-à-vis Britain. This brought the rebels on the international plane *durante bello*, although

W. Tucker, *The Law of War and Neutrality at Sea* (Washington: United States Government Printing Office, 1955), 200.

89 See 11 July 1827, FO 83/2385.

90 23 January 1822, FO 83/2366. See also McNair, *International Law Opinions*, 362–363; Pitt Cobbett, *Cases and Opinions of International Law, and various points of English law connected therewith*, vol. 3 (London: Stevens and Haynes, 1913), 365–368.

91 De Wütz v Hendricks, 2 Bing 314 (1824). Due to such judicial reasoning the Provisional Government of Greece found ways to circumvent the connection of the loans to insurgent activities by obtaining loans through intermediaries, such as the London Philhellenic Committee. Greece raised two big loans in 1824 and 1825. For a detailed account on this see John A. Levandis, *The Greek Foreign Debt and The Great Powers, 1821–1898* (New York: Columbia University Press, 1944), 1–28.

they were characterised by only a functional personality of a limited scope. Moreover, analysis of early practice of secessionist wars oftentimes reveals association of the legal right to wage war with a recognition of independence. To the Ottoman Porte, Canning justified its position on the basis of the fact that according to the rules and principles of international law, other nations had no alternative but to grasp the social reality and recognise the belligerency of the Greeks. According to him, the determination of the existence of belligerency was 'not so much a principle, as a fact'.[92] A 'community', then, which exercises its war powers must be acknowledged as a 'belligerent' or a 'pirate', but 'what monstrous consequences would follow from treating as pirates a population of millions of souls, to whom, by that very treatment, the right would be conveyed, and on whom (according to the natural right of self-defence) the obligation would be imposed, of making terrible reprisals?'[93] To the Greeks, Canning explained that by discharging its duties as a neutral, Britain contributed to reducing a barbarous system of warfare but also prevented other powers 'from making common cause against the Greeks as insurgents not entitled to privileges of legitimate warfare'.[94] However, he added, Britain could not go beyond this line and intervene on their behalf as that would constitute a violation of the system of treaties. First, intervention would violate the ancient treaties between Britain and the Ottoman Empire, which protected British interests in the Ottoman dominions.[95] Second, by doing so Britain would depart from the general treaties between the European powers, which prevented any territorial aggrandisement by way of creating new protectorates in Europe.[96]

In sum, when faced with a foreign civil war whose consequences affected the lives and property of British subjects, Britain resorted to traditional categories of the law of neutrality. The operative challenges, however, of applying those inter-state rules to non-state actors laid the ground for legal adjustments and solutions *de lege ferenda.* On an international level, changes occurred from bottom to top; while on a domestic level, changes were implemented from top

92 Harold Temperley, *The Foreign Policy of Canning 1822–1827: England, the Neo-Holy Alliance, and the New World* (London: G. Bell and Sons, 1925), 326.

93 *Ibid.*

94 Memorandum of Conference with the Greek Deputies, Messr. Orlando, Spaniolacki, and Luriottis, 29 September 1825, FO 352/11/3.

95 Ibid. See also Canning to M. Rodios, 1 December 1824, 12 BFSP 900–903.

96 Memorandum of Conference 1825. See also Act of the Provisional Government of Greece, proposing to place the Greek Nation under the Protection of Great Britain, in Foreign Office, 12 BFSP 904–906.

to bottom. In many instances – and especially on a domestic level – duties of neutrality converged with the principle of non-intervention.

5 Collective Security, Mediation, Intervention

By 1825, Britain was in isolation from the pro-interventionist continental powers of Europe. As argued above, Britain considered the principle of non-intervention as a general rule, which allowed only strict exceptions justified by the 'strongest necessity'. In this way, Britain would not object to claims of intervention from principle if these were based on threats to the 'immediate security' of the intervening state, or to an allied intervention based on larger threats to peace and security of Europe. In any of the allowed cases for intervention, however, aggrandisement subversive to the territorial system of Europe would be deemed unacceptable.

The British government initially rejected any invitation by the continental powers to engage in the Greek affair. In 1826, however, Britain felt called upon to intervene. First, the security situation in the eastern Mediterranean deteriorated causing serious breakdown of law and order, and the region turned into a breeding ground for piracy. Second, Britain wanted to contain the Russian attempt at a unilateral resolution of the Greek question, which now became part of the ongoing Russo-Ottoman negotiations.[97] Circumstances thus arose to shift the British attitude to a pro-active interventionist policy to restore peace and security in Greece.

But if Britain was to take a pro-active role in the Greek affairs, then form was to be respected. Thus the sole basis from which Britain would derive authority to speak on the matter was to be invited by one of the parties to the contest.[98] After obtaining a formal request for 'good offices' by the Greeks, Britain negotiated a protocol with Russia which carried in its essence proposals for mediation and a clause of disinterestedness for Greece.[99] The protocol contained two parts: first, in case mediation was accepted by the Porte, the allied powers

97 The Protocol of St Petersburg between Great Britain and Russia was concluded on 23 March 1826 and the Convention of Akkerman between the Russian and the Ottoman Empire on 7 October 1826.

98 See Canning to Lieven, 4 September 1826, reproduced in Augustus G. Stapleton, *The Political Life of the Right Honourable George Canning* (London: Longman, Rees, Orme, Brown and Green, 1831), vol. 3, 263.

99 Protocol of Conference between the British and Russian Plenipotentiaries relative to the Mediation of Great Britain, between the Ottoman Empire and the Greeks, 4 April 1826, 14 BFSP 629–632.

would propose Greece to remain a dependency of the Ottoman Empire but governed by its own elected authorities; and second, in case mediation was rejected, the terms of the protocol would remain unaltered in further efforts of reconciliation, unilaterally or in concert.[100] Moreover, conscious of the possible risks of misuse of the protocol, Article 5 contracted a self-denying clause saying that the parties 'will not seek any increase of territory, exclusive influence nor advantage in commerce for their subjects, which shall not be equally attainable by all other nations'.[101]

Canning hailed the protocol as timely and proper. First, time was ripe to mediate since Greece had shown a flexible disposition to accommodate to its terms short of absolute independence.[102] Second, mediation would be based on a formal invitation of one party to the conflict; hence, Britain's action greatly differed from the principle of intervention as advocated by the Holy Alliance.[103] Lastly, and most importantly, the self-denying obligations alleviated the consequences of a possible war between the allies and Turkey.[104] The goal was therefore to tame any pretensions to enlargement. The protocol, however, did not envisage any concrete measures in case the proposal for pacification was refused. Canning used this silence to discuss the possibilities and limits of such measures with his Russian counterpart. First, he explicitly stated that the British government would not consider the refusal of mediation as a just cause for war.[105] However, he asserted, 'the continuance of a contest so ferocious in its details, so hopeless of termination, and leading to excesses of piracy and plunder intolerable to civilized Europe, to be an evil of extraordinary character as *to justify extraordinary interposition, and to render lawful any expedients, short of positive hostility*'.[106] He made two propositions for such measures: first, simultaneous withdrawal of the ambassadors from Constantinople,[107] and second, a closer alignment with the Greeks accompanied by the eventual recognition of Greek independence.[108]

100 *Ibid.*

101 *Ibid.*

102 Canning to Mr. Temple, in Augustus G. Stapleton, *George Canning and His Times* (London: J.W. Parker, 1859), 481–484.

103 *Ibid.*

104 *Ibid.*

105 Canning to Lieven, 4 September 1826, reproduced in Stapleton, *Political life of Canning*, 263.

106 Ibid. Emphasis added.

107 Ibid. This measure was envisaged as collective and was to be executed only if all powers adhered to it.

108 The measure was suggested by Austria during the unsuccessful negotiation for a pacification of Greece in St. Petersburg in 1825 between Russia, Austria and Prussia. It was

Shortly after the conclusion of the protocol, Britain and Russia sent invitations to the other European great powers – Austria, France and Prussia – to participate in an even more ambitious attempt for pacification of Greece and by that give the intervention a collective character. France accepted, while Austria and Prussia dissented from the proposal. A Treaty for the Pacification of Greece was finally concluded in London and contained almost identical provisions to the ones found in the St. Petersburg Protocol, but reinforced with one secret additional article.[109] The adoption of the protocol and the treaty were justified on the basis of, first, formal invitation of one party to the conflict, and second, 'sentiments of humanity' and 'interests for the tranquillity of Europe'. The preamble of the Treaty of London spelled out that

> the necessity of putting an end to the sanguinary struggle which, while it abandons the Greek provinces and islands of the Archipelago to all the disorders of the anarchy, daily causes fresh impediments to the commerce of the States of Europe, and gives opportunity for acts of piracy which not only expose the subjects of the high-contracting parties to grievous losses, but also renders necessary measures which are burdensome for their observation and suppression.[110]

The justification for intervention was thus not framed as saving foreigners abroad, but rather as saving own nationals and property from the continuation of hostilities. In sum, to justify their intervention in the civil war, the allies invoked the right of self-preservation but also relied on the invitation of the one party to the conflict.[111]

Interestingly, British officials pursued two lines of justifications. In the official diplomatic correspondence with the Ottoman Porte, Britain frequently invoked the right of self-preservation. For instance, the British Ambassador in Constantinople complained of the dangers that Britain incurred from 'piratical

justified on the basis of the duration of the conflict and the capability of the Greeks to maintain the struggle for independence. See ibid.

109 Treaty between Britain, France and Russia, for Pacification of Greece, 6 of July 1827, 14 BFSP 632–639.

110 Protocole de la Conférence tenue au Foreign Office, 12 July 1827 – Forme de Première Déclaration à la Porte Ottomane, convenue entre les Plénipotentiaires des Hautes Puissances Contractantes, à Londres, 12 July 1827, *Papers relative to the affairs of Greece, 1826–1832* (London: J.Harrison and Son, 1835), 5; Forme de Déclaration à addresser a la Commission du Govrenment Provisiore de la Grèce, convenue entre les Plénipotentiaires des Hautes Puissances Contractantes, à Londres, 12 July 1827, *Ibid.*, 8.

111 For the same conclusion see Davide Rodogno, *Against Massacre*, 88; Chesterman, *Just War or Just Peace?*, 29; Smiley, 'War without War', 57.

excesses'.[112] He invoked the law of nations and the Capitulations – which objective was the protection of British commerce in Ottoman ports and territorial waters –[113] to complain of the obstacles and lack of justice for British subjects affected by the violence, and the considerable expenditure of employing navy squadrons in the Levant to protect its trade.[114] Furthermore, when the Treaty of London was presented to the Porte, the allies deplored the Ottoman Empire's role in the conflict as 'incompatible avec les véritables intérêts de la Porte, avec la sûreté du commerce en general, et la parfaite tranquillité de l'Europe'.[115]

In Parliament, government officials defended their policy as one of preservation of peace. Despite the fierce debates from the Whig opposition on the need to intervene to avert humanitarian catastrophe,[116] the line of justification adopted by government officials reveals that prevention of war between Russia and Turkey was the main objective for Britain to engage in the conflict. The Prime Minister stated that the principle upon which Britain signed the protocol was 'not to rescue the Greeks from the domination of Turkey, but to prevent universal war'.[117] He went on to say that 'the great object of the Treaty of July, 1827 was to settle the affairs of Greece, without the necessity of going to war'.[118] According to the Duke of Wellington – the official negotiator of the Protocol of St. Petersburg – 'the transaction of the 6th of July was founded on an anxious desire to maintain peace between [the Turkish and the Russian] empires'.[119] In the governmental instructions upon which he negotiated the

112 Mr. Stratford Canning to the Reis Effendi, 13 June 1826.

113 Capitulations and Articles of peace between the Majesty of the King of Great Britain, France, and Ireland and the Sultan of the Ottoman Empire, as they have been augmented and altered in the Times of several Ambassadors, 1641 (Pap.Off.U., No 2), Art. XIX: 'If the pirates, or Levents, who infest the seas with their frigates, shall be found to have taken any English vessel or to have robbed or spoiled their goods and faculties; also, if it shall be found, that in any of our dominions, any shall have violently taken goods of any Englishman, our ministers shall *with diligence* seek out such offenders, and severely punish them, and cause that all such goods, ships, monies, and whatsoever hath been taken away from the English nation, shall be presently, justly, and absolutely restored to them'.

114 Mr. S Canning to the Reis Effendi, FO 78/143.

115 'Première Déclaration à la Porte Ottomane', *Papers relative to the affairs of Greece*, 5.

116 Yet the government promptly resorted to verification of such information, and eventually dismissed them as false. Viscount Goderich later revealed that Britain received an explicit disavowal from both Ibrahim Pasha and the Porte of the alleged news of enslaving a large population of the Morea. Earl Bathurst – a then Secretary of War – confirmed this. Lord Ellenborough – a Tory and close friend to the Duke of Wellington – also confirmed the false rumour: see *Mirror of Parliament*, 18 February 1830, 106–107.

117 Hansard, House of Lords, 16 July 1828, vol 19 cc 1709–41.

118 *Ibid.*

119 *Ibid.*

Protocol 'presentation of peace was not only the great object specified, but it was, in point of fact, laid down as the *sine qua non* of any arrangement that might be entered into'.[120]

International legal language in public discourse – parliament and newspapers – relied on 'bundled justifications'.[121] In newspapers, Britain's international obligations were framed in religious, civilizational and humanitarian imperatives. Debates before the adoption of the protocol and the treaty revolved around the mistreatment of the Greeks under Ottoman rule and the alleged news of the intention of the Porte to transport part of the Greek population from the Morea to Egypt.[122]

The Treaty of London contained a twofold proposal for the warring parties: meditation and an immediate armistice to enable negotiations. The proposal was immediately accepted by Greece,[123] but repeatedly rejected by the Ottoman Empire as an unlawful intervention.[124] As a matter of law, the Porte invoked the principle of independence and the laws that emanate from its sovereignty as fully and exclusively applicable to its revolted subjects:

> the Greek affair is an internal affair of the Sublime Porte, and she alone is to deal with it; henceforth no Power should interfere with this affair, and if anyone would do it, we would ask for his reason of doing so, for the interest of the preservation of the rights of the Governments, and the Laws of the Nation.[125]

120 *Ibid.*

121 The term 'bundled justifications' is borrowed from Maddeliane Chiam to signify 'a collective of differentiated standards, including those of law, morality, strategy, economics and ethics'. See Madalaine S. Chiam, *International Law in Australian Public Debate 2003, 1965, 1916* (Melbourne: unpublished thesis, 2017), 45.

122 Temperley, *The Foreign Policy of Canning*, 349.

123 Proclamation of the Provisional Government of Greece, accepting the Armistice with the Ottoman Empire, proposed by the Mediating Powers, Great Britain, France, and Russia, *British and Foreign State Papers*, 1048–1049.

124 Manifesto of the Sublime Porte, declining the Pacification with the Greeks, proposed by the Mediating Powers, 9 June 1827, Ibid., 1042–1047; Proclamation of the Ottoman Porte, declining the Mediation of the Allied Powers, and the Proposed Armistice with the Greeks, 20 December 1827, Ibid., 1052–1057.

125 Manifesto of the Sublime Porte, *Papers relative to the affairs of Greece*, 1046: 'l'affaire Grecque est une affaire interne de la Sublime Porte, et que c'est à elle seule à s'en occuper; que désormais auncune Puissance ne doit plus se mêler de cette affaire, et que dans le cas où quelqu'une le ferait on lui en demanderait raison, et cela dans l'intérêt de la conservation des droits des Gouvernments, et des Lois des Nations' (translated by the author).

It further delved into the inappropriate usage of the terms 'mediation', 'armistice' and 'pacification' to the conflict. According to the Porte, these terms belonged to diplomatic vocabulary as applied between states and were thus inoperative in a situation where a state was criminally punishing its own 'deviant' subjects.[126]

Notwithstanding the assurance of the allies that the measures offered in the treaty would not affect the friendly relations with the Porte,[127] their legality was indeed doubtful. First, there was a lack of state consent about the allied squadrons deployed in the territorial waters of the Ottoman Empire. Second, the adopted measures were clearly not compatible with Britain's professed neutrality. Indeed, during the treaty negotiations Britain was contemplating the nature of the measures envisaged in the additional article. It therefore requested a prompt opinion from the Law Officers whether such measures contained an obligation which Britain could not contract with reference to its domestic laws of neutrality or the law of nations.[128] The King's Advocate underlined that the British government should be cautious in adopting measures which exceeded the offices of friendly mediation and warned that 'such compulsory influence is not reconcilable with 'amity and neutrality' as professed by Britain:

> [t]he objection appears to me to remain as to the right of forcible interference in the events of War between Belligerent Powers…I think such stipulations far exceed the offices of friendly mediation as far as the Confederate Powers allege their own interests as a motive for exercising such compulsory influence; an act not reconcilable with the independence of the Belligerent States and of variance with the Principles which have been maintained by this Country respecting the Duties and Obligations of Neutral Powers in their relations to States of War. The same objection will be in my humble opinion to the demonstration of an armed force as contemplated in the Treaty for the purposes there described; and the provisions of amity and neutrality only make the interference more possibly objectionable.[129]

Moreover, the protocols of action adopted subsequently developed but also expanded the treaty articles. First, they stipulated that the conduct of the allied squadrons in the eastern Mediterranean should consist of, inter alia, closer

126 *Ibid.*, 1047.

127 Forme de Seconde Déclaration à la Porte Ottomane, convenue entre les Plénipotentiaires des Hautes Puissances Contractantes, à Londres, 12 July 1827, 14 BFSP.

128 25 June 1827, FO 83/2385.

129 3 July 1827, FO 83/2385.

alignment with the Greeks and interception of all ships carrying troops, arms, ammunition and stores for the use of Ottoman force in Greece without interfering with neutral shipping.[130] If interruption nevertheless occurred, it should be strictly confined to neutrals sailing under the convoy of the Ottoman fleet.[131] The navy was instructed not to use force except in self-defence.[132] Second, the initial mandate was expanded to include certain enforcement measures against the unlicensed Greek corsairs.[133] The justification for imposing such measures was the infancy and inability of the Greek authorities to deal with robbery and plunder and to protect neutral commerce at sea.[134] Thus despite the lack of Porte's consent to mediate, the allied war ships entered and patrolled the territorial waters of the Ottoman Empire subjecting both parties of the conflict to enforcement measures.

The first major use of force by the allies, at the Bay of Navarino, occurred allegedly in response to an attack by the Ottoman-Egyptian fleet after a provisional cessation of hostilities.[135] The magnitude of the collision, however, completely de-legitimised the British claims that it acted neutrally and friendly. The Porte lodged protests condemning such acts as aggression and called them a declaration of war.[136] It asked the allies to (1) immediately cease to pursue

130 Instruction commune aux Ambassadeurs d'Angleterre, de France, et au Ministre de Russie, de Constantinople, convenue entre les Plénipotentiaires des Hautes Puissances Contractantes, 12 July 1827 and Seconde Instruction commune aux Officiers Commandans, dans les Mers du Levant, les Escadres respectives des Hautes Puisances Contractantes; convenue entre les Plénipotentiaires de ces meme Hautes Puissances, 12 July 1827, *Papers relative to the affairs of Greece*, 1, 9–10.

131 Protocole réserve de la Conférence du 15 Octobre, 1827 – Secret instructions to be addressed to the Admirals commanding the Squadrons of the three Powers in the Mediterranean, *Ibid.*, 17.

132 *Ibid.* In a confidential letter, the British Ambassador in Constantinople wrote to Admiral Codrington that force was allowed as a last resort: 'On the subject of collision for instance, we agree that although the measures to be executed by you are not to be adopted in a hostile spirit, and although it is clearly the intention of the Allied Governments to avoid, if possible, anything that may bring on war, yet the prevention of supplies, as states in your instructions, is ultimately to be enforced, if necessary; and when all other means are exhausted, *by cannon shot'* Edward Codrington: *Queries and Answers* (London: J.Cowell, 1828), 13 [emphasis added].

133 Protocole réserve de la Conférence du 15 Octobre 1827, *Papers relative to the affairs of Greece*. See further Rubin, *Piracy*, 216–220.

134 British Order in Council, relative to the prevention of certain Armed Vessels under the Greek Flag, from committing depredations on British Commerce, 16 November 1827, 14 BFSP 784.

135 See further Christopher M. Woodhouse, *The Battle of Navarino* (London: Hodder & Stoughton, 1965); Smiley, 'War without War', 42–69.

136 Proclamation of the Ottoman Porte, declining the Mediation of the Allied Powers, and the Proposed Armistice with the Greeks, 20 December 1827, 14 BFSP 1052, 1055.

the Greek question; (2) pay indemnities for the damages caused to the Ottoman fleet; and (3) provide satisfaction to the Sublime Porte and the sultan.[137] Great Britain, on its part, justified the battle as self-defence and called it an 'untoward' event.[138] The prime minister, Viscount Goderich (1782–1859), stated that the possibility of collision of the allied and Ottoman fleets was predicted with the protocol and the treaty, for if the British government was justified in adopting these instruments to preserve British interests then it was 'no less justified in adopting that more direct and coercive interference'.[139] The request for reparation was rejected on the basis that the allied squadrons were acting in self-defence upon an attack by the Ottoman-Egyptian fleet.[140]

In the aftermath of the battle, the nature and purpose of the collective intervention was seriously challenged. First, there was much criticism against the enforcement actions of the allies from other European states.[141] Second, the British efforts for collective response to the crisis were undermined when Russia declared war on the Ottoman Empire.[142] Britain declined a Russian invitation to join. For Britain, the 'ulterior measures' envisaged in the Treaty of London 'do not exclude hostilities', but they also not necessarily lead to such a consequence.[143] According to the Foreign Office, the *travaux préparatoires* and the subsequent developments to the treaty led to the conclusion that its objective would be best achieved by 'measures short of war', and only in last instance by measures of coercion only in the territory of Greece.[144] Thus a general war effort against the Ottoman Empire, although legally justifiable for Russia,[145] was not compatible with British interests.

All of the above suggests that for the first time in the aftermath of the Vienna Congress of 1815, Great Britain has classified a civil war as a 'threat to

137 M. le Général Guilleminot à M. le Baron de Damas, 11 Novembre 1827, *Papers relative to the affairs of Greece*, 19.

138 Speech of the Lords Commissioners, to both Houses of Parliament, on Tuesday, 29 January 1828, 15 BFSP 1.

139 *Ibid.*

140 Note adressée a son Excellence le Reis Effendi, par les Ambassadeurs des trois Cours, 10 Novembre 1827, *Papers relative to the affairs of Greece*, 22.

141 For example, for Austria the blockade and battle of Navarino constituted an act of war: see Metternich to Esterhazy, 29 October 1827, in Prince Richard Metternich (ed.), *Memoirs of Prince Metternich, 1815–1829* (London: Richard Bentley & Son, New Burlington Street, 1881), 413.

142 Russian Declaration of War against Turkey, 14 April 1828, 15 BFSP 656–662.

143 The Earl of Dudley to Prience Lieven, 6 March 1828, *Papers relative to the affairs of Greece*, 39.

144 *Ibid.*

145 Earl of Aberdeen to Prince Lieven, 6 June 1828, *Papers relative to the Affairs of Greece*, 78.

European peace and tranquillity'. The threat, according to Britain, consisted of the wide repercussions of the civil war beyond the borders accompanied with the humanitarian consequences of the conflict in total.

6 Conclusion

The early nineteenth century was a formative period for international law with regards civil war. This chapter, through a case study, tried to show the maladies of a century often idealistically perceived as an era of peace, and in particular, the intensity of enforcement actions of the great powers in the so-called 'semi-peripheral' parts of the world. For Britain, the Greek question was part of the 'burning' Russo-Ottoman relations and British actions have to be read against its desire for containment of that conflict. The following conclusions unfold.

First, Britain discovered that the legal consequences of piracy could not be attached to foreigners whose degree of organisation and ability to conform with the laws of war were insufficient to justify the classification of 'belligerency', but could not properly be classified as 'piracy' in the British municipal admiralty law sense because of the lack of an *animus furandi*. Second, Britain only gradually resorted to neutral rights and duties. This largely depended on the capacity of the rebels to effectively practice the usages and customs of warfare. Third, Britain's pro-active role in the Greek conflict was not based on humanitarian principles. The analysis above shows that Britain did not intervene to save foreign subjects from their own government, but primarily to save its own nationals and their property when the territorial state was unable to do so. Further, every intent to intervene was collective and founded on the right of self-preservation. The British argument for collective action seems to rest on the Vattelian conception of the possibility of an international law enforcement against disturbers of the peace and the balance of power, and the insistence that such measures should be taken collectively rather than be left to individual avengers.[146] Another important element that resurfaced in every justification for intervention was the self-denying clause for territorial expansion.

Finally, the chapter unpacked the role of international law in the governmental decision-making by looking *whether* and *when* a legal advice was sought and given by the Law Officers of the Crown. The paper showed that the King's Advocate and the other Law Officers of the Crown were frequently consulted but their legal advice did not often factor into policy.

146 Walter Rech, *Enemies of Mankind. Vattel's Theory of Collective Security* (Leiden: Martinus Nijhoff, 2013), 125–127.

Acknowledgements

Many thanks to Randall Lesaffer and Inge Van Hulle for their useful comments on the first draft. I am also indebted to the Laureate Programme of International Law at the University of Melbourne where I did a great amount of research and was given the opportunity to present the findings of the paper. All errors and omissions remain my own.

PART 2

International Law and Empire

CHAPTER 4

Equality of Non-European Nations in International Law

Andrew Fitzmaurice

The return of empire in historical scholarship has had an extraordinary impact upon the history of international law over the past twenty years. Numerous studies have shown that international law was an instrument of empire. International law, we are told, established a hierarchy of states. At the top were European states and the new states of America, while certain supposedly 'semi-civilised' nations held a middling position and so-called 'uncivilised' territories sat at the bottom. This hierarchy licensed the states at the top, European states, to act in ways that were deemed appropriate in order to bring civility and commerce to those peoples at other points of the hierarchy. Different degrees of intervention in and control over non-European nations were justified according to their position in the hierarchy. Guardianship was justified over 'semi-civilised' peoples, with existing property relations, allowing the protection of commerce; such guardianship might include control over sovereignty. Over 'uncivilised' nations, believed to possess no property or sovereignty, colonisation was justified.

This system, if we can describe it as such, was largely a creation of nineteenth-century international law and it gained momentum during the course of that century. Prior to that, historians have argued, the natural law theories which dominated the law of nations permitted some Europeans to treat non-European nations as of more or less equal standing in the society of nations.[1] Growing nationalism in the nineteenth century encouraged a view of the law of nations that excluded non-European nations from possessing equal status, and its practitioners frequently referred to it as the European Law of Nations as though, we are told, there was no other (although the epithet 'European' might just as easily imply that there was another more universal law

1 The most noted example of this argument is in the work of Alexandrowicz, see: Charles H. Alexandrowicz, *The Law of Nations in Global History*, David Armitage and Jennifer Pitts (eds.) (Oxford: Oxford University Press, 2017).

 | DOI:10.1163/9789004412088_005

of nations, one with less detail than that which applied to Europe, and that, as we shall see, is precisely what Lord Stowell, and Sir Travers Twiss, argued).[2] Nineteenth-century international lawyers therefore argued for an unequal hierarchy in international society which, in turn, justified further imperial interventions by European states in the non-European world.

This portrayal of the inequality of non-European nations in international law does not hold up to close examination. It is true that it conforms to the ideas of certain nineteenth-century jurists, such as James Lorimer, the Regius Professor of Public Law, the Law of Nature and of Nations at the University of Edinburgh, but there was a diversity of views on the status of non-European nations in the society of nations amongst nineteenth-century jurists.[3] A number of nineteenth-century jurists argued for the equality of non-European nations in international law. This chapter focuses upon one of those jurists, Travers Twiss (1809–1897), and his reasons for arguing for the *equality* of what he described as 'Oriental' nations in international society.

1 King's College and the Ottomans

Travers Twiss was a prominent Victorian ecclesiastical and international lawyer. He held positions in Oxford, as a teacher of civil law, which was the common basis for ecclesiastical and international law, and he reached the position of Regius Professor of Civil Law in 1856. He also held positions in London, where he worked in the college of civil lawyers, the Doctors Commons, and he held prominent legal posts both in the Church of England, notably as Vicar General to the Archbishop of Canterbury, and as an advocate in the Admiralty courts, rising to Queen's Advocate in 1867. Over the course of his career, there were many occasions upon which he was engaged with non-European people – real people – on questions of international law.

Twiss' first professional office in international law was at King's College, London, which had been founded in 1829. On 19 January 1849, Richard Jelf (1791–1871), principal of King's College London, pointed out to the governing Council of the college that 'three Egyptian gentleman' had recently been admitted to the College 'with the view of being educated as Diplomatists'.[4]

2 See Jennifer Pitts, 'Empire and legal universalisms in the eighteenth century', *American Historical Review* 117 (2012), 92–121.

3 James Lorimer, *The Institutes of the Law of Nations* (2 vols., Edinburgh: William Blackwood and Sons, 1883).

4 College Minutes, 19 January 1849, King's College Archive, MS KA/IC/M5, 46–47.

In fact, the college Calendar from 1849 reveals that there were in total, during the course of the year, 'eight young Egyptians, sent over by the Viceroy of Egypt' to King's College and who were to be trained for a career of 'Diplomatic Service'.[5] Since the expulsion of Napoleon in 1801, Egypt had exercised a great degree of autonomy under the rule of Muhammed Ali who, through to 1848, embarked upon a programme of modernisation combined with territorial expansion, a combination also characteristic of a number of nineteenth-century European states. That programme included sending students to Europe for training in industrial, military and diplomatic arts. The policy was strongly supported by Britain, particularly with Viscount Palmerston as Foreign Secretary and Prime Minister, because it furthered Palmerston's vision of a strong Ottoman Empire which could serve as a bulwark against the Russian Empire, preventing its feared spread south as far as the Bosporus or even further, through Syria, where it could imperil British trade routes to the East. Rather than seeking to influence the Ottomans through expensive direct controls, Palmerston and British policy more generally encouraged free trade and liberal reforms in the Ottoman Empire, including Egypt, which they believed would strengthen Ottoman power as well as advance British trade.[6]

In 1848, Muhammed Ali had been replaced first by his son and then by his grandson, Abbas I, who tried to undo many of his reforms, but in 1849 Egyptian students were still being trained in Europe, including by being sent to study the law of nations at King's College. The principal of King's College argued accordingly that the College needed a chair of the law of nations in order to provide the necessary training for these students. The College Calendar added that 'it is thought probably that such a Professorship may ultimately be made available to English students with a view to the same profession'.[7] Jelf proposed to the College Council that Travers Twiss, 'who until lately had filled the Chair of Political Economy at Oxford', was 'a gentleman now in London who is fully competent to fill this Chair'. The Council agreed to establish a 'Professorship of the Law of Nations' and to offer the post to Twiss who, in turn, heartily accepted by return of post.[8] It is worth pausing to note here that one of the first professional positions in international law established in Britain in the nineteenth century was created, contrary to our image of the 'European' law of nations, in order to teach non-European students.

---

5 *The Calendar of King's College London for 1849–50* (London: John W. Parker, 1849), 24.

6 Ronald Robinson, John Gallagher and Alice Denny, *Africa and the Victorians: The Official Mind of Imperialism* (London: Macmillan Press, 1961), 77–78.

7 *Ibid.*

8 Twiss to Jelf, 20 January 1849, King's College Archive, KA/IC/T25.

In 1855, Twiss published his lectures given at King's College. That publication became his first general statement of the principles of international law: namely, his *Two Introductory Lectures on the Science of International Law*. These may have been the lectures that the College *Annual Report* mentions Twiss 'very kindly gave' to students in the Department of Civil Service and Commerce, and 'to the public generally', in 1854.[9] Although the Report does not mention whether the Egyptian students were present on that occasion, their presence in the College and role in the justification for Twiss' position form part of the context for the publication of that text. To accept a post to train Egyptian diplomats in the law of nations was to accept the application of the law of nations to Egypt. Following the Crimean War and the 1856 Treaty of Paris, Twiss would explicitly state, as we shall see, that the Ottoman Empire, which formally included Egypt, *was* a member of the society of nations. Clearly, for the Palmerstonians in Britain, there were strategic advantages to admitting the Ottomans into that society.

Twiss resigned from King's College in 1855 to take the position as Regius Professor at Oxford. One of his jobs as Regius Professor was, at Oxford's annual founder's day ceremony, to award honorary Doctorates of Civil Law, or DCLs, to eminent figures. In his first year as Regius Professor, in June 1856, Twiss awarded DCLs to representatives of the victorious powers in the Crimean War, which had only been concluded the previous March with the Treaty of Paris, as well as to celebrated generals of the war. The recipients included Prince Frederick William of Prussia, the Prince of Baden, and the war hero Major-General Fenwick Williams, all of whom were greeted with great cheers from the auditorium. A further recipient was the ambassador Constantine Musurus Bey, the representative of Britain's ally, the Ottoman Sultan. Twiss presented Musurus Bey to the audience in the Sheldonian as the 'first Christian subject of the Porte' to have held the post of ambassador. Christian subjects of the sultan were useful for easing relations with Europe and it may also have been the case that some or all of the Egyptian students sent to King's College were Coptic or hailed from other Christian sects in Egypt. Twiss also praised the sultan for having granted full privileges to his Christian subjects (the absence of which had been a pretext for the Russians to go to war in 1853), although a call for cheers for the sultan and Omar Pasha, the Ottoman general, reportedly 'fell flat' because they 'were rather abstract ideas'.[10] Twiss' encomium of the

---

9 *The Calendar of King's College London for 1855–56* (London: John W. Parker, 1849), 44–45.

10 'The Oxford Commemoration', *Carlisle Patriot* (7 June 1856), 5. For further reports on Twiss in this ceremony, see: *London Evening Standard* (5 June 1856), 1; *Oxford Journal* (7 June 1856), 5.

Turks on this occasion anticipated the publication five years later, in 1861, of his most important work on international law, *The Law of Nations*, in which he declared that the 1856 Treaty of Paris 'may be considered as the formal Act of Reception of the Sublime Porte into the Fellowship of European Nations'.[11] At issue here, for Twiss, as for his contemporaries, was the crucial question of the scope of international law. Whereas the Ottomans had been completely outside the 1815 Congress of Vienna, Twiss pointed out that, by virtue of the Treaty of Paris, the contracting powers had guaranteed the 'independence and integrity of the Ottoman Empire' and its inclusion within international law. At the same time, the Ottomans had accepted that regulations established in the Congress of Vienna, governing open navigation of the great rivers of Europe, would be extended to the Danube.[12]

2 India

The age of revolutions was not restricted to Europe, it was global, and Twiss engaged with it beyond the European stage and, in particular, in the British Empire. The Empire was not spared the turbulence from which Britain itself was supposedly free.[13] A notable instance of Twiss' engagement with those revolutions was when he was employed in 1857 by the King of Awadh, the northern Indian state just south of Nepal, to provide an opinion on the legality of the kingdom's annexation by the British East India Company in 1856. The East India Company had ruled much of India since the mid-eighteenth century through a system of indirect control, leaving local rulers in power but under Company domination through a system of unequal treaties. By the 1840s, the Company had grown impatient with that system, seeking direct British administration, and began a series of annexations of Indian states and cities. The last of those annexations was Awadh, which was a large state, approximately four hundred kilometres from north to south and two hundred east to west. It was a buffer between East India Company territories and Nepal and was ruled by Nawabs, or kings, of Persian origin, from their capital at Lucknow. The seizure

11 Travers Twiss, *The Law of Nations Considered as Independent Communities: On the right and duties of nations in time of peace* (Oxford: Clarendon Press, 1861), 105.

12 *Ibid.*, 106.

13 Miles Taylor, 'The 1848 Revolutions in the British Empire', *Past and Present* 166 (2000), 146–181. For the age of revolutions in global context, see: Chris Bayly, *The Birth of the Modern World, 1780–1914* (Malden: Blackwell Publishing, 2004); David Armitage and Sanjay Subrahmanyam (eds.), *The Age of Revolutions in Global Context* (Basingstoke: Palgrave, 2010).

of Awadh on 11 February 1856 was a trigger for the 1857 Sepoy Rebellion, or the 'Indian Mutiny' to the British and the 'First War of Independence' to some Indian nationalists. The rebellion began amongst sepoys, or Indian soldiers, in the East India Company army, many of whom were concerned by the series of annexations and the potential loss, as a consequence of the suppression of local laws, of their own privileges. The rebellion spread rapidly throughout northern India and continued from May in 1857 through to July the following year. In that time, many thousands were killed on both sides and many atrocities were committed. The massacre of the British in Cawnpore (or Kanpur) and the siege of Lucknow hardened British attitudes, leading to reprisals after the war in which many more thousands of Indians were massacred.

On the eve of these events, just months prior to the rebellion, Wajid Ali Shah, the deposed King of Awadh, now in exile in Calcutta, resolved to appeal to British justice against the annexation of Awadh. Due to his own ill health, he sent to England his mother, the 'Queen Dowager' or 'Queen Mother', as the English described her, his brother, his son and a large retinue. The English press closely followed the procession of the Queen Dowager and her retinue from Calcutta to Suez, through Egypt and on to England, where they arrived in August 1856.[14] While there, they made a petition to parliament, gained an audience with the queen, and requested, on behalf of Wajid Ali Shah, Travers Twiss' opinion on the standing of the annexation of Awadh in the law of nations. Twiss' response was consistent with his more general insistence in his writings and lectures on the need for respect for sovereignty and, in this case, sovereign agreements. He found that the annexation was a violation of the law of nations. Following his usual historical methodology, he carefully recounted the history of the case. He explained that prior to 1798, the 'Sovereigns of Oude [ie.Awadh]' had made treaties of 'equal alliance' with the East India Government, but thereafter the treaties had been unequal: that is, they involved a degree of dependence of the Awadh Sovereigns upon the Company government. The first of these later treaties in 1798 was one of 'offensive and defensive alliance' on both sides whereby the Awadh government agreed to a financial 'subsidy' to the Company in return for 'protection'.[15] According to the terms of the second, in 1801, the East India Company provided a 'territorial guaranty' in return for a large territorial cession.[16] In this treaty, the 'Sovereign of Oude' also engaged to establish

14 See, for example: *Worcestershire Chronicle* (13 August 1856), 4; *Westmorland Gazette* (16 August 1856), 3.

15 *Case of his Majesty the King of Oude: Copy Opinion of Dr Twiss*, Paris, Bibliothèque nationale de France, Fol.-NT-333, fols.1–2.

16 *Ibid.*, fols. 2–3.

a 'system of administration' that would be 'conducive to the prosperity of his subjects and be calculated to secure the lives and property of the inhabitants'.[17] He undertook, that is, to provide the conditions for security and prosperity that were regarded, according to the law of nations, to be the responsibility of all sovereigns. The treaty of 1837 pointed out, however, that the 1801 treaty provided 'no remedy for the neglect of that solemn and paramount obligation' to provide security and prosperity. The 1837 treaty therefore stipulated that if 'gross and systematic oppression should prevail within the Oude dominions', the British Government reserved the right to appoint its own officers to administer the territory to the extent necessary to restore order at the expense of the Oude treasuries.[18] Article 8 of that treaty stipulated that if the governor general of India should be compelled to resort to this measure, he would 'endeavour, as far as possible, to maintain… the native institutions and forms of administration… so as to facilitate the restoration of those territories to the Sovereign of Oude when the proper period for such restoration should arrive'.[19]

This article in the treaty was an obstacle to the policy of annexation, what was called 'the doctrine of lapse', that had been pursued since the 1840s, because no such consideration to 'native institutions' and administration was given under those annexations. The governor general, James Broun-Ramsey, Lord Dalhousie, therefore insisted, when he annexed Awadh, that the treaty of 1837 was 'null and void' and that only the treaty of 1801 prevailed which contained no obstacles to annexation.[20] His grounds for that claim were that the Secret Committee of the Court of Directors of the East India Company had disallowed the treaty when they received it in 1838.[21] Twiss pointed out that this fact had not been transmitted either to the Court of Awadh or to British officers in India who continued to refer to the provisions of the treaty between 1837 and the moment when the governor general declared it null and void in 1855.[22] The question, therefore, was whether a treaty was valid when it had not been formally ratified but had been treated as valid by both parties to it. Twiss cited Grotius to point out that 'if the Sovereign power is silent', as it had been in this case by failing to communicate its will, then certain acts performed by the executive government would provide 'virtual ratification' if those acts 'cannot

17 *Ibid.*, fol.3.

18 *Ibid.*, fol.4. On the history of the claim to a responsibility to protect used to justify imperial expansion, see: Andrew Fitzmaurice, 'Sovereign Trusteeship and Empire', *Theoretical Inquiries in Law* 16 (2015), 447–471.

19 *Case of his Majesty the King of Oude*, fols.3–4.

20 *Ibid.*, fol.5.

21 *Ibid.*, fol.5.

22 *Ibid.*, fols.6–8.

be referred to any other source than the treaty'. In this case, he argued that executive government on both sides had indeed behaved in ways that implied the validity of the treaty. He terminated his opinion with the following judgement on 24 February 1857:

> I am constrained to come to the conclusion that the Governor-General of India, in Council, was not authorised by the Law of Nations to set aside the treaty of 1837 as inoperative, and to look exclusively to the treaty of 1801 as the instrument by which the mutual relations of the East India Company and the Rulers of Oude were regulated.[23]

For Twiss, the concern was probably less the sovereignty of Awadh, which he noted had been forced into unequal alliances, and was therefore a dependent sovereign, and rather respect for sovereign agreements. He had argued in the case of Schleswig and Holstein that dependent states were virtually no sovereigns at all, although in consistently referring to the 'Sovereign of Oude' he appeared to believe the degree of dependence of Awadh to be less than that for Schleswig and Holstein. The dukes of Schleswig and Holstein, he argued, were not sovereigns during the periods in which the duchies were dependent states of the empires of Denmark and Germany.[24] At the same time, dependant states were nevertheless subject to sovereign agreements, or treaties, and such agreements must be respected. Twiss' opinion was cited at great length in newspapers and, in one such article, John Davenport, a strong critic of British policy in India, cited Vattel on the 'sacred and inviolable' nature of treaties.[25] They were sacred, as Vattel argued, because they secured the 'safety and repose' of nations and all things that tended to the preservation of states were sacred, as it were, because self-preservation was the first law of nature. These were sentiments precisely in accord with Twiss's own views, so that it comes as no surprise that he found in favour of the 'King of Oude' and against the actions of the Company. That Twiss also ruled against a colonising company with sovereign pretensions is particularly striking given the great efforts he made, later in life, to substantiate precisely such sovereign claims by colonising companies, notably King Leopold II's International Association for the Congo.

In addition to newspaper coverage critical of the annexation of Awadh, Twiss' opinion was also reproduced in a tract calling for the restitution of

---

23 *Ibid.*, fol.10.

24 Travers Twiss, *The Relations of the Duchies of Schleswig and Holstein to the Crown of Denmark and the Germanic Confederation* (London: Longman, Brown, Green, and Longmans, 1848), 65–66.

25 *Morning Chronicle* (25 July 1857), 3. See also: *London Evening Standard* (13 May 1858), 5.

Awadh to the 'family of Oude', written by Samuel Lucas, the anti-slavery campaigner and newspaper editor. Lucas also demanded reparation and an investigation into whether annexation was a benefit to commerce.[26] Such demands were not met, and the petition to the House of Commons did not succeed, but the East India Company was seen as responsible for the events that provoked the 1857 'Rebellion', including the annexation of Awadh, so that the government passed the Government of India Act in 1858, ending more than 250 years of Company activities and transferring its functions to the Crown with the establishment of the British Raj. At the same time, the soldiers who resisted the Indian Rebellion were celebrated as heroes in England and were feted upon their return. Prominent amongst those celebrations was the annual Encaenia, or commemoration of founders at Oxford, held in the Sheldonian Theatre, in which DCL's were awarded to distinguished figures, which frequently meant to heroes of the Empire. The first Encaenia to celebrate the heroes of the Indian Mutiny, as it was then called, was on Wednesday 16 June 1858, just four days before the rebellion came to an end with the fall of Gwalior. On this occasion, Sir John Inglis was presented at the ceremony for the award of the DCL. Inglis had been responsible for the defence of the British garrison at Lucknow, taking over the command after the commanding officer, Sir Henry Lawrence, had died from a shell during the defence. The defence of Lucknow had captured the public imagination in Britain as several hundred British officers and soldiers, the vast majority of them Indian, had held out against several thousand sepoy rebels for 87 days. The man who presented Inglis for the honorary degree was the Regius Professor of Civil Law, Travers Twiss:

> Dr Twiss, in the course of a Latin speech, dwelt upon the meritorious services of General Inglis and adverted to Lady Inglis [women had been portrayed as particular victims of the rebellion], Havelock and Outram [Major General Henry Havelock and Sir James Outram who both relieved Lucknow], the mention of each being the signal for further applause.[27]

Another report eulogised:

> When General Inglis appeared, with the effects of indisposition still traceable upon his pallid features, thunders of applause burst from area and gallery, and for some time proceedings were utterly at a standstill.[28]

26 [Samuel Lucas], *Dacoitee in Excelcis* (London, 1859), 200. For Twiss's Opinion, see: 192–199.

27 *Birmingham Daily Post*, (18 June 1858), 1.

28 *Essex Standard* (18 June 1858), 3.

A year later, in July 1859, with the Rebellion fully concluded, the celebrations at the commemoration day continued. On this occasion, three of the 'Indian heroes' were presented to the ceremony: namely, Sir John Lawrence who had captured Delhi from the sepoys; Sir Archdale Wilson who had commanded the British troops during the siege of Delhi after his superior died of cholera; and Brigadier Edward Greathead who had also helped capture Delhi and led troops in Agra, Cawnpore and Lucknow, while being responsible for punitive attacks on Indian villages. Travers Twiss performed his customary duty, presenting each of the DCL recipients 'individually in an elegant Latin speech in which their public services, virtues and good qualities were adverted to in glowing and eulogistic language'.[29] The reception was 'remarkable... and will long be remembered by those who witnessed it. The whole theatre rose – the doctors waved their caps like undergraduates – ladies clapped their small hands with all their might, the area was a sea of waving arms'.

3 Admiralty Cases

The Admiralty Courts were the forum in which the everyday business of the law of nations was conducted and, as an Admiralty advocate, Twiss provided opinions on relations between European and non-European powers on hundreds of occasions. Moreover, as Queen's Advocate from 1867 – the equivalent, that is, of an attorney general for international law – he advised the government on a daily basis on matters touching the law of nations. More often than not, as one would expect in the government of a vast empire, those matters touched the interests of non-European nations. The fact that non-European sovereigns were frequently subjects within the Admiralty courts, or central to problems to be considered by the Queen's Advocate, reflected an acknowledgement in practice, regardless of what some jurists maintained in theory, that those sovereigns belonged, at some level, to the society of nations. Twiss' opinion for Wajid Ali Shah was one of only a number of occasions in which he provided legal judgements for or about Indian sovereigns. In April 1863, he wrote an opinion concerning the 'Rajah of Mysore', Krishnaraja Wadiyar III. This opinion may either have been commissioned directly by Krishnaraja Wadiyar or, more likely, was in response to a request from the newly established India Office. The opinion addressed whether Krishnaraja Wadiyar could adopt a successor to his territories. The Wadiyar dynasty had ruled Mysore since the fourteenth

29 *Oxford Chronicle and Reading Gazette* (9 July 1859), 2. See also: *Oxford University and City Herald* (9 July 1859), 11, 12.

century and passed through an inherited male line of succession. In the second half of the eighteenth century, the kingdom had fallen under the control of Hyder Ali and his son Tipu Sultan who, through an expansionism which aggravated their neighbours and through resistance to the East India Company, provoked the Anglo-Mysore wars. Those, wars led to much of Mysore being broken up between the Nizam of Hyderabad, the Maratha Confederacy, and the East India Company, while the Wadiyars were restored to the remaining rump.[30] In 1831, the East India Company argued that Mysore was badly governed and seized control of the administration, leaving Krishnaraja Wadiyar III with little power. A further threat to the Wadiyar dynasty arose from Krishnaraja Wadiyar not having a male heir, raising the danger that the British or the Nizam of Hyderbad could invoke the doctrine of lapse to annex the state entirely. In February 1863, Krishnaraja Wadiyar's son-in-law, Sardar Chikka Krishnaraj Urs, died and, several days later, his daughter gave birth to a boy. Only weeks later, Twiss was consulted on whether, according to the terms of the treaties which concluded the Anglo-Mysore wars and re-established the rule of the Wadiyars, Krishnaraja Wadiyar could name his grandson as the heir to his title. Twiss responded that 'the territory ceded to the Rajah of Mysore, by the Treaty of Mysore, was ceded in absolute sovereignty descendible to his heirs'.[31] The whole purpose of this treaty, and the Treaty of Seringapatam, he argued, was a 'settlement of the dominions' of the Tipu Sultan and the 'effectual establishment' of the maharajah, the Wadiyars, in the government of Mysore. Twiss was therefore 'of [the] opinion that, as a Sovereign Prince, the rajah of Mysore can adopt a successor to his dominions' and there was 'nothing in the language of the treaties to prevent the exercise of such a right'. He warned, however, that if the maharajah died without naming a successor, his territories would revert to the nizam of Hyderbad and to the British government, who had reinstalled the Wadiyars in Mysore. On the 25 April, Twiss further clarified his opinion, stating that the Maharajah could not establish his successor through a last will and testament but must do so by law and that, if he did so, he would effectively block any claims from the nizam of Hyderbad upon Mysore.[32]

The complex treaty relations and lines of succession in India provided a number of occasions in which Twiss' expertise was employed. Again, in October 1864, the British Government sought his opinion on the nawabship of the

30 For background to the treaties arising from the Anglo-Mysore wars, see: Robert Travers, 'A British Empire by Treaty in Eighteenth Century India', in Saliha Belmessous (ed.), *Empire by Treaty* (Oxford: Oxford University Press, 2015), 132–160.

31 Travers Twiss, 'Ex parte. The Rajah of Mysore. 23 April 1863', *Law Officer's Opinions, 1862–1886*, Harvard Law Library, MS 1110, vol.1, 9–10.

32 Travers Twiss, 'Further opinion on the above. 25 April 1863', *Ibid.*, 10.

Carnatic, in South India, which had become vacant in 1855 when the Nawab Ghouse Khan died. Azim Jah, the brother of Azam Jah, the eleventh nawab, who preceded Ghouse Khan, claimed the title to the throne. However, his claim was not approved by the British until 1867. Twiss' view may well have been critical to that recognition as in his 1864 opinion he argued that, under the law of nations, the Carnatic Treaty of 1801 obliged the British East India Company, and its successor the British Raj, to respect the hereditary succession of the nawabs of the Carnatic and to provide them with twenty percent of the territory's revenue in exchange for their own assumption of authority and the remaining eighty percent of revenue.[33]

Twiss also regularly provided opinions on jurisdiction and administration in areas within which Britain exercised extraterritorial power, including under the Ottoman capitulations. In a joint opinion, he advised the British Government on whether British subjects in Turkey should take advantage of the Ottoman offer to allow the possession of real property in Turkey in exchange for the same subjects relinquishing their extraterritorial privileges, an offer already taken up by many French residents but one that Twiss noted came at a high cost.[34] In a further joint opinion with three other law officers, Twiss responded to the complaint by Ali Pasha Mubarak, the senior minister in the Egyptian government, while visiting London in 1868, that reform was needed in the judicial system in Egypt in cases concerning 'natives and foreigners'. Ali Pasha pointed out that in many cases foreigners resident in Egypt withdrew themselves from the jurisdiction of the 'native tribunals' and insisted upon being tried by their consuls. This was an abuse, as Twiss and his colleagues noted, of the principle in the law of nations that 'actor sequitur forum rei': namely, that cases should be tried in the forum in which the grievance occurred. These abuses, moreover, were inconsistent with the 'letter of the capitulations'. The complaints of Ali Mubarak, therefore, 'appear to us to be only too well founded' and the 'usurped Consular jurisdiction' was 'most galling and offensive'.[35]

On questions regarding Asian sovereigns, Twiss provided diverse opinions including on the drafting of a treaty between Britain and the Rajah of Kedah, a dependency of Siam (and now a northern state of present-day Malaysia). This treaty outlined the obligations of the Rajah to protect British subjects from crime, specifically 'gang robbery', 'great personal violence', murder, arson, rape

33 Travers Twiss, 'In re the Nawaubship of the Carnatic: Opinion. 15 October 1864', *Ibid.*, 42–44.

34 Travers Twiss, 'Turkey. Tenure of land by foreigners. 29 June 1868', *Ibid.*, vol. 2, 50.

35 Travers Twiss et al., 'Egypt. Judicial system in, as to alteration of, in cases where natives and foreigners are concerned. 25 June 1868', *Ibid.*, 45–49.

and burglary.[36] He also provided opinions on jurisdiction in Japanese ports, the suppression of piracy in China and the legality of Chinese stations imposing tax upon the opium trade.[37] Regarding Africa, he provided numerous opinions, including on the creation of a vice-admiralty court in Zanzibar, as well as an admiring account of the ad hoc equity courts that had been established between foreign traders and West African sovereigns.[38] In all these cases he took seriously the notion of non-European sovereigns as actors in the law of nations.

4 The Institute of International Law and 'Oriental' Nations

By the 1870s, Twiss had established a reputation as one of the outstanding international lawyers of his generation, a reputation built on his early work on the *Oregon Question* (1846), his Professorship in International Law at King's College, his Regius Professorship of Civil Law at Oxford, as well as upon his appointment in 1867 to the position in the Admiralty Courts as Queen's Advocate, upon his *Law of Nations* in two volumes, *Peace* and *War*, and, in the 1870s, his work on the *Black Book of the Admiralty*. In the 1870s he consolidated that reputation with prolific publication of a series of articles on international law in the *Law Magazine and Review*, the *Revue de droit international*, and the *Annuaire de l'Institut de Droit International*. With this standing, Twiss was elected as a member of the Institute of International Law at its August and September meeting in Geneva in 1874, which he attended. He immediately set about involving himself in its affairs and one of his first duties was to address himself to the question of the applicability of the law of nations to non-European nations,

36 Travers Twiss et al., 'Draft of Convention between Her Majesty and the Rajah of Queddah. 10 December 1868', *Ibid.*, 272–273.

37 Travers Twiss et al., 'Japan. Vice-Admiralty Jurisdiction in Consular Courts, 12 September 1868', *Ibid.*, 180; Travers Twiss et al., 'Regulations drawn up by H.M's Minister in Japan on opening of the ports of Hiogo and Osaka, 29 February 1868', *Ibid.*, vol.3, 253–254; Travers Twiss et al., 'As to suppression of piracy in the Chinese seas, 28 August 1868', *Ibid.*, vol.2, 151; Travers Twiss et al., 'As to rendition to the Chinese Govt. of pirates captures by H.M's Cruizers, 12 September 1868', *Ibid.*, 181; Travers Twiss et al., 'As to the establishment of Opium Tax Stations in the vicinity of Hong Kong by Chinese Govt. 5th January, 1869', *Ibid.*, 299.

38 Travers Twiss et al., 'Zanzibar. As to the establishment of a Vice-Admiralty Court at. 30th September, 1869', *Ibid.*, vol.3, 35–38; Travers Twiss et al., 'As to the legality of certain courts of equity established beyond HM's jurisdiction on the West Coast of Africa, August, 1870', *Ibid.*, vol.6, 337–339; Travers Twiss et al., 'Extension of jurisdiction in certain territory on the West Coast of Africa, 15 January 1872', *Ibid.*, vol.7, 423–424.

a question brought to the Institute by David Dudley Field. In 1874, Field, an American law reformer who was deeply committed to the codification of law, presented the Institute with a memorandum in which he posed the question of whether, and in what conditions, the 'unwritten' European law of nations was applicable to 'oriental nations'.[39] By 'unwritten', Field appeared to mean the fundamental principles. He explained that during a recent voyage around the world he had the opportunity to observe the law of nations in practice. He discovered that those countries that had not been submitted to Christian powers found themselves in an 'abnormal' condition from the point of view of international law. What we call the 'law of nations' was just, he said, an 'assemblage of juridical rules' which Christianity had made to sanction Christian peoples and from whose authority 'the greatest part of the world escapes'. He conceded that this European 'international law' was not completely unknown outside Europe and that it was invoked, for example, in relations between China and Japan. Nevertheless, he pointed out that the international relations that prevailed between non-European nations were very different from those between Christian states. To the degree that it was recognised, the law of nations in the Ottoman Empire, in Asia, with the exception of Siberia and 'Hindustan', and in all of Africa, with the exception of Liberia (a colony of freed United States' slaves), was practiced with many exceptions and modifications.[40]

In general, Field observed, it can be said that the law of nations, as it was understood in the Christian world, had not reached the rest of the world in its fullest expression ('plenitude').[41] The reason for this limitation, he argued, was evident. This system of law had been developed in Europe with the purpose of aiding commerce and community between nations. By contrast, non-Christian nations were isolationist, uninterested in community with the rest of the world. A consequence of this contrast was that when people came from Europe and America to live in these non-Christian nations they were obliged to live apart and to conduct their commerce apart. In other words, this difference necessitated the creation of extraterritorial enclaves. This separation also necessitated those enclaves creating their own laws and conditions of security. Turning back to the question of the applicability of the European law of nations to 'oriental nations', he argued that the fact that it had not been adopted more generally was 'purely historic'. This was a system of rights born in Europe, applied in Europe, and fashioned for Europe, before any considerable

39 David Dudley Field, 'De la possibilité d'appliquer le droit international Européen aux nations Orientales', *Revue de droit international et de législation comparèe* 7 (1875), 659–668.

40 Ibid., 659.

41 Ibid., 662.

relations existed with countries outside Europe.[42] The important differences were not religious but more generally cultural. These were not differences of civilisation, or a dichotomy between the civilised and 'non-civilised'. Is it possible, he asked in reference to China, to call a country that had a regular system of government for thousands of years uncivilised?[43] The question of the applicability of the law of nations cannot, he argued, be answered by the matter of civilisation. It was necessary, therefore, that oriental nations enjoy all the privileges and duties of the law of nations, including those of sovereignty, equality, perpetuity, territory and property. At the same time, as long as the legal institutions and practices of those countries remained repugnant to Europeans, it was necessary that Europeans carry their extraterritorial powers with them while in those countries. While visiting China, Field declared, he had witnessed first-hand legal practices in which witnesses were tortured if they refused to admit to crimes, in which there was no legal representation, in which women did not possess the same rights that they enjoyed in European and American nations. It would be 'revolting', he concluded, to submit 'our own' citizens to such justice.[44] The way forward, until such time as Oriental nations had 'assimilated' to Occidental norms, would be to submit all legal questions involving European and American nationals in Oriental nations to mixed tribunals which followed European standards but were presided over by both consuls and an 'indigenous judge'.[45] It was in the interests of 'humanity' and 'civilisation' that 'oriental nations' be 'as quickly as possible submitted to the empire of international law'.[46] This would mean, he noted in a subsequent statement of this ambition, that they would be admitted to the enjoyment of all the 'rights' and all the 'duties' 'determined by international law'.[47]

In their meeting at The Hague in August 1875, the members of the Institute decided to establish a commission to examine the question put by Dudley Field's memorandum on 'Oriental nations'. They formulated the question of that commission as: 'In what conditions and to what point are the customary laws of Europe applicable to Oriental nations?'[48] The meeting agreed that seven of its members would examine this question, including Dudley Field, James Lorimer, and Joseph Hornung, and that the committee would be chaired by Travers Twiss who would write the report. Twiss insisted that a questionnaire

42 Ibid., 665.
43 Ibid., 664.
44 Ibid., 667.
45 *Annuaire de l'institut de droit international* (1878), 13.1.
46 Field, 'De la possibilité', 667.
47 *Annuaire* (1878), 131.
48 *Annuaire* 1 (1877), 9, 37.

regarding the issues should be printed and sent to 'competent persons' in 'various countries'.[49] The questions were as follows: Question one: 'Is there between the ideas and beliefs of the nationals of oriental countries, on the one hand, and those of Christian nations, on the other hand, touching their obligations, in relation to foreign peoples and individuals, a difference that is so radical that it makes it impossible to contemplate admitting oriental nations to the general community of international law?'; Question two: 'Are the notions of oriental nations regarding the observation of the stipulations of treaties fundamentally different from those of Christian nations on the same subject?'; Question three: 'Do you think it is necessary for Christian governments to accord special protection to missionaries manifested in direct interventions?'. This question was qualified by 'two generally accepted propositions': namely, that 'Christian nations do not have the right to impose upon non-Christian nations their religion and civilization'; and, to paraphrase, that subjects of non-Christian powers do not remove themselves from subjection to the government and laws of their country by virtue of having embraced Christianity. The first question revealed that concern about the universality of the principles underlying the law of nations motivated jurists to reject any suggestion that it was a projection of European religion. The law of nations had been developed during and following the wars of religion in Europe and had, as a consequence, routinely been presented as a system of values that were independent of religion. Grotius had famously boasted in the *Prolegomena* to his *On the Law of War and Peace* that the laws he described, based upon the principle of self-preservation, would have 'validity' even in circumstances 'which cannot be conceded without the utmost wickedness': namely, that 'there is no God'.[50] Twiss' first proposition shows a similar desire for the law of nations to be free of cultural prejudice arising from the civilising mission. The second question, that the Christianity of the subjects of non-Christian powers did not remove them from the duty of subjection to those powers, was likely to have been motivated by the Russian intervention into the Ottoman Empire to supposedly protect Christian subjects (an intervention to which the Swiss jurist, Joseph Hornung, objected).[51]

Question four was 'Does the conduct of Christian missionaries in the country of which you have a special knowledge provide an occasion or pretext for

49 *Ibid.* See also 140–141.

50 Hugo Grotius, *De Jure Belli ac Pacis libri tres* (1625, text of 1646, Classics of International Law, Oxford: Clarendon Press, 1925), Prol. 11.

51 On Hornung and his objection, see: Andrew Fitzmaurice, 'Scepticism of the civilizing mission in international law', in Martti Koskenniemi, Walter Rech and Manuel Jiménez Fonseca (eds.), *International Law and Empire: Historical Explorations* (Oxford: Oxford University Press, 2017), 359–381.

hostile sentiments towards Christian countries?'. Question five: 'Does the social state of Oriental peoples, notably in Persia, Egypt, China, Turkey, and Japan etc, justify the maintenance of consular jurisdiction or other exceptional jurisdiction with the forms of protection that accompany capitulations? In what ways and in what measure could those jurisdictions be modified?'; Question six: 'Is the right of jurisdiction that European countries exercise in the Orient accompanied by a duty to organise courts, consular or otherwise, in a way that will guarantee good and impartial justice?'[52]

In the 1877 meeting of the Institute at Zurich, Twiss reported that he had received some 'interesting' answers to his questionnaire, including from 'Persia', China and Egypt, but that the inquiry remained incomplete.[53] The commission was therefore prolonged. He finally presented his report to the meeting of the Institute at Ghent in 1879.[54] He noted that he had received few responses to his questionnaire because of confidentiality. He commented that questioning retired diplomats was useless because of the speed with which 'oriental' nations were changing, so their advice would be outdated. He observed that it was necessary to distinguish between different degrees of civilisation amongst the non-European nations.[55] Some such as China, Japan and Turkey were civilised and recognised the law of nations, others were cannibals or pagans with little civility.[56] For the first two questions he obtained information on the 'ideas and beliefs of Oriental nations' from 'European experts' and 'even from Asian diplomats accredited to European courts'. From those sources he had 'been assured' that: 1. The difference between Oriental ideas and beliefs and 'ours' is not so great that it is impossible to contemplate admitting 'them' to the community of international law; '2. That the ideas of beliefs of Oriental peoples concerning the observation of treaties are not fundamentally different from those of Christian peoples'. There were differences, he argued, between countries such as China and Japan in their ability to respond quickly to diplomatic issues, but their understanding of their treaty obligations was nevertheless the same. On questions three to six, he found evidence that missionaries had been the cause for hostility to Christian powers.[57] On extraterritorial jurisdiction he found that 'the time has not arrived when European nations can dispense with the forms of protection' which they had obtained by virtue of capitulations but, he added, 'we demand with reason' an improvement in those systems of

52 'Questionaire', *Annuaire* 1 (1880), 298–299.
53 *Annuaire* (1878), 131.
54 *Annuaire* 2 (1880), 314.
55 'Rapport', *Annuaire* 1 (1880), 301.
56 Ibid., 302.
57 Ibid., 304.

justice. His conclusion here was consistent with his advice on Egypt more than ten years earlier as an Admiralty advocate.

To Twiss' report, Joseph Hornung, who had been in the commission, added a dissenting report. Hornung declared that he could not 'prevent himself from making a remark prejudicial to the question'.[58] 'As much', he observed, 'as we wanted to occupy ourselves with Oriental nations, we are always doing so from our own interests and our own point of view'. We think only about 'our commerce, our nationals and coreligionists'. The 'question of the Orient is just a pretext for certain powers who wish to expand. In our rapport with the non-European world we only see our own interests'. The 'opium affair' and the even greater brutality with which Russia had expelled the peoples of the Caucasus region were sufficient to prove 'the inferiority' of civilised states. The European powers 'forced China to open her ports: was that in the interest of China?' 'Everything that happens in Egypt' was 'uniquely for the profit' of Europeans.[59] And with the question with which we are now concerned we are only addressing 'the interests of our nationals'. Hornung's vision was paternalistic. He argued that 'intelligent peoples' should only use their strength to aid the 'weak'.[60] But it was more than merely paternalistic. He looked forward to the creation of the 'world state' that had been 'dreamed of by Kant' which could not be realised until civilised humanity looked to a greater moral purpose than its own interests or those of its nationals or coreligionists.[61] Hornung promised to expand further upon this question in a forthcoming article in the *Revue de droit international* which duly appeared as a series of papers on 'Civilisés et barbares'.[62]

Twiss' report was sandwiched by the sharply contrasting views of two members of his committee. Hornung, on the one hand, who rejected the question posed by the committee and argued that they should address themselves to what duties European states owed 'Oriental' nations, and James Lorimer, on the other, who supported one of the most radically racial interpretations of the law of nations amongst nineteenth-century jurists. Lorimer distinguished between progressive Europeans and non-progressive races, which were everybody else. Writing just three years after the report of the committee on the status of 'Oriental' nations in international society, he observed that the great question facing the future of international law was whether 'the entire

58 Ibid., 305.
59 Ibid.
60 Ibid., 306.
61 Ibid., 307.
62 For Hornung's 'Civilisés et barbares', see Fitzmaurice, 'Scepticism of the civilizing mission'.

subjection of these [non-progressive] races' would be necessary, or whether it was possible there would be 'the gradual development of some oriental form of political organisation hitherto unknown to the history of politics'.[63] He was pessimistic about this second possibility, particularly insofar as the 'Mahommedan' races were concerned. 'The Turks, as a race', he wrote, 'are probably incapable of the political development which would render their adoption of constitutional government possible'.[64] The Koran 'stood between' Muslim countries and the 'world without', 'unless we are all to become Mahometans'.[65]

Twiss steered a course between Lorimer and Hornung. He agreed with Lorimer that there was a hierarchy within the society of nations but, in contrast to Lorimer, he placed a large number of 'Oriental' nations in the top level of that hierarchy. He agreed with Hornung on the equality of many non-European peoples and he similarly rejected the civilising mission as a basis for the law of nations. Twiss was not, however, like Hornung a sceptic of empire. He insisted upon equality in order to extend extraterritorial rule and to impose upon non-European peoples an international jurisdiction which guaranteed the navigation and commerce of European states. He made clear his impatience with the anti-imperial views of jurists such as Hornung in a private commentary he provided upon his own report on the status of 'Oriental nations' in international law. That commentary was contained in a letter he wrote to Sir Austen Henry Layard in 1880, the same year in which the *Annuaire* published his report. Layard was a celebrated archaeologist and Orientalist. He had excavated the ancient Assyrian cities of Nimrud and Ninevah in the 1840s and 1850s and discovered the library of Ashurbanipal which included, amongst its thousands of tablets, the *Epic of Gilgamesh*. In 1877, Prime Minister Disraeli appointed Layard as the British Ambassador to Constantinople against the background of the 1877–1878 Russian and Turkish war in which Russia claimed to be intervening in the Ottoman Empire in order to protect its Christian subjects from massacres perpetrated by the Ottomans.[66] It was precisely such interventions in the name of coreligionists to which Hornung had objected in his dissenting report to the Institute and which had been condemned by the Institute more generally as against the principles of the law of nations. William

63 Lorimer, *Institutes*, vol.1, 100. For Lorimer, see: Jennifer Pitts, 'Boundaries of Victorian International Law', in Duncan Bell (ed.), *Victorian Visions of Global Order* (Cambridge: Cambridge University Press, 2007), 67–88; and Jennifer Pitts, *Boundaries of the International: Law and Empire* (Cambridge MA: Harvard University Press, 2018), 171–173.

64 Lorimer, *Institutes*, vol.1, 123.

65 *Ibid.*, 123–124.

66 Jonathan Parry, 'Sir Austen Henry Layard', in *Oxford Dictionary of National Biography* (Oxford: Oxford University Press, 2004–2016).

Gladstone, in Britain, had used the conflict in the Ottoman Empire to attack the Disraeli government and argued in his 1867 pamphlet *Bulgarian Horrors and the Question of the East* that outside powers *should* intervene to support Christians in the empire. Layard strongly opposed Gladstone's perspective but eventually found himself in opposition, also, to Sultan Abdul Hamid II, who suspected the British of being complicit in the diminution of Ottoman power after the Berlin Congress of 1878. In 1880, Layard wrote a pessimistic and overheated dispatch regarding the state of the Ottoman Empire which was published by Gladstone, who had returned to government in April of that year. Layard was then recalled from Constantinople and he retired to Venice where he moved into a palazzo, the Ca' Cappello, on the Grand Canal (now known as Ca' Cappello Layard), where Twiss wrote to him in September 1880. Twiss would have known Layard from the late 1840s and 1850s, when they were both members of the Royal Geographic Society and of the Athenaeum Club (Twiss was elected to the Athenaeum in 1845, Layard in 1848), as well as from a period in which Layard was under-Secretary for Foreign Affairs in the 1860s, when Twiss was Advocate General and constantly consulted by the Foreign Office. But Layard's position as ambassador to Constantinople brought him to Twiss' attention when he was writing his Report on 'Oriental nations' in international law.[67] In a candid statement of his views, Twiss wrote to Layard that he was enclosing a copy of his 'memoir' on 'jurisdiction in the Levant, which I have had to study as Rapporteur for the Institute de droit international'.[68] Twiss said that he discovered 'on enquiring at the Foreign Office that your address is at Venice'. After some pleasantries – 'I hardly venture', he noted, 'that Ca. Capello means Casa Capello' – he turned to his subject: 'Now I must beg pardon, when you are immersed in the study of Great Matters of Colour, for recalling your attention to a subject which is perhaps … marked by you as of no colour, or black, in your memory'. 'The modern attempt', Twiss observed, 'to wash the blackamoor white is after all only a new Crusade'. For Twiss, therefore, cosmopolitan and humanitarian arguments were merely an attempt to impose European authority upon non-Europeans and most twenty-first-century historians would agree with that aspect of his argument. He argued, instead, that Europeans and 'the Blackamoor' were 'oil and vinegar', albeit that some regarded them as 'indivisible'. When the work of integrating Europeans and non-Europeans 'is accomplished who shall sup on the salad? which the French do and seem inclined

67 For Layard and Twiss as members of the Athenaeum Club, see *Athenaeum. Rules and Regulations and List of Members. 1868* (London: Athenaeum Club, 1868).

68 'Travers Twiss to Austen Henry Layard', September 1880, *British Library*, Layard Papers, Additional MS. 39034/170 recto–171 verso.

to do'. He concluded by extending his sympathy for what he believed was Layard's rough treatment by Gladstone: 'Hoping you are well after all the ill requited labour of your post further East'. From this letter, it is apparent that Twiss' arguments for the equality of 'Oriental nations' did not prevent him from employing a racialised perspective upon international relations, although it is also evident that his racialised perspective did not prevent, and indeed encouraged, his arguments for equality.

5 International Duties and Extraterritorial Powers

While Twiss' idea for international jurisdiction over non-European states was evident in his report to the Institute of International Law, it was stated more clearly in a series of articles and pamphlets he published in the *Law and Magazine Review* while preparing that report, particularly in the articles on the 'Applicability of the European Law of Nations to African Slave States', in 1876, and in the address he gave to the seventh annual conference of Dudley Field's Association for the Reform and Codification of the Law of Nations held in the Guildhall of the City of London in 1879, entitled: 'On international conventions for the maintenance of sea lights' which the Association published as a pamphlet in the same year.[69] In 'Applicability of the European Law of Nations to African Slave States', published the year after the Institute of International Law established the commission charged with examining the position of 'Oriental nations' in international law, Twiss pointed out that the countries which the Institute had 'chiefly in view' for that question were Turkey, Egypt, Persia, China and Japan. They had not foreseen, he observed, that 'the first difficulty in the way of the Mahommedan races being admitted to a full participation in the European Concert of Public Law would arise in respect of the Arab States on the East Coast of South Africa'.[70]

The context for this remark was the crisis over what were known as the Fugitive Slave Circulars issued by the Admiralty under instruction from the British Government in 1875 and 1876. It was a relatively common occurrence that slaves in ports visited by British naval vessels would swim to the ships and take refuge on them claiming protection under British law. British naval vessels claimed extraterritorial powers when in the territorial waters of non-British

69 Travers Twiss, *On International Conventions for the Maintenance of Sea Lights* (London: William Clowes and Sons, 1879).

70 Travers Twiss, 'Applicability of the European law of nations to African slave states', *Law Magazine and Review* (May 1876), 409.

nations and, because slavery was not recognised in British law, it had been common for British ships to protect escaping slaves and put them down in another port where they would be free. In the 1860s and 1870s, this policy came under increasing pressure, particularly after the opening of the Suez Canal in 1869, which brought British ships travelling to India and Australia through the ports of slave-owning societies in the Red Sea, the Persian Gulf, the Gulf of Oman and on the east coast of Africa. Benjamin Disraeli's government was concerned that the protection of slaves by warships when visiting the ports of foreign governments would antagonise the people and governments of friendly powers. Enslaved pearl divers in the Persian Gulf, for example, could take refuge on British ships bringing the viability of their masters' enterprises into peril.[71] Extraterritoriality, argued a government report, should not be allowed 'to set aside the law' of another country.[72] In fact, that is precisely what extraterritoriality was intended to do, but this was one of many instances of contradiction and difficulty to which the idea of extraterritoriality gave rise. The policy of the government, and the Admiralty instructions issued in the Fugitive Slave Circulars were intended to guarantee stability in areas of British interest abroad, in what has been described as its informal empire, but it succeeded in reviving anti-slavery interests at home.

Twiss, however, wrote in protest at the Fugitive Slave Circulars out of motives other than anti-slavery. For Twiss, at the heart of the crisis, which dominated political debate in Britain in late 1875 and in 1876, was the question which the Institute of International Law had commissioned him to report upon: namely, what was the status of 'Oriental nations' in international law? In contrast to some anti-slavery advocates, Twiss did not point to the institution of slavery as evidence of the inequality of certain non-European states in the society of nations.[73] As we have seen, he argued in his 1861 *Law of Nations* that the 1856 Treaty of Paris was a 'formal act of reception' whereby the Ottoman Empire was admitted to the 'Fellowship of European Nations'.[74] He repeated this claim in his article on the African 'Slave States', adding that even prior to the 1856 treaty the 'Ottoman Porte' had, from a 'Christian point of view', been 'received as a Peer into the European Parliament of States' when its ambassadors were admitted into the courts of 'Two Great European Powers' as well as through treaties that it had made with European states since the first sixteenth-century

71 William Mulligan, 'The Fugitive Slave Circulars, 1875–1876', *Journal of Imperial and Commonwealth History* 37 (2009), 183–205, 188.

72 Ibid., 187.

73 On anti-slavery activists' perceptions of slave states, see Ibid., 193.

74 Twiss, *Law of Nations*, 105; Twiss, 'Applicability', 410.

treaty with the French.[75] Nevertheless, he argued, recent years had seen a 'growing desire on the part of the Mussulman Races to place themselves on the same platform of Public Law with the Christian Races of Europe'. Twiss asked, therefore, to what degree 'Mahommedan Governments' were subject to the rules of international law – a subject in which he was deeply engrossed given his work on the commission for the *Institut*. He observed that William Scott, Lord Stowell, in whose footsteps he had in many ways followed since his days at University College, Oxford (Stowell's own college), had addressed the same question in 1800 in the Admiralty Prize Court. Stowell had argued that it would be 'extremely hard' on persons who lived in the Kingdom of Morocco if they were held to be 'bound by all the rules of the Law of Nations as it is practised amongst European States'.[76] The European law of nations, he said, was a 'pretty artificial system', which was unfamiliar to Moroccans and so should not be applied 'in its full rigour'. They could, however, be expected to be familiar with conventions that were 'universal' and 'simple', in this instance the observance of a blockade in war, and could be held to such an 'elementary principle'.[77] Twiss took two principles from Stowell's judgement. Firstly, that European nations could not 'extract' from 'African nations a strict compliance' with European international norms. Secondly, that European nations could require African nations to observe 'European usages' where those usages were in accordance with 'natural right and where the African Nations cannot be ignorant of them'. Any other basis for deepening relations between European and African nations would lead to a 'humiliation' of the African nations and a 'degradation' of the Europeans. Centuries of treaties between Europeans and Africans, he added, had supplied African nations with a 'knowledge of European Usages'.[78] Twiss then declared that a further principle must govern relations between European and African nations: namely, that if African nations were to have the 'benefit' of 'European usages of international intercourse' they must also 'submit to the inconvenience of them'.[79] To this end he cited the maxim 'Qui sentit beneficium sentire debet et onus': that is, whoever has the benefit of something must also accept the burden. As an example, he said that an African nation could not 'claim from an European Nation the recognition of its right to the free navigation of the High Seas' without conceding the same right to European nations as well as committing to the restraint of piracy.[80]

75 Twiss, 'Applicability', 410.
76 Ibid., 411.
77 Ibid., 412.
78 Ibid.
79 Ibid., 413.
80 Ibid.

Now, reasoned Twiss, 'A good deal has been said' about the 'Fugitive Slave Circulars' and the 'personal *status* of the African slave'. The slave, he said, reminding his audience that he was an expert on the subject of legal personality, has 'properly speaking, no *personal status*. The slave, in fact, has no *personality*'.[81] The slave was a 'thing, a chattel', who, like an ox or an ass, was the property of his master. When 'he' escapes slavery, on the other hand, he 'becomes once more a man'.[82] Slavery, he pointed out, was a 'local institution' and a 'local law' to which slaves were 'accidentally subject'. The 'Mahommedan Powers' had accordingly accepted, through numerous treaties, that it was a 'rule of the Common Law of nations' that if a slave 'escaped beyond the jurisdiction of the law, in virtue of which he is a slave' he becomes once more a man. These treaties, Twiss argued, were something to which African nations were bound 'if they wish to be admitted within the pale of the European State-System'.[83] The provisions of the treaties were 'based on the recognition' of a 'jus commune gentium' (a common law of nations) which was 'applicable equally to African as to European States' and upon which 'a young bud of positive law' was growing upon an 'old stock of natural right'. Here Twiss was making the quite remarkable claim for equality between European states and the Muslim nations of Africa in international law. The reason he was doing so, however, was not because, like Hornung, he was a Kantian cosmopolitan or some other kind of opponent of empire.

Twiss proceeded in this article to go into a detailed account of the treaties that had for centuries past been established between Muslim African nations and European states. In these treaties, for example those between Britain and Morocco, or Denmark and Tunis, he found the recognition of two principles: firstly, that if a slave escapes beyond the 'jurisdiction of the law in virtue of which he is a slave', the state under whose jurisdiction he places himself is entitled to protect him; and, secondly, that a slave has placed 'himself' in the jurisdiction of another state when he has escaped on board 'one of its public Ships of War'.[84] The plea of 'comity' between nations, which the Disraeli government had used to justify the return of slaves to their masters in the hope of not antagonising foreign powers, was, Twiss said 'out of place'. Comity was no ground for why the 'Free Nations of Europe should submit to abandon the exercise of their rights of Sovereignty within their own Public Ships of War under conditions in which they have hitherto persistently maintained those rights in

81 Ibid., 415.
82 Ibid., 416.
83 Ibid., 417.
84 Ibid., 418.

their intercourse with the Slave States of Africa'.[85] If Britain were to abandon the practice of protecting fugitive slaves it would place itself in conflict with its 'sister Christian states'.[86] And yet, the Lord Chancellor, Hugh Cairns, addressing the House of Lords, had 'expressed a difficulty' in 'accepting the doctrine of the extraterritoriality of a British ship of war in the sense… that she carries with her the juridical attributes of British soil, wherever she goes'.[87] The Lord Chancellor, he said, had been misled by the fact that 'the term "Extraterritoriality" is a metaphor' and that it did not signify the same thing in the case of a ship of war and an ambassador's house. The creation of resident embassies was, Twiss observed, a recent development in international relations and the 'doctrine of the immunity of the Ambassador's house from the local law was an innovation' from a generally accepted principle that the laws of a nation bind all people within that territory.[88] On the other hand, the doctrine that the sea within three miles of a coast is part of that country's territory employed the idea of 'territory' as a metaphor in order to explain empire over the sea. When we speak of the extraterritoriality of ships of war in territorial waters we 'array metaphor against metaphor'. The idea of territorial waters was the more misleading of the two metaphors because nations do not have the same absolute right to determine law in the waters that border their territory as they do when persons travers their territory.[89] The extraterritoriality of ships trumped territorial waters. Returning, therefore, to the 'position of European Public Ships of War in the so-called territorial waters of African Slave States', Twiss reached the 'ready answer' that if the African states 'are desirous to live under a Common Law with the European Nations' they must concede the extraterritorial powers of European ships of war.[90] Pointing to the maritime nature of Britain's empire, Twiss concluded that 'no nation is more interested' than Britain in maintaining the 'authority of *international usage* in all matters which regard the navigation of the High Seas'.[91]

In his article, Twiss asserted the equality of African nations in international law in order to argue for their obligations in maintaining principles of extraterritoriality, which, he claimed, had been recognised by centuries of practice. Those powers of extraterritoriality, not least the extraterritoriality of gunboats, were precisely the means by which European nations were, from

85 Ibid., 421.
86 Ibid., 428.
87 Ibid., 430.
88 Ibid., 435.
89 Ibid., 436.
90 Ibid.
91 Ibid., 437.

the mid-nineteenth century, once more expanding their empires across the globe, in Asia, Africa, the Pacific and, closer to Europe, in the Ottoman empire. More important, however, than the claim to portable extraterritoriality, was the broader notion that these African peoples had obligations under the law of nations. Twiss further developed this idea of the equality of non-European states in international law and their corresponding obligations in his 1879 pamphlet 'On international conventions for the maintenance of sea lights' which he had delivered to the Association for the Reform and Codification of the Law of Nations in London. He began this article by pointing out that for all nations that were 'members of the European family' there was a 'primary duty on the part of each nation to light up its coasts to passing vessels' in order to meet their larger commitment to freedom of the seas.[92] He pointed out, however, that 'hardly anything' had been said of this duty by writers on international law. Nevertheless, he observed, the question of lighthouses was all the more urgent since the invention of steamships, 'the great maritime discovery of the present century'.[93] He proceeded to provide a detailed history of lighthouses, from ancient times to the present, in order to demonstrate that: 'the modern lighthouse is an institution capable in certain cases of producing such great international benefit, that its erection and maintenance may well deserve the co-operative action of civilized states'.[94] Here, therefore, was a duty, alongside the provision of channel markers and actions against piracy, that lay upon all peoples who wished to participate in the society of nations and he articulated it in precisely those terms: that is, as 'the international duty of states to light up their sea-coasts'.[95]

Having established this duty that lay upon members of the society of nations, Twiss turned to examining in what ways it was incumbent upon non-European nations. Repeating the claims he made in previous publications and in the Institute commission on the place of 'Oriental nations' in international law, he declared that 'Asiatic and African states' had 'recently been admitted into the European concert of public law'.[96] The Ottoman Empire, he observed, had 'farmed out' its lighthouse keeping duties to a French company.[97] The 1858 Treaty of Tientsin, which ended the Opium Wars, obliged China to provide sea lights and placed the 'administration of the maritime customs… entirely under

92 Twiss, *Sea Lights*, 3.
93 *Ibid.*, 3.
94 *Ibid.*, 9.
95 *Ibid.*, 12.
96 *Ibid.*, 13.
97 *Ibid.*, 14.

the direction of European officers'.[98] In 1866, Japan had signed a common tariff convention which guaranteed the provision of navigational aids that were then provided by British engineers at a cost of over one million pounds.[99] These agreements had all guaranteed European commerce. The 'two great civilised nations of the far East' had 'acceded effectively to the established practice of the nations of the Western world'.[100] In other words, for Twiss, the admission of these 'Oriental nations' into the law of nations brought with it duties which they were obliged to perform, such as the provision of lighthouses, and also sanctioned their submission to an international regime, where necessary, in order to meet those obligations.

There were other countries, however, with which 'Europe has been brought into contact under a system of trade' but which did not have the means to 'meet the expenditure' necessary to 'light up their coasts'. Moreover there were 'some countries' in which no civilized government exists'.[101] 'How', he asked, 'shall we provide for the safe navigation of the steamship along coasts, and amidst islands which are not under the sovereignty of any civilized power'.[102] He enumerated the various sites on the eastern side of the Suez Canal, which required lighthouses but were not under the control of any power who would provide them, including in the Gulf of Aden, islands in the Indian Ocean, the Arafura Sea and Torres Straits, north of Australia, and the east coast of Africa, including the coast of Somalia. Many of these places, according to Twiss, were under systems of government but unable to provide navigational aids. The 'Somali Arabs', for example, were the 'lords of the soil' but were not a people who could be treated with.[103] What was necessary in such countries, or in countries with 'no civilized government', was a system of 'international lighthouses' protected, if necessary, by 'a fort' and 'a strong garrison of soldiers'.[104] He held out, as an example of international cooperation to create such lighthouses, the 1865 Cape Spartel Convention, in which the Sultan of Morocco handed the administration of the lighthouse on Cape Spartel, below the Straits of Gibraltar, to a concert of European and American powers. 'Why should we not hope', he asked, 'to the see the day arrive when INTERNATIONAL LIGHTHOUSES shall be amongst the trophies of peace, which the civilization of Europe shall

98 *Ibid.*
99 *Ibid.*, 14–15.
100 *Ibid.*, 15.
101 *Ibid.*
102 *Ibid.*, 16.
103 *Ibid.*, 17.
104 *Ibid.*

set up amidst the islands of the far East?'[105] He concluded by observing that 'we are in the present day only on the threshold of the East African question'. Indeed, in 1879, when he wrote, European powers were turning their attention to Africa as a new field for colonisation, in part because advances in medicine enabled the settlement of tropical latitudes and because steam power enabled the navigation of fast-flowing rivers that had previously been impenetrable. 'If the civilization of Europe is to penetrate into the heart of Africa from the east', Twiss concluded, 'the first great step will be to secure to the European mariner a safe approach to its shores, and this may be materially furnished by an international concert'.[106]

On 21 August 1879, Twiss sent two copies of his article on lighthouses to the chief of staff, Baron Paul de Borchgrave d'Altena, to King Leopold II of Belgium. Alongside many European states, Leopold had been developing an interest in Africa throughout the 1870s. Twiss wrote to Borchgrave, to say that his article on 'International Conventions on the Maintenance of Sea Lights' had 'an immediate bearing on the attempt to civilize Africa from the East Coast in which his Majesty is taking so noble a lead, and in which I am desirous to cooperate in a very humble manner by suggesting an international concert to light up the seaway along the East African Coast'.[107] It would transpire that Leopold colonised Africa from the west, rather than the east, but Twiss proved to be a key figure in making the legal case for the claim of Leopold's colonial corporation to become a state, the Congo Free State. One of the pillars of that case was the claim that African peoples possessed sovereignty that they could cede to Leopold's company and, for that argument to succeed, it was necessary first to establish, as Twiss had, the standing of 'Oriental' peoples in the law of nations.

6 Conclusion

In his article on sea-lights, Twiss clarified two developing streams of his thought in the 1870s and 1880s. Firstly, he argued for the equality of many non-European nations in international society and international law. He, secondly, did so because he viewed membership of society as something that comes with both rights and duties. He understood that granting membership to non-European governments, such as the Turks, Chinese, Japanese, or even the 'Slave-states'

105 *Ibid.*, 24.
106 *Ibid.*
107 'Travers Twiss to Baron Paul de Borchgrave d'Altena', *Archives du Palais royal*, Brussels, A96 – CDG XI/22.

of Africa, meant that Europeans could demand that those governments meet certain standards of behaviour and, if they failed to do so, they could be held to account and have certain 'duties' imposed upon them, for example in the imposition of extraterritoriality by foreign powers. This idea of the equality of 'Oriental nations' can be contrasted with common representations of nineteenth-century perceptions of the inequality of nations in international law. It is frequently argued that in order to extend their empires, Europeans developed a system of international law, which assumed a fundamental inequality between European and non-European powers and which enabled them to impose their sovereignty upon the non-European world. There is no question that such a characterisation holds true for certain jurists, such as James Lorimer, who developed highly racialised and hierarchical theories of international law. But that vision of inequality was just one amongst a number of understandings of the relations between Europeans and non-Europeans in international law. Some jurists, such as Hornung, argued for the equality of certain non-European nations in international law in order to restrain European imperialism, even if they did so in the context of a paternalistic view.

Highly influential voices, such as Dudley Field and Twiss, argued for the equality of non-European nations precisely in order to extend European and American empires, or 'informal empires'. Historians have perhaps been deaf to these arguments because they were based upon the idea of duties. Knowing that Europeans used international law as an instrument of expansion, we have tended to assume that an argument for expansion must be based upon dominance and dominance must be based upon inequality, and most probably, from a twenty-first-century perspective, inequality in the possession of rights. The arguments Twiss made for the dominance of Europeans, however, were based upon the assumption of equality and the duties that equality brought with it. Failure to meet those duties led to accountability and the extension of sovereignty over the recalcitrant powers. Twiss's position in many ways gave a legal voice to Palmerston's policy of free-trade imperialism. Twiss was a frequent guest at Palmerston's house and it was Palmerston, as prime minister, who presented Twiss to the queen when he was appointed Regius Professor of Civil Law at Oxford in 1856.[108] Although Twiss had at some points in his career been critical of Palmerston on particular points of policy, he was more frequently in accord with him.

108 On the presentation to the Queen: 'University and Clerical Intelligence', *Oxford Journal* (15 March 1856), 5. For Twiss dining at Palmerston's house, see: 'Fashionable and political reunion', *Morning Post* (March 3 1851), 5; 'Fashionable entertainments', *Morning Post* (23 July 1860), 5.

Twiss's argument for the equality of 'Oriental nations' in the society of nations were consistent with broader movements for the expansion of the franchise, for example in the Reform Act of 1867 which extended the vote to working class men. Just as male subjects of the state were increasingly granted political standing, and there were even arguments made to extend that standing to women, Twiss endorsed a broader franchise for the subjects of international society.[109] One might ask whether, in all such instances, arguments for equality could also become premises of dependence.

Acknowledgements

I would like to thank Saliha Belmessous, Joanna Innes, Jon Parry and Natasha Wheatley for extensive comments on earlier versions of this paper.

---

109 Instead, however, of basing that franchise upon rights, or negative liberty, as was the case with the 1867 Reform Act, he based it upon both rights and duties. For the centrality of negative liberty to the 1867 Reform Act, see: Philip Harling, 'The Powers of the Victorian State', in Peter Mandler (ed.) *Liberty and Authority in Victorian Britain* (Oxford: Oxford University Press, 2006), 33.

CHAPTER 5

British Humanitarianism, International Law and Human Sacrifice in West Africa

Inge Van Hulle

1 Introduction

Within the history of international law and imperialism during the nineteenth century, the resort to the civilising mission played an essential role as a justification for taking legal measures that targeted the rights of non-Western peoples.[1] 'Civilisation'[2] became a lens through which the West viewed its own cultural superiority and constructed its own identity in opposition to the 'Other'.[3] In order to become equal participants in the family of nations, non-Western states needed to pass a test of civilisation that was entirely predicated on Christian-inspired political, legal and cultural values.[4] In the legal arena, externally, non-Western states needed to demonstrate their ability to conduct reciprocal international relations and adhere to standards of Western diplomacy that included the protection of foreigners.[5] Internally, they needed a – to Western eyes – recognisable sovereign state structure founded on Western-style constitutional politics that would guarantee the protection of fundamental rights to its citizens and that was built on enlightened criminal and private law principles.

In recent years, the Western imposition of its own cultural framework through international law has been explored specifically with regard to the Ottoman Empire, Japan, China and Siam. There is a burgeoning literature

1 Brett Bowden, *The Empire of Civilization: The Evolution of an Imperial Idea* (Chicago: University of Chicago Press, 2014); Gerrit Gong, *The Standard of 'Civilization' in International Society* (Oxford: Clarendon Press, 1984).

2 The use of terms such as 'civilisation', 'tribes' or 'barbarous' in this chapter do not reflect the author's personal opinions, yet are merely a reflection of nineteenth-century discourse that was found in the source material consulted for this chapter.

3 Edward W. Said, *Orientalism* (London: Penguin, 2003).

4 Luigi Nuzzo, 'Territory, Sovereignty and the Construction of the Colonial Space', in Martti Koskenniemi, Walter Rech and Manuel Jiménez Fonseca (eds.), *International Law and Empire: Historical Explorations* (Oxford: Oxford University Press, 2017), 263–292, 266–267.

5 Inge Van Hulle, 'Unequal Treaties', in Gordon Martel (ed.) *The Encyclopedia of Diplomacy* (New York: Wiley, 2018), [forthcoming].

 | DOI:10.1163/9789004412088_006

with respect to extraterritoriality, unequal treaties and the imperialism of free trade.[6] However, this limited geographical focus has led to a virtual association between these regions and the nineteenth- and early twentieth-century so- called 'standard of civilisation' to a point where they now have become almost synonymous,[7] while the last word has certainly not been written with respect to the application of the concept of civilisation as an imperial strategy to the above-mentioned regions. Their predominance in scholarship when it comes to this particular topic nevertheless detracts from the fact that similar processes of imperial reform were undertaken by Western powers in other parts of the world under the guise of civilisation.

One of these regions is Africa. Here the near-exclusive focus of scholars has been on the abolition of the slave trade and the late nineteenth-century Euro-African treaties that ceded sovereignty or territory to Western powers.[8] The focus on the abolition of the slave trade as a condition imposed on African rulers for cultural 'improvement' has obscured the fact that Africa was subjected to a litany of civilizational requirements of which abolition was just

6 See for a representative selection: Eliana Augusti, 'From Capitulations to Unequal Treaties: The Matter of an Extraterritorial Jurisdiction in the Ottoman Empire', *Journal of Civil Law Studies* 4 (2011), 285–307; Michael R. Auslin, *Negotiating with Imperialism: The Unequal Treaties and the Culture of Japanese Diplomacy* (Cambridge, MA: Harvard University Press, 2006); Johannes Berchtold, *Recht und Gerechtigkeit in der Konsulargerichtsbarkeit: Britische Exterritorialität im Osmanischen Reich, 1825–1914* (Munich: R. Oldenbourg, 2009); Pär K. Cassel, *Grounds of Judgment: Extraterritoriality and Imperial Power in Nineteenth-Century China and Japan* (Oxford: Oxford University Press, 2012); Turan Kayaoğlu, *Legal Imperialism: Sovereignty and Extraterritoriality in Japan, the Ottoman Empire, and China* (Cambridge: Cambridge University Press, 2010); Teemu Ruskola, *Legal Orientalism: China, the United States, and Modern Law* (Cambridge, MA: Harvard University Press, 2013).

7 See a similar critique by Hailegabriel G. Feyissa, 'European Extraterritoriality in Semicolonial Ethiopia', *Melbourne Journal of International Law* 17 (2016), 107–134, 108.

8 See for a selection on the slave trade: Lauren Benton, 'Abolition and Imperial Law, 1790–1820', *The Journal of Imperial and Commonwealth History* 39 (2011), 355–374; Jenny Martinez, *The Slave Trade and the Origins of International Human Rights Law* (Oxford: Oxford University Press, 2012); Edward Keene, 'A Case-Study of the Construction of International Hierarchy: British Treaty-Making Against the Slave Trade in the Early Nineteenth Century', *International Organization* 61 (2007), 311–339; Robin Law, 'International Law and the British Suppression of the Atlantic Slave Trade', in Derek R. Peterson (ed.), *Abolitionism and Imperialism in Britain, Africa and the Atlantic* (Cambridge: Cambridge University Press, 2010), 150–174. See for treaties: Charles H. Alexandrowicz, *The European-African Confrontation. A Study in Treaty Making* (Leiden: A.W. Sijthoff, 1973); Mieke van der Linden, *The Acquisition of Africa (1870–1914). The Nature of International Law* (Leiden and Boston: Brill/Nijhoff, 2017). See for an excellent exception: Rebecca Shumway, 'Palavers and Treaty Making in the British Acquisition of the Gold Coast Colony (West Africa)', in Saliha Belmessous (ed.), *Empire by Treaty. Negotiating European Expansion, 1600–1900* (Cambridge: Cambridge University Press, 2015), 161–185.

one. This chapter, instead, focuses on one particular instance of cultural imperialism, namely British efforts to abolish human sacrifice during the mid- and late nineteenth century through the conclusion of treaties with African rulers and use of force.

The confrontation between international law and the practice of human sacrifice reached an early and dramatic climax at the conference of Valladolid in 1550 and 1551. The conference was organised to address the Spanish legal methods used to create dominion and to spread the Catholic faith in South America, yet quickly hinged on whether the Spanish Crown had a right to wage a just war against the South American indigenous population.[9] The question of human sacrifice took centre-stage as Juan Ginés de Sepúlveda (1494–1573) argued that human sacrifice constituted a violation of natural law, which required punishment and the protection of its potential victims through use of force. His adversary, Bartolomé de Las Casas (1484–1566) argued that it did not violate natural law, yet his opinion represented a minority position, as most of his imminent colleagues, such as, for example, Francisco de Vitoria (1492–1546), Domingo de Soto (1494–1560) and, later, Francisco Suárez (1548–1617) would disagree.

As this chapter shows, human sacrifice never ceased to exercise a powerful hold on the Western imagination and was equally present when it came to the imperial regard and cultural taxation by Europeans of the indigenous population of West Africa. The operationalisation of the concept of civilisation through the creation of legal techniques such as unequal treaties and extraterritoriality in the Middle East and South-East Asia must be placed within a wider justificatory scheme employed by Western powers in various imperial arenas around the globe to mould indigenous customs. While the language employed to argue against the use of human sacrifice was no longer that of natural law, the humanitarian turn of the late eighteenth and early nineteenth centuries precipitated arguments of intervention against human sacrifice. The historical examples of British interference through law with human sacrifice in West Africa are vast. This chapter limits itself to a discussion of interventions in Dahomey, Asante and Benin. These interventions took the form first and foremost of treaties, yet were inherently connected with the use of force. Treaties constituted a written record of enforceable rights, which upon nonfulfilment provided a ready excuse for the violent suppression of human sacrifice. While the underlying motives for the resort to force were often economic

9 Glen Carman, 'Human Sacrifice and Natural Law in Las Casas's Apologia', *Colonial Latin American Review* 25 (2016), 278–299, 278–279.

or political in nature, they were couched in humanitarian cries for saving the victims of human sacrifice.

2 Human Sacrifice in the Nineteenth-Century European Imagination

Until the last quarter of the nineteenth century, British formal presence in West Africa was largely limited to a number of settlements and factories near the coast. The concerted drive by the British government towards the global abolition of the slave trade from 1807 onwards; combined with a heightened scientific interest into West Africa's fauna and flora and with its potential for British commercial expansion led to more European incursions.[10] Experimentation with resettled ex-slaves in Granville Sharpe's 'Province of Freedom' would eventually lead to the creation of Sierra Leone.[11] It was turned into a Crown Colony in 1808 following the administrative transfer by the Sierra Leone Company to the British government and became the centre of the British activities for the abolition of the slave trade on the west coast. At the Gold Coast, the Company of Merchants Trading to Africa administered the British forts and held its administrative centre at Cape Coast Castle. Apart from a brief period of Crown rule between 1821 and 1827, merchants continued to administer the forts until 1843. Following complaints of corruption and the existence of an illegal trade in slaves the forts were finally taken over by the British government in 1843.[12] Since the second half of the eighteenth century, the settlements along the river Gambia had formed a bone of contention between Britain and France. After the Napoleonic Wars, the First Treaty of Paris of 1814 seemed to have settled the matter for once and for all: the captured territories of Senegal and Gorée were returned to France, whereas the river Gámbia remained under the exclusive control of Britain.[13] Nevertheless, the British position in the

10 Robert A. Stafford, 'Scientific Exploration and Empire', in Andrew Porter (ed.), *The Oxford History of the British Empire: The Nineteenth Century* (Oxford: Oxford University Press, 2006), 294–319, 296.

11 See on the early history of Sierra Leone: J. Braidwood, *Black Poor and White Philanthropists: London's Blacks and the Foundation of the Sierra Leone Settlement, 1786–1791* (Liverpool: Liverpool University Press, 1994); Bronwen Everill, *Abolition and Empire in Sierra Leone and Liberia* (Basingstoke: Palgrave Macmillan, 2013); Padraic X. Scanlan, *British Freedom's Debtors: British antislavery in Sierra Leone in the Age of Revolution* (Yale: Yale University Press, 2017).

12 Rebecca Shumway, *The Fante and the Transatlantic Slave Trade* (Rochester: University of Rochester Press, 2011).

13 Convention for a Suspension of Hostilities between Austria. Great Britain, Prussia, Russia and Spain, and France, 23 April 1814, *Hertslet's Commercial Treaties* 1 (1840), 247.

Gambia remained a precarious one: surrounded on all sides by French territory, it was difficult for British merchants to acquire a foothold in what from the 1820s onwards became a flowering trade in gum.[14] Abolition efforts, missionary activities and merchants involved in legitimate trade also brought the heightened presence of British imperial agents in the Bights of Benin, Biafra and there especially, the Niger Delta.[15]

Since the earliest presence of Europeans on the West African coast, rumours of human sacrifice circulated. The actual practice of human sacrifice in nineteenth-century West Africa remains understudied.[16] While many regional variations existed, historians and anthropologists have associated the existence of human sacrifice in societies in West Africa with state centralisation, social stratification and the exercise of royal authority.[17] In kingdoms such as Asante and Dahomey, human sacrifice of prisoners of war, slaves or other selected individuals was used to communicate with deities, solidify state power, secure social standing in the afterlife and to ward off evil.[18] The eventual disappearance of human sacrifice in West Africa was by no means solely attributable to European agitation, but rather depended on a variety of factors that included resistance by slaves against the practice, the rise of Islam, missionary efforts and British official abolition efforts and coercion.[19]

Part of the reason for the tentativeness on the part of scholars to engage with the history of human sacrifice is the abundance of folktales as a leftover of the

14 James F. Searing, *West African Slavery and Atlantic Commerce: The Senegal River Valley, 1700–1860* (Cambridge: Cambridge University Press, 2002), 75; Judith B. Williams, 'The Development of British Trade with West Africa, 1750 to 1850', *Political Science Quarterly* 50 (1935), 194–213, 196.

15 See generally on legitimate trade and the Benin and Niger region: Martin Lynn, *Commerce and Economic Change in West Africa. The Palm Oil Trade in the Nineteenth Century* (Cambridge: Cambridge University Press, 2002); Robin Law, *Ouidah: The Social History of a Slaving 'Port', 1727–1892* (Athens, Ohio: Ohio University Press, 1727–1892); Kenneth O. Dike, *Trade and Politics in the Niger Delta, 1830–1885: An Introduction to the Economic and Political History of Nigeria* (Oxford: Clarendon Press, 1956).

16 Lawrence E.Y. Mbogoni, *Human Sacrifice and the Supernatural in African History* (Dar es Salaam: Mkuki na Nyota Publishers, 2013), 1.

17 Olantunji Ojo, 'Slavery and Human Sacrifice in Yorubaland: Ondo, c. 1870–94', *Journal of African History* 46 (2005), 379–404, 379–380.

18 Robin Law, 'Human Sacrifice in Pre-Colonial West Africa', *African Affairs* 84 (1985), 78–86; Clifford Williams, 'Human Sacrifice or Capital Punishment? An Assessment of the Period 1807–1874', *International Journal of African Historical Studies* 21 (1988), 433–441, 436; Ivor Wilks, 'Asante: Human Sacrifice or Capital Punishment? A Rejoinder', *International Journal of African Historical Studies* 21 (1988), 443–452.

19 Law, 'Human Sacrifice in Pre-Colonial West Africa', 78–86; Ojo, 'Slavery and Human Sacrifice in Yorubaland', 379–380.

colonial era that distorted the reality of human sacrifice with respect to its frequency and nature. European travellers often did not understand the cultural distinctions between various types of sacrifice for either religious, criminal or political reasons. Tales of human sacrifice in West Africa steadily reached Western audiences from the eighteenth century onwards through travel literature composed by European traders, explorers, missionaries, imperial personnel or naval officers. Many of them were tailored to the more sensationalist expectations of their readership by focusing on the gory details of execution or by grossly exaggerating the numbers involved in human sacrifice.[20]

The kingdoms of Dahomey, Asante and Benin bore the brunt of these inflated reports. According to Edna Bay, Dahomey 'epitomized everything negative that the Euro-American imagination of the nineteenth and twentieth centuries wanted to believe about Africa'.[21] It was depicted as a militarist and despotically ruled state that depended on regular slave-hunts, which terrorised neighbouring tribes in order to provide a regular supply of war captives.[22] Its moral depravity was further illustrated by the presence of female soldiers[23] and, especially, the annual and grand customs in which, by some accounts, thousands were said to perish through sacrifice.[24] Even the king himself was aware of the existence of these wild tales and in his eagerness to rectify them told British Commodore Wilmot in 1863: 'You have seen that only a few are sacrificed, and not the thousands that wicked men have told the world'.[25]

The kingdom of Asante, which lay geographically close to the British possessions on the Gold Coast, exercised a similar hold on the British imagination. It too was depicted as a slave- and gold trading empire, whose king exercised human sacrifice in an arbitrary and particularly gruesome manner.[26] Since the

20 Philip D. Curtin, *The Image of Africa. British Ideas and Action, 1780–1850* (Madison: University of Wisconsin Press, 1973), vol. 1, 24.

21 Edna G. Bay, *Wives of the Leopard: Gender, Politics and Culture in the Kingdom of Dahomey* (Charlottesville: University of Virginia Press, 1998), 1.

22 Robert Norris, *Memoirs of the Reign of Bossa Ahadee* (London: Lowndes, 1789), 130–131, 137–138.

23 Archibald Dalzel, *The History of Dahomy, an Inland Kingdom of Africa* (London: T. Spilbury and Son, 1793), ix; William Snelgrave, *A New Account of Some Parts of Guinea and the Slave Trade* (London: J.J. and P. Knapton, 1739), 126.

24 Dalzel, *History of Dahomy*, 202.

25 Commodore Wilmot to Rear-Admiral Sir B. Walker, January 29 1863 in Richard Burton, *A Mission to Gelele, King of Dahome* (London: Tinsley Brothers, 1864), vol. 1, 359.

26 Frederick Boyle, *Through Fanteeland to Coomassie, a Diary of the Ashantee Expedition* (London: Chapman and Hall, 1874), 342, 355; Rev. Thomas B. Freeman, *Journal of Various Visits to the Kingdoms of Ashanti, Aku and Dahomi, in Western Africa* (London: s.n., 1844), 32, 47.

early nineteenth century, its relationship with Britain was particularly fraught which repeatedly led to violent confrontation and outright war.[27] The administrators of the British forts on the Gold Coast and Asante were locked into discussions that mainly concerned access to trade and the legal status of the Fante, who lived in the immediate vicinity of the British forts and over which Britain made ill-defined claims of 'protection'.[28] In 1824, tensions escalated and the British governor of Sierra Leone and the Gold Coast, Charles MacCarthy led an expeditionary force against Asante in which he perished. Wild tales surrounding his alleged decapitation by Asante and the subsequent ceremonial fate of his remains would haunt the British imagination for the coming decades and would become firmly associated with Asante's thirst for human sacrifice and its aptitude to display human skulls as a method of intimidation.[29]

More dispassionate accounts of human sacrifice by, for example, Thomas Bowdich, Joseph Dupuis, William Hutton and Richard Burton surfaced that nuanced previous tales of horror and explicitly condemned exaggerated numbers of victims.[30] These writings must nevertheless be placed within a burgeoning intellectual framework that increasingly considered Africans as uncivilised and that to varying degrees evolved towards the depiction of Africans as racially inferior. The Scottish Enlightenment gave rise to stadial theories of history that divided the evolution of civil society into different stages of development.[31] As primitive societies moved towards free trade capitalism, so would they develop towards more complex political organisation. Also, the introduction of new findings in the natural sciences stimulated the development of racial thinking about non-Western peoples whereby, similar to the construction of a natural history of plants and animals, it was deemed possible to construct

27 Ivor Wilks, *Asante in the Nineteenth Century: The Structure and Evolution of a Political Order* (Cambridge: Cambridge University Press, 1975), 207–242.

28 Inge Van Hulle, 'British Protection, Extraterritoriality, and Protectorates in West Africa, 1807–80' in Lauren Benton, Adam Clulow and Bain Attwood (eds.), *Protection and Empire. A Global History* (Cambridge: Cambridge University Press, 2018), 194–210.

29 Padriac X. Scanlan, *Freedom's Debtors: British Antislavery in Sierra Leone in the Age of Revolution* (New Haven: Yale University Press, 2017), 210–224.

30 Thomas E. Bowdich, *Mission from Cape Coast Castle to Ashantee* (London: John Murray, 1819); Burton, *A Mission to Gelele, King of Dahome*, vol. 1, xv; Joseph Dupuis, *Journal of a Residence in Ashantee* (London: Henry Colburn, 1824); William Hutton, *A Voyage to Africa* (London: Longman, 1821).

31 Silvia Sebastiani, *The Scottish Enlightenment: Race, Gender and the Limits of Progress* (New York: Palgrave Macmillan, 2013), 46.

a natural history of the human species, whereby Europeans were the standard against which others were negatively compared.[32]

Andrew Curran has pointed out that this 'general blindness to the biopolitics of representation' penetrated all intellectual fields.[33] It should come as little surprise then that Richard Burton, for example, who was vice-consul of Fernando Po and who criticised previous authors for their wrongful reports of human sacrifice at Dahomey, also stands as the author of particularly poisonous accounts of human sacrifice in Benin. Benin was a centralised state at the head of which stood the sacred king, the Oba. While the commercial and political confrontations between Britain, Dahomey and Asante steadily increased during the course of the nineteenth century, the kingdom of Benin had managed to remain off the official radar until the end of the century. While commerce between British merchants and Benin existed, it was not until Burton's exploratory visit to the kingdom and the subsequent publication of his travel account, that the wider audience became acquainted with Benin. Burton described the sight of human sacrifice through crucifixion in vivid details and used terms such as 'City of Blood', 'Field of Death' and 'Golgotha' to illustrate Benin's depravity.[34] In fact, Burton's writings would become known as one of the most vitriolic nineteenth-century accounts of West Africa's degeneracy, coming to the conclusion in 1863 – when abolition of the slave trade was in full sway – that it was unsurprising that the 'Caucasian man' should have taught himself to think of Africans as the 'servants of servants'.[35]

3 Treaties and the Abolition of Human Sacrifice

These above-mentioned 'biopolitics of representation' and the gory anecdotes of human sacrifice in West Africa would also filter into the discourse of the humanitarians that would spur the British government into legal action against human sacrifice. British efforts to suppress human sacrifice in West Africa were a direct result of the ambiguous relationship between Western imperial expansion and a real concern for the perceived suffering of non-Western peoples.

32 Nicholas Hudson, 'From "Nation" to "Race": The Origin of Racial Classification in Eighteenth-Century Thought', *Eighteenth-Century Studies* 29 (1996), 247–264, 252.

33 Andrew S. Curran, *The Anatomy of Blackness. Science and Slavery in an Age of Enlightenment* (Baltimore: John Hopkins University Press, 2011), 220.

34 Richard Burton, *Wanderings in West Africa from Liverpool to Fernando Po* (London: Tinsley Brothers, 1863), vol. 2, 287–288.

35 Ibid., vol. 1, 178. See on Richard Burton's legacy: Dane Kennedy, *The Highly Civilized Man: Richard Burton and the Victorian World* (Cambridge, MA: Harvard University Press, 2007).

This concern was founded on the pervasiveness of what Alan Lester and Fae Dussart have termed a 'humanitarian register' that was based on empathy, pity and commiseration for the seemingly oppressed.[36] With respect to West Africa, this humanitarian register would lead to activism against the slave trade and against other practices that were considered to require suppression so as to save their potential victims. These concerned human sacrifice but also the killing of twin children and trial by ordeal. Through humanitarian activism the British government was also urged to re-examine the manner in which its subjects behaved in its overseas territories and focused on the treatment of 'aborigines' or the indigenous population by white settlers, epitomised by the Parliamentary Select Committee on Aboriginal Tribes in 1837.[37]

The origins of this activism can be traced back to a late eighteenth-century Evangelical awakening that emphasised a Christian duty of compassion and personal benevolence.[38] This Christian revival intersected with continued discussions on which elements best constituted progress and civilisation.[39] To the British mind, these elements were grafted onto English values, such as political liberty and good government, but also free commerce. Britain's rapid rise to industrial predominance and its relatively unscathed emergence from the devastation wrecked on Europe by the Napoleonic wars had illustrated not just the value of trade, but also the predestined fate of Britain to carry its particular brand of civilisation in the form of commerce, Christianity and civilisation across the seas.[40] The humanitarian register permeated the discourse of activists but also extended to the desks of the Colonial and Foreign Office. In turn,

36 Alan Lester and Fae Dussart, *Colonization and the Origins of Humanitarian Governance. Protecting Aborigines across the Nineteenth-Century British Empire* (Cambridge: Cambridge University Press, 2016), 5. See also: Michael Barnett, *Empire of Humanity: A History of Humanitarianism* (London: Cornell University Press, 2011); Fabian Klose, 'Enforcing Abolition: The Entanglement of Civil Society, Humanitarian Norm-Setting, and Military Intervention', in Fabian Klose (ed.), *The Emergence of Humanitarian Intervention: Ideas and Practice from the Nineteenth Century to the Present* (Cambridge: Cambridge University Press, 2015), 91–120, 94–96.

37 *Report of the Parliamentary Select Committee on Aboriginal Tribes* (London, s.n., 1837); James Heartfield, *The Aborigines' Protection Society: Humanitarian Imperialism in Australia, New Zealand, Fiji, Canada, South Africa, and the Congo, 1836–1909* (New York: Columbia University Press, 2011),

38 Catherine Hall, *Civilising Subjects: Metropole and Colony in the English Imagination, 1830–1867* (Cambridge: Polity, 2001), 301–109.

39 Andrew Porter, *Religion versus Empire? British Protestant Missionaries and Overseas Expansion, 1700–1914* (Manchester: Manchester University Press, 2004), 92–94.

40 There remained uncertainty, however, about which of these elements should be introduced first: Andrew Porter, 'Commerce and Christianity: The Rise and Fall of a Missionary Slogan', *The Historical Journal* 28 (1985), 597–621, 597–600.

their subordinate counterparts in West Africa composed correspondence that was drenched in humanitarian calls for the conclusion of treaties, the extension of extraterritorial jurisdiction or use of force, all for the enhancement of the African.

Within this context, exaggerated depictions of human sacrifice served a variety of contradictory political purposes. Robin Law has shown that during the eighteenth century such anecdotes were often composed by individuals who engaged in the slave trade and who instrumentalised their accounts of African atrocities as part of the battle between proponents and opponents of the slave trade.[41] Enthusiasts of the slave trade saw in – what they perceived as – the despondent submission of Africans to tyrannical domestic rule proof of their natural propensity to being slaves. Also, the export of Africans from the African continent as slaves was cloaked as a humanitarian favour as it would save slaves from the likelihood of human sacrifice.

From the 1840s onwards, such politically charged discussions concerning the cause and effect of African human sacrifice intersected with new humanitarian ideas that evolved around the most effective method of abolishing the slave trade. Under the instigation of Thomas Fowell Buxton (1786–1845), the Anti-Slavery Society began pressuring the British government into adopting a more stringent approach towards the suppression of the slave trade. The existing international legal framework that depended primarily on bilateral inter-European treaties for the suppression of the slave trade was found to be lacking in effectiveness as the rising numbers of slave exports illustrated.[42] Buxton argued in favour of the replacement of the slave trade by the introduction of legitimate commerce, Christianity and civilisation in Africa. In order to achieve this, he proposed enhancing the efficiency of the British navy in capturing slave vessels and the conclusion of treaties with African rulers in which they promised to abolish the slave trade and cede portions of their land to Britain for the establishment of commercial factories. His more immediate suggestion consisted of sending an expedition to the river Niger in order to put his plan into action.

In his popular two-part work *The African Slave Trade and Its Remedy*, Buxton urged the inclusion of the abolition of human sacrifice in the proposed

41 Robin Law, 'Dahomey and the Slave Trade: Reflections on the Historiography of the Rise of Dahomey', *Journal of African History* 27 (1986), 237–267, 250–251.

42 John Gallagher, 'Fowell Buxton and the New African Policy, 1838–1842', *Cambridge Historical Journal* 10 (1950), 36–58, 37; David Turley, 'Anti-Slavery Activists and Officials. "Influence", Lobbying and the Slave Trade', in Keith Hamilton and Patrick Salmon (eds.), *Slavery, Diplomacy and Empire. Britain and the Suppression of the Slave Trade, 1807–1975* (Eastbourne: Sussex Academy Press, 2009), 81–90, 84–85.

treaties. In a chapter tellingly entitled 'Superstitions and Cruelties of the Africans', he presented an overview of the various accounts concerning the seeming omnipresence of human sacrifice in Africa, with a particular focus on the kingdoms of Dahomey and Asante. His reasons for this reiteration were to refute arguments in favour of the slave trade based on the pro-slavery idea that an excess of slaves would result in their sacrifice so that the best methods to save Africans from this cruel fate was to export them from the continent.[43] In fact, according to Buxton, the prevalence of human sacrifice *co-existed* with the presence of the slave trade and was owed to the 'low rate at which human life is valued' generally in Africa due to havoc wreaked on it by the traffic in slaves in which humans were treated as commodities.[44] The task for Britain was to protest against the practice of human sacrifice 'in all (…) official transactions' with African rulers by addressing its abolition 'by stipulations in our treaties'.[45]

After some initial hesitation, the British government agreed to sponsor Buxton's plan for the Niger expedition and for the conclusion of treaties with African rulers. James Bandinel, the senior clerk of the slave trade department within the Foreign Office was requested by the Colonial Secretary, Lord Glenelg (1835–1839) to draft a model agreement for the purpose.[46] The main objective of the twelve-clause agreement was stated in the preamble and was both to 'put down the slave trade forever' and to establish a commercial relationship between Britain and the African treaty partner.[47] One of the additional articles to the agreement – the inclusion of which was left to the discretion of the negotiators – provided for the abolition of the practice of human sacrifice. It was not inserted into the main body of the text as 'the prejudices of the Natives may be so strong in favour of the Custom' that the fear existed that insisting on its absolute abolition would jeopardise successful negotiations for the abolition of the slave trade.[48] However, it was advised that in all instances negotiators should use their 'earnest exhortation' and 'affectionate advice' against

43 Thomas F. Buxton, *The African Slave Trade and Its Remedy* (London: John Murray, 1840), 230.

44 *Ibid.*, 238.

45 *Ibid.*, 230, 244.

46 Keith Hamilton, 'Zealots and Helots. The Slave Trade Department of the Nineteenth-Century Foreign Office', in Keith Hamilton and Patrick Salmon (eds.), *Slavery, Diplomacy and Empire. Britain and the Suppression of the Slave Trade, 1807–1975* (Eastbourne: Sussex Academy Press, 2009), 20–42, 23.

47 Draft of Agreement Proposed to be entered into with African Chiefs, FO 84/336, TNA. See for an exhaustive account of the model agreement: Inge Van Hulle, *Britain, West Africa and Imperial International Law, 1807–1885* (Leuven: unpublished thesis, 2016).

48 James Bandinel to James Stephen, 10 April 1840, London, The National Archive [hereinafter TNA], FO 84/336.

the practice of human sacrifice and to not relinquish their attempts until they had 'fully ascertained the impossibility of obtaining even a mitigation of the Practice'.

Already during the 1840s and 1850s, as a result of the government's commitment to suppress human sacrifice, Dahomey became the focus of several diplomatic journeys in which British representatives tried to convince the king to abolish the slave trade. In 1849, instructions for negotiations with King Gezo of Dahomey explicitly stated that if the opportunity should avail itself, the king should be told that the practice of human sacrifice was reprehensible to the Christian religion and that it would be 'gratifying' to the British queen to know that 'the king had ordered it to be discontinued'.[49] While in 1877 a promise was exacted from the new king, Glele, that at least British subjects should no longer 'be compelled to attend any of the customs of the country of Dahomey where any human sacrifices are held' the final blow to human sacrifice at Dahomey was dealt by the military conquest of the kingdom by France.[50]

Treaties with African rulers featured standard clauses that described the abolition of human sacrifice in the following terms:

> The King and Chiefs of Jaboo declare that no human beings shall, at any time, be sacrificed within their territories, on account of religious or other ceremonies, and that they will prevent the barbarous practice of murdering prisoners in war.[51]

However, the above remarks made by James Bandinel illustrate that while the suppression of human sacrifice was considered an important objective, it took second place to the abolition of the slave trade. This reflects the theory that underlay abolitionist efforts that in order for Africa to become truly civilised, the slave trade needed to be expunged first. State practice reflected this approach as the number of treaties that included clauses for the abolition of human sacrifice were comparatively less than those that focused exclusively on the slave trade. While treaties providing for the abolition of the slave trade were stated in absolute terms, the agreements concerning the abolition of human sacrifice

49 Commodore Fanshawe to Lieutenant Forbes, 9 September 1849, *Papers relative to the Reduction of Lagos by Her Majesty's Forces on the West Coast of Africa* 1852 (1455), 215.

50 Art. 5, Treaty between Great Britain and Dahomey, 12 May 1877, *British and Foreign State Papers* (170 vols., London: HMSO, 1844–1977), vol. 68, 674 [hereinafter BFSP].

51 Art. 7, Engagement for the Abolition of the Traffic in Slaves between Great Britain and the King and Chiefs of Jaboo, 25 February 1852, 42 BFSP 691. See also: Engagement for the Abolition of the Traffic in Slaves between Great Britain and the Chiefs of Grand Popoe, 2 February 1852 and Engagement for the Abolition of the Traffic in Slaves between Great Britain and the Chiefs of Aghwey, 2 February 1852, 42 BFSP 689 and 687.

often took the form – next to the above-quoted clause – of 'solemn promises' whereby African rulers pledged to use their 'utmost influence and power' to induce their subjects to abandon human sacrifice.[52] The precise obligation of African rulers was therefore described in terms that seemed much more open-ended than slave trade provisions that forced them to enact legislation concerning the slave trade, to prohibit the residence of foreign slave traders on their territory and that made the failure to uphold these provisions punishable by force.[53]

One of the reasons put forward by British negotiators seemed to have been inspired by a certain dejection as to the feasibility of the project as the practice of human sacrifice seemed 'so inveterate, that even the arbitrary power of an African King is not sufficient to put at once an end to the evil'.[54] However, the rationale behind the conclusion of treaties in which the prohibition of human sacrifice was engraved was nevertheless the same as that which underpinned the abolition of the slave trade through treaties. Bilateral agreements shifted the burden of obligations towards African rulers and left a tool in the hands of British imperial agents to enforce prohibition through other means than mere moral persuasion.[55] Despite the vague descriptions of the terms of these 'solemn promises', stipulations against human sacrifice would be used for the purpose of violent interventions that were justified on humanitarian grounds and the non-fulfilment of treaty obligations.

4 Treaties as Facilitators for the Use of Force

These humanitarian justifications penetrated all aspects of the treaty-making process. The legal discourse used in the treaties, for example, clearly reflected the cultural apprehensions harboured against the practice of human sacrifice as it was described as 'abominable, inhuman, and un-Christian-like'.[56]

52 Promise made by King Eyo of Old Calabar, and by his Chiefs of Duke Town and Creek Town, 18/29 March 1848, BFSP 36 (1847–1848), 865.

53 Agreement with the Chiefs of Ivory Bay, 2 March 1848, BFSP 36 (1847–1848), 863; Engagement entered into by King Pepple, River Bonny, 2 December 1849, BFSP 39 (1849–1850), 18.

54 Commodore Murray to Commodore Sir Charles Hotham, 24 March 1848, *Report from the Select Committee of the House of Lords Appointed to Consider the Best Means which Great Britain can adopt of the Final Extinction of the African Slave Trade and to Report thereon to the House*, Session 1849, 405.

55 Arthur Westeijn, '"Love Alone is not Enough". Treaties in Seventeenth-Century Dutch Colonial Expansion', in Saliha Belmessous (ed.), *Empire by Treaty. Negotiating European Expansion, 1600–1900* (Oxford: Oxford University Press, 2014), 19–44, 19.

56 Promise made by King Eyo of Old Calabar, and by his Chiefs of Duke Town and Creek Town, 18/29 March 1848, 36 BFSP 865.

Oftentimes, the abolition of human sacrifice formed part of what might be termed a 'humanitarian package-deal' to expunge local customs that did not accord with Christian morality. This deal included the abolition of human sacrifice together with that of the slave trade and all other customs that were deemed as uncivilised to Europeans. Next to the slave trade, prohibition clauses could, for example, entail the ritual killing of twin children, trial by ordeal or panyarring, which was a form of debt slavery.[57] In the 1844 Bonds concluded with Fante rulers on the Gold Coast, the abolition of human sacrifice was prescribed in a sweeping, all-encompassing clause that read that 'Human sacrifices, and other barbarous customs, such as panyarring, are abominations, and contrary to law'.[58] The general nature of the clause can be explained by the fact that the relationship between the British authorities on the Gold Coast and the surrounding Fante had for a number of decades been progressing towards the gradual extension of British extraterritorial jurisdiction, especially in the field of criminal law. It also underscores the British idea that the cultural progress of Africans could not limit itself to ending the slave trade or human sacrifice.[59]

The creation and implementation of treaties or other legal instruments in the imperial arena was the result of a complex interplay between, on the one hand indigenous actors, and, on the other hand the central organs of government situated in London, imperial agents that operated on the ground consisting of naval officers, judicial commissioners, colonial governors, consular agents and various individuals who had a stake in the advance of British influence, such as merchants or missionaries. This amalgam of intermediate officials has been variably described as 'men on the spot',[60] 'imperial bridgeheads'[61] or 'middle power'.[62]

57 On the differences between slavery, pawnship and panyarring: Paul E. Lovejoy, 'The Business of Slaving: Pawnship in Western Africa, c. 1600–1810', *Journal of African History* 42 (2001), 67–89, 75.

58 Bond, 6 March 1844; Bond, 18 March 1844; Bond, 12 April 1844; Bond, 8 May 1844; Bond, 29 May 1844; Bond, 2 July 1844. All to be found in TNA, CO 96/4.

59 Van Hulle, 'British Protection, Extraterritoriality, and Protectorates', 194–210.

60 John S. Galbraith, *Reluctant Empire: British Policy on the South African Frontier, 1834–1854* (Berkeley: University of California Press, 1963); Ronald Hyam, *Understanding the British Empire* (Cambridge: Cambridge University Press, 2010).

61 Bronwen Everill, 'Bridgeheads of Empire? Liberated African Missionaries in West Africa', *Journal of Imperial and Commonwealth History* 40 (2012), 789–805, 790; John Darwin, 'Imperialism and the Victorians: The Dynamics of Territorial Expansion', *English Historical Review* 112 (1997), 614–642.

62 Lauren Benton and Lisa Ford, *Rage for Order: The British Empire and the Origins of International Law, 1800–1850* (Cambridge, MA: Harvard University Press, 2016).

Many of the treaties that prescribed the prohibition of human sacrifice and the circumstances that surrounded their conclusion betray the particularly important role of missionaries. In West Africa, missions had with mixed degrees of success been present since the late eighteenth century, yet their interest in West Africa was heightened during the course of the nineteenth century due to the evangelical revival in England. Susan Thorne has aptly described missionaries as the 'advance column of imperialism's cultural assault on indigenous subjectivities' as missionaries often spearheaded British influence and advocated against 'un-Christian' cultural practices.[63] Some of the missionaries were of African descent. African bureaucrats in the service of empire have been described by Benjamin Lawrance, Emily Lynn Osborn and Richard Roberts as the 'hidden lynchpins of colonial rule'.[64] They functioned as intermediates between European colonial officials and the indigenous populations as they were able to bridge the racial and cultural divides established by colonial rule.[65] As missionaries frequently established bases outside of the official boundaries of British jurisdiction, they could implement their civilizational agenda on a daily basis through persuasion and education, while benefiting from the protection of Britain's coercive capabilities if need be as British subjects.

Many treaties betray the presence and persuasive force of missionaries in steering the conclusion of treaties that provided for the abolition of human sacrifice as they were often mentioned as witnesses in the process of negotiation and signature.[66] For example, in 1848 in Old Calabar, missionary lobbying and press campaigns paved the way for the Royal Navy's extraction of a written promise of several African rulers to use their influence to suppress human sacrifice.[67] Two years later, they took the initiative to gather support for the formation of a 'permanent society for the suppression of human sacrifices' and urged the need for King Eyo to create an Egbo law officially outlawing the practice of human sacrifice. However, it was not until one of the naval officers present in the town declared to have been so appalled by what had transpired in the region that 'all friendly intercourse between them must cease', that the

63 Susan Thorne, *Congregational Missions & the Making of an Imperial Culture in Nineteenth-Century England* (Stanford: Stanford University Press, 1999), 9.

64 Benjamin N. Lawrance, Emily Lynn Osborn and Richard L. Roberts, 'African Intermediaries and the 'Bargain' of Collaboration', in Benjamin N. Lawrance, Emily Lynn Osborn and Richard L. Roberts (eds.) *Intermediaries, Interpreters, and Clerks* (Madison: The University of Wisconsin Press, 2006), 3–34, 4–5.

65 Everill, 'Bridgeheads of Empire? Liberated African Missionaries in West Africa', 790.

66 Promise made by King Eyo, of Old Calabar, 36 BFSP 865.

67 Article from the Patriot, s.d., Ibid., 652.

king conceded to the proposal.[68] The promulgation of the law was confirmed by treaty.

Several years later, the continued presence of human sacrifice in spite of the treaty was used as a pretext by British supercargoes who held a monopoly position in the trade in palm oil to demand intervention.[69] They felt threatened by the fact that attempts had been made by local merchants to circumvent them in order to trade palm oil directly to Britain.[70] The inexperienced acting consul Lynslager, ignorant with respect to African politics, was easily manipulated. In a display of disproportionate force he, 'completely riddled the town' and 'set fire to every part of it' in reprisal to the breach of treaty obligations.[71] The British permission to rebuild Old Town was made conditional on the conclusion of a further treaty which outlawed human sacrifice on the basis of Egbo law and which included the prohibition of trial by ordeal and the ritual killing of twin children.[72]

The example of Old Calabar illustrates that the conclusion of treaties within the colonial sphere held the constant potential for violent confrontation. This potential was two-fold. Firstly, if the signature of an African chief could not be secured through diplomatic persuasion, duress was at times applied instead. The justification for such use of duress was often found within the same racist discourse that vilified African customs as 'barbarous' as outlined above. Africans could not be trusted to find the path to true civilisation themselves and needed to be 'guided', i.e. forcefully dragged in the right direction by Britain. Secondly, once treaties were secured, they provided a legal basis for intervention when African rulers neglected to adhere to their obligations.

68 Extract from the 'Missionary Record' for July 1850, *Class (B.) Correspondence with British Ministers and Agents in Foreign Countries, and with Foreign Ministers in England, relating to the Slave Trade, from 1 April 1850 to 31 March 1851* 26 (1850), 5.

69 The Masters and Supercargoes in the Bonny Rover to Acting-Consul Lynslager, 18 January 1855, 45 BFSP 1024.

70 Rosalind J. Hackett, *Religion in Calabar: the Religious Life and History of a Nigerian Town* (Berkin: New York, 1989), 63; M. Efiong Noah, 'Political History of the City States of Old Calabar, 1820–60', in Boniface I. Obichere (ed.), *Studies in Southern Nigerian History. A Festschrift for Joseph Christopher Okwudili Anene, 1918–68* (London: Routledge, 1982), 37–68, 47–49.

71 Lieutenant Young to Commodore Adams, 24 January 1855, 45 BFSP 1023.

72 Treaty with the Chiefs of Old Town, Old Calabar, for the Abolition of Human Sacrifices, the Use of the Poison-nut, and the Practice of Killing Twin Children, in Lewis Hertslet (ed.), *A Complete Collection of the Treaties and Conventions and Reciprocal Regulations at Present Subsisting between Great Britain and Foreign Powers* (London: Buttersworth, 1859), vol. 10, 33.

5 Annexation and the Abolition of Human Sacrifice

The most blatant examples for the abuse of treaty-rights that were based on the abolition of human sacrifice exist in the outright annexation of African territories as a form of reprisal for the failure of African rulers to uphold treaties. These calls for reprisals intersected with British aspirations, as a civilised nation, to instruct Africans in the ways of cultural progress. For example, James Irvine, a prominent Liverpool palm oil trader with multiple stakes in West Africa likened Africans to recalcitrant children who needed forceful instruction. In a speech that condemned human sacrifice, he argued that the duty of civilised nations was 'to force them to recognise law, and if necessary, proceed even to the extent of conquest'.[73] Similar justifications for the use of force based on the need to expunge human sacrifice reigned in France, which annexed Dahomey in 1892. Here, mass hysteria in the press regarding human sacrifice had bolstered the French resolve to send expeditions in 1890 and 1892.[74] At the Paris World Fair of 1900, the Dahomean pavilion took shape as an actual 'Tower of Sacrifice', which was adorned with human skulls that had allegedly been sacrificed by King Behanzin.[75]

The final subjugation in 1897 by Britain of the Kingdom of Benin was also clouded by humanitarian rhetoric that emphasised human sacrifice as a deeply engrained custom in Benin's culture. The immediate reason for intervention was nevertheless more prosaic, as the ruler of Benin, Oba Ovonramwen, refused to relax trade restrictions, which increasingly proved a thorn in Britain's commercial eye. Religious practice at Benin centred on the notion of sacred kingship and the seemingly discretionary powers ascribed to his office were seen as the greatest obstacle to greater political and commercial influence.[76] In 1892, Vice-Consul H.L. Gallwey attempted to negotiate a treaty with the Oba that would place Benin under the protection of Britain and that entailed – amongst others – a provision for the abolition of human sacrifice.[77] The conditions surrounding the conclusion of the treaty were obscure and the Oba contested ever having signed the document. Finally, in 1896 an expedition under the

73 James Irvine, *The Ashantee Difficulty. A Paper Read to the Birkenhead Literary and Scientific Society* (Liverpool: Benson and Holme, 1873), 30.

74 Véronique Campion-Vincent, 'L'image du Dahomey dans la presse française (1890–1895): Les sacrifices humains', *Cahiers d'Etudes Africaines* 25 (1967), 27–58, 29–30.

75 Neil Macmaster, *Racism in Europe: 1870–200* (London: Macmillan, 2001), 75.

76 Flora Edouwaye S. Kaplan, 'Understanding Sacrifice and Sanctity in Benin Indigenous Religion, Nigeria: A Case Study' in Jacob K. Olupona (ed.), *Beyond primitivism: Indigenous Religious Traditions and Modernity* (London: Routledge, 2003), 181–199, 183.

77 Alan F.C. Ryder, *Benin and the Europeans, 1485–1897* (London: Longmans, 1969), 268.

leadership of the acting Consul-General, James Phillips, was sent to secure the deposition of the Oba, yet was ambushed by a subordinate chief. In retaliation for both the ambush and the non-compliance with the contested treaty, a punitive expedition was launched which left the city of Benin burnt to the ground and the Oba kneeling in submission. Several pictures that evidenced the practice of human sacrifice taken during the expedition which were supposed to illustrated the justness of the intervention were later reproduced in H.L. Roth's tellingly entitled 'Great Benin: its Customs, Art and Horrors'.[78]

In 1871, tensions with Asante came once more to a head when the Dutch and the British government agreed to the cession of the Dutch forts to British rule. The cession highlighted a number of outstanding political concerns for Asante. These included rights of sovereignty over the Dutch forts which revolved around the legal status of the 'kostbrief' that the Dutch government paid to Asante for its occupation of the forts, which the Asante king, Kofi Karikari (1867–1874) considered to constitute a rent.[79] Furthermore, the loss of influence over the Dutch forts, and especially over Elmina, would once again complicate Asante access to the sea.[80] The resulting campaign, which stood under the leadership of Sir Garnet Wolseley, who was to make a name for himself as a 'specialist' in African warfare, was the first West African war between an African and European nation that attracted substantial attention in Europe.[81] The main objectives of the campaign were to force Asante to relinquish its claims over all tribes previously under Dutch influence and to abolish the payment of the 'rent'. Wolseley was also instructed to put an end 'if possible' to the 'human sacrifices and the slave-hunting which, with other barbarities, prevail in the Ashanti kingdom'.[82]

78 Henry Ling Roth, *Great Benin: its Customs, Art and Horrors* (Halifax: F. King and Sons, Ltd, 1903).

79 Kennedy to Nagtglas, 9 October 1870, enclosed in Kennedy to Kimberley, 10 October 1870, TNA, CO 879/3. Also contained in *Correspondence Relative to the Cession by the Netherlands Government to the British Government of the Dutch Settlements on the West Coast of Africa*, Parliamentary Papers, 1872 (670), 1–2. See generally on the legal status of the Kostbrief: Harvey Feinberg, 'There was an Elmina Note, But…'. *International Journal of African Historical Studies* 9 (1976), 618–630; Larry Yarak, 'The "Elmina Note:" Myth and Reality of Asante-Dutch Relations', *History in Africa* 13 (1986), 365–382.

80 William D. McIntyre, 'British Policy in West Africa: The Ashanti Expedition of 1873–4', *Historical Journal* 5 (1962), 19–46, 30.

81 Ian F.W. Beckett, 'Manipulating the Modern Curse of Armies: Wolseley, the Press and the Ashanti War, 1873–1874', in Stephen Miller (ed.), *Soldiers and Settlers in Africa, 1850–1918* (Leiden: Brill, 2009), 219–234, 219.

82 Lord Kimberley to Sir Garnet Wolesley, 10 September 1873, TNA, CO 879/5.

While the conditional phrasing of the instructions of the foreign secretary to Wolseley with respect to human sacrifice seem to have been included almost as an afterthought, the prohibition of human sacrifice in the resulting Treaty of Fomena would have important consequences for the political fate of Asante.[83] To the British official beholder an independent Asante in Britain's West African backyard presented a dangerous wildcard. The years following the British campaign were tarnished by internal political upheaval and civil war in Asante. By the 1890s, British influence needed to contend with encroachments by Germany and France. Repeated offers of British protection and the establishment of a British resident were rejected.[84] When the newly enstooled king, Prempeh (1888–1896), sent an embassy to Britain to negotiate an agreement for the exploitation of Asante's mineral resources with private investors in circumvention of the Gold Coast government, the British government was shocked into action. The final acceptance by Prempeh of the British resident under threats of war could no longer deter the resolve of foreign secretary, Joseph Chamberlain (1895–1903), to turn Asante into a puppet state.

The result of the expedition was the formal submission of Prempeh and the queen mother, their prostration to Governor Maxwell and the exile of Prempeh and his family members.[85] Prempeh had advised against forceful resistance in order to safeguard the survival of the nation. Officially the government justified its forceful action on the basis of the neglect on the part of Asante to carry out the terms of the Treaty of Fomena. In the debates surrounding the legality of the war, several clauses of the Fomena Treaty were said to have been violated, which included the obligation to pay an indemnity and the promise to keep the roads open for commerce. However, it was primarily the continued practice of human sacrifice in spite of the Treaty of Fomena that acted as a smokescreen behind which the British government could hide its true political objectives. Pro-interventionists repeatedly appealed to how British control would now finally 'put a stop to the barbarous practices that had hitherto prevailed'.[86] It was alleged that human sacrifices had been continued up to the

83 Treaty of Peace between Great Britain and Ashantee, 13 February 1874, 75 BFSP 471.

84 Tom McCaskie, 'Prempeh before the Exile', in Emmanuel Akyeampong, Adu Boahen, Nancy Lawler, Tom McCaskie, Ivor Wilks (eds.), *The History of Ashanti Kings and the Whole Country Itself and Other Writings by Otumfuo, Nana Agyeman Prempeh I* (Oxford: Oxford University Press), 3–20, 16–18.

85 Emmanuel Akyeampong, 'Christianity, Modernity and the Weight of Tradition in the Life of "Asantehne" Agyeman Prempeh I, c. 1888–1931', *Africa: Journal of the International African Institute* 69 (1999), 279–311, 287.

86 Hansard, House of Commons, 2 April 1897, vol. 48, cc 436.

very entry of British troops into Comassie, where 'the remains of thousands of persons' were found.

The resort to justifications that were cloaked under the guise of saving the victims of human sacrifice were not universally accepted. Both with respect to the expeditions against Benin and Asante critical voices that questioned governmental interference or annexation could be heard. The real commercial and political motives of use of force did not pass unnoticed or 'would the attempt to put it down ever have been made if of the tyrant of Benin had not interfered with trade'?[87] The criticism levied against the expedition to Comassie only heightened the reliance on a humanitarian discourse that applauded the contribution of the British to the abolition of human sacrifice in Asante through force. Wolseley himself attested that 'if we could look forward to no other result from this war' than the end of human sacrifice in Asante, then all 'the blood we had shed, the lives we had lost, and the treasure we had expended' would not have been in vain.[88]

6 Conclusion

The use of legal measures to suppress cultural practices of human sacrifice by Britain did not limit itself to West Africa, but also extended, for example, to India.[89] Such legal interventions formed part of a wider nineteenth-century imperialist trend for the gradual expulsion of all indigenous cultural institutions that did not accord to Christian worldviews and can therefore not be separated from European practices of extraterritoriality and unequal treaties imposed on South-East Asia and the Ottoman Empire.

The focus on the abolition of the slave trade has overshadowed the importance of the European concerns over human sacrifice and how these functioned as justifications for intervention in West Africa. Europeans associated many of the African kingdoms, most notably Benin, Dahomey and Asante with the tales of horror and bloodshed that circulated through travel literature. Next to the slave trade, the abolition of human sacrifice became part of a civilizational agenda that sought to mould African indigenous customs in which Britain and its imperial agents played a leading role. Under pressure

87 Ibid., cc 446.

88 Comments by Sir Garnet Wolseley, *Proceedings of the Royal Geographical Society* (session 1878–1874), 259.

89 Andrea Major, *Sovereignty and Social Reform in India: British Colonialism and the Campaign against Sati, 1830–1860* (London: Routledge, 2011).

of humanitarians, including missionaries, treaties were concluded with African rulers that prohibited human sacrifice. These treaties in turn laid the legal foundations for the resort to forcible measures couched in humanitarian language. The widespread use of treaties for the formalisation of international relations in West Africa, of which the suppression of human sacrifice was merely one objective, gave imperial agents the ability to appeal to the binding force of written obligations as a basis for intervention. In their most abject forms, such measures amounted to the full annexation of African territories.

CHAPTER 6

The Mahmoud Ben Ayad Case and the Transformation of International Law

Raphaël Cahen

1 Introduction

In these times of neo-liberalism, globalisation and digital revolution, the Panama Papers and corruption scandals have become daily news. In the long nineteenth century and especially in its second half, the relationships between finance and international law, as well as between individual actors and state finance, became closer and stronger. This can be partly explained by growing global capitalism and the Industrial Revolution as well as the decline of old empires, the emergence of new empires and nation-states and the opening of new markets, as in South America.[1] Many scandals formed the daily bread of public opinion in a world without internet and social media.[2]

The specific case this chapter focuses on has never been fully studied even though, or maybe because, a massive amount of information and sources is available concerning its facts. There is, for example, an independent section of 382 boxes in the Tunisian State Archive pertaining to it.[3] However, this chapter is based on the materials available in the archives of the French Foreign Ministry as well as the private papers from Joseph-Marie Portalis who served as president of the 'committee of litigation' in charge of the Ben Ayad case.

Constrained by the use of exclusively French materials, I hope to give a first extensive insight on this affair which had 'une importance et un retentissement extraordinaires en France' and beyond.[4] The case had not only many juridical

1 Jürgen Osterhammel, *Die Verwandlung der Welt. Eine Geschichte des 19. Jahrhunderts* (Munich: C.H. Beck, 2009); Lea Heimbeck, *Die Abwicklung von Staatsbankrotten im Völkerrecht. Verrechtlichung und Rechtsvermeidung zwischen 1824 und 1907* (Baden-Baden: Nomos Verlag, 2013).

2 In France, mostly during the Third Republic, many finance scandals occurred, see Jean Garrigues, *Les Scandales de la Républiques. De Panama à l'affaire Cahuzac* (Paris: Nouveau monde, 2013).

3 Série 'Affaire Mahmoud Ben Ayad', Archives Nationales de Tunisie.

4 Mohamed Salah Mzali et Jean Pignon (eds.), *Kheredine. Homme d'état, Mémoires* (Tunis: Maison tunisienne de l'édition, 1971), 21.

 | DOI:10.1163/9789004412088_007

peculiarities and political and historical ramifications, but was also directly related to the transformation of international law in the long nineteenth century as it involved an arbitration given by Napoleon III (November 1856).

In 1852, Ben Ayad, one of the most powerful and richest members of the Tunisian elite, returned to France, where he obtained the French nationality and decided to settle.[5] In May 1853, for various reasons and after the refusal of Ben Ayad to come back to the regency, the bey of Tunis sent a letter to all European consulates stating that Ben Ayad had escaped the regency after robbing half of the Tunisian treasury.[6] A dispute started between Ben Ayad and the Tunisian government which led to an arbitration of the dispute by Napoleon III in November 1856, after two years of work by his litigation committee.[7]

This dispute and the arbitration constituted important steps toward the recognition of the sovereignty of Tunisia and led to the increase of European and especially French interference and control on what was essentially a vassal state of the Ottoman Empire. The dispute started some months before the Crimean War and the arbitration was given just after the Congress of Paris (1856) in the same new building of the French Foreign Ministry at the Quai D'Orsay. The case also is relevant to the history of arbitration or mediation in the nineteenth century. Even if the final decision took place in form of a 'sentence arbitrale', it was not a common international arbitration as it did not involve two states. Therefore, the Ben Ayad case is not to be found in various collections of international arbitration of the nineteenth century.[8] However, it can be seen as an international arbitration since the dispute related to 'pecuniary damages suffered by a state, or its nationals, as a consequence of illegal actions or negligence on the part of another state or its nationals'.[9]

---

5 See for the Archives, Paris, Archives du Ministère des Affaires Etrangères [herineafter AMAE], Contentieux 430, folder 1.

6 In the press different articles were also published. See for instance in *La Presse*, 1 September 1853, and a novel by Alphonse Daudet, Le Nabab, Paris 1877.

7 AMAE, Contentieux 430, 431, 432. There are several versions of the 'Sentence Arbitrale' to be found. See AMAE, 482 PAAP/16 dossier 2 or AMAE, Contentieux 431. *Sentence arbitrale rendue par Sa Majesté l'empereur des Français sur les réclamations réciproques de Son Altesse le Bey de Tunis et du général Benaïad*, 30 November 1856, signed by le Comte Portalis, Marquis de Gabriac, Duvergier, A. Marchand, Armand Lefebvre and A. Walewski.

8 A. de Lapradelle, N. Politis, *Recueil des Arbitrages Internationaux* (Paris: Pedone, 1923); H. la Fontaine, *Pasicrisie internationale 1794–1900. Histoire documentaire des arbitrages internationaux* (The Hague: Brill, 1997).

9 See Randall Lesaffer, 'Peace Through Law: The Hague Peace Conferences and the Rise of Ius Contra Bellum', in Maartje H. Abbenhuis, Christopher Ernest Barber and Annalise R. Higgins (eds.), *War, Peace and International Order?: The Legacies of the Hague Conferences of 1899 and 1907* (Abingdon, Oxon.: Routledge, 2017), 31–52.

The litigation committee of the French foreign minister had to deal with an increasing number of cases after 1830 arising from France's imperial interests. Despite the growing number of cases around the world, the practice of arbitration has not been studied extensively for the period between the famous Jay Treaty of 1794 and the codification of principles and procedure in The Hague in 1899.[10]

In this chapter, firstly, the actors of the case and its historical and contextual backgrounds will be discussed. Secondly, the chapter will analyse the result and the impact of Napoleon III's arbitration on the transformation of international law.

2 Context and Actors of the Case

First of all, it is important to recall that the juridical status of Tunisia was unclear in terms of international law in the long nineteenth century. The so-called 'regency of Tunis' was, since the sixteenth century, like Algiers or Tripoli, administrated by Pashas in the name of the Sultan of Constantinople and fell theoretically under the sovereignty of the Ottoman Empire.[11] But the three *barbaresque* states gained more and more autonomy during the eighteenth century. In Tunis, the Husainid dynasty managed to stay in power from 1705 until the proclamation of the Republic by Habib Bourguiba in 1957.[12] During that long period of dynastic stability, Tunis gained a quasi-independent status from the Ottoman Empire and would eventually be treated as a quasi-full sovereign state by the community of nations before becoming a protectorate of France in 1881.[13]

10 Dominique Gaurier, *Histoire du droit international. De l'Antiquité à la création de l'ONU* (Rennes: Presses Universitaires de Rennes, 2014), 640–668.

11 A. Guellouz, A. Masmoudi, M. Smida, A. Saadaoui, *Histoire générale de la Tunisie: Les temps modernes* (Tunis: Sud éditions, 2007), 260–312; Christian Windler, 'Towards the Empire of a Civilizing Nation: the French Revolution and its Impact on Relations with the Ottoman Regencies in the Maghreb', in Martti Koskenniemi, Walter Rech, and Manuel Jiménez Fonseca (ed.), *International Law and Empire. Historical Explorations* (Oxford: Oxford University Press, 2017), 201–223.

12 Guellouz et alii, *Histoire générale de la Tunisie*, 327–328; Windler, 'Towards the Empire of a Civilizing Nation', 207–208. Windler stressed that for the French Consuls at the end of the eighteenth century Tunis was already regarded as an independent Kingdom.

13 Guellouz et alii, *Histoire générale de la Tunisie*, 327–400. For Smida it is hard to tell what the exact juridical status of Tunisia was; Karim Rahmouni, *L'Etat beylical et le droit: une transition vers la modernité? (1705–1881)* (Aix-Marseille Université: unpublished thesis, 2007). The author refers to the great 'autonomy', from 1600 and onwards, see 42–46; André

During the Vienna Congress, one of the issues that had been raised and linked to the question of slavery, but had never been solved, concerned the activity of piracy of the *barbaresque* states which was extremely damaging for European commerce.[14] An anti-corsair league was formed in Europe and different actions were made against the regency of Tunis and against Algiers, such as the bombing of the city of Algiers in 1816.[15]

At the same time, the Ottoman Empire had started its decline with the gradual loss of some of its territories. Greece became independent in the 1820s. In 1830, France under Charles X (1824–1830) conquered Algiers. Ever since, France shared a common border with Tunisia. A Franco-Tunisian treaty was signed in August 1830.[16]

In the 1840s, Mahmoud Ben Ayad was sent as an ambassador of the bey to Paris like his father had been before him.[17] He prepared the state visit of the French King Louis Philippe's sons to Tunis and Cartago in the summer of 1846 as well as the return-visit of Ahmed I to Paris in November of the same year. That was the first visit of the bey of Tunis to Europe as well as the first state visit of a Muslim monarch to Europe in peacetime. Ibrahim Pasha of Egypt, son of Mehmet Ali, would likewise pay a visit to Europe around the same time.[18]

Those new cultural and political encounters were certainly signs of what historians often call the growing 'modernisation' and 'westernisation' that was undertaken for Tunisia by Ahmed I (1837–1855) as well as Mohammed Bey II (1855–1859), in the same spirit as the *Tanzimat* in the heart of the Ottoman

---

Raymond, 'Les provinces arabes (XVIe–XVIIIe siècle)', in Robert Mantran (ed.), *Histoire de l'Empire Ottoman* (Paris: Fayard, 1989), 404–420. Here for André Raymond, the Maghreb provinces were 'quasi-independent'.

14 See Brian E. Vick, *The Congress of Vienna. Power and Politics after Napoleon* (Cambridge: Harvard University Press, 2014), 17, 194–195, 212–224.

15 Vick, *The Congress of Vienna*, 223–224; Daniel Panzac, *Barbary Corsairs. The End of a Legend, 1800–1820* (Leiden: Brill, 2005), 270–292.

16 Jacques-Alain de Sedouy, *Le Concert européen aux origines de l'Europe 1814–1914* (Paris: Fayard 2009); Anouard Chahed, *Un tournant dans l'histoire de la régence de Tunis le règne du Muschir Muhammad Pacha Bey (1855–1859)* (Nice : unpublished thesis, 2000), 183–194.

17 Leon Carl Brown, *The Tunisia of Ahmad Bey, 1837–1855* (Princeton: Princeton University Press, 1974), 83. The author stressed the importance of the Ben Ayads by writing that 'the history of Tunisia cannot be without the Bin Ayads'. Brown wrote as well that 'Bin Ayad was to Ahmad Bey comparable to what Colbert was to Louis XIV', 336.

18 *Ibid.*, 325–341; Mohamed Salah Mzali, *Les beys de Tunis et le roi des français* (Tunis: Maison tunisienne de l'édition, 1976); See also Jules Burgy, *A son Altesse le bey de Tunis, Ahmed, ami du genre humain* (Paris: s.n., 1846). The Bey did not go to London after Paris since the Queen was not willing to receive him without the Ambassador of the Sublime Porte.

Empire or in Egypt.[19] The Tunisian army was modernised and slavery was fully abolished, hereby seriously decreasing the control of the Mamelukes.[20] Tunisian troops took part in the Crimean War in 1854–1856 under their own flag.[21] All these events as well as many diplomatic and symbolic measures such as the creation of its own currency, its own 'Order of Glory' (the *Nichan iftikar*) or the fact that the seal of the bey was to be found in all international papers and treaties gave Tunisia increasing autonomy and independence from the Ottoman Empire.[22]

In the 1860s and 1870s, modernisation continued with the adoption of the Fundamental Pact, which gave equal rights and freedom to all inhabitants of the regency.[23] The first Tunisian constitution was adopted, exactly 150 years before the recent Tunisian revolution.[24] But these modernisations were accompanied by growing European imperialism as a European finance commission took control over the Tunisian government at the end of the 1860s, much like it happened in Egypt and later in Istanbul.[25] The Ben Ayad Case played an important role in that transition period.

Mahmoud Ben Ayad, was a member of an important family of Caïds – provincial governors – and corsairs from Djerba.[26] Close to the court of Bey Ahmed I and holding the rank of a minister, he was in charge of various state

19 Guellouz et alii, *Histoire générale de la Tunisie*, 327–328; Donald Quataert, 'The Age of Reforms, 1812–1914', in Halil Inalcik and Donald Quataert (eds.), *An Economic and Social History of the Ottoman Empire, 1300–1914* (Cambridge: Cambridge University Press, 1996), 759–946; Brown, *The Tunisia of Ahmad Bey*, 336; Chahed, *Un tournant dans l'histoire de la régence*, 183–194. Robert Mantran, 'Les débuts de la Question d'Orient (1774–1839)', in Mantran (ed.), *Histoire de l'Empire Ottoman*, 451–500.

20 Guellouz et alii, *Histoire générale de la Tunisie*, 327–328.

21 *Ibid.*; F. Arnoulet, 'Participation tunisienne a la guerre de Crimée (1854–1856)', *Les cahiers de Tunisie* 20 (1972), 10–19. Tunis had already send some Troops at the battle of Navarino in 1827.

22 Guellouz et alii, *Histoire générale de la Tunisie*, 327–328; Raymond, *les provinces arabes* 1989, 416–417.

23 Guellouz et alii, *Histoire générale de la Tunisie*, 327–328; Rahmouni, *L'Etat beylical et le droit*, 214–287.

24 On the 2010–2011 Revolution see Pierre Avril, 'La Tunisie', *Pouvoirs. Revue française d'études constitutionnelles et politiques* 156 (2016), 137–145.

25 Guellouz et alii, *Histoire générale de la Tunisie*, 327–328; Heimbeck, *Die Abwicklung von Staatsbankrotten im Völkerrecht*; Malak Labib, 'Crise de la dette publique et missions financières européennes en Egypte, 1878–1879', *Monde(s)* 4 (2013/2), 23–43. DOI: 10.3917/mond.132.0023. URL: https://www.cairn.info/revue-mondes1-2013-2-page-23.htm; See also Jean Ganiage, 'France, England and the Tunisian Affair', in Prosser Gifford and WM. Roger Louis (eds.) *France and Britain in Africa. Imperial Rivalry and Colonial Rule* (New Haven: Yale University Press, 1971), 35–72.

26 See on Mahmoud ben Ayad or Benaïad, *Notice sur le general Benaïd, sa famille et son administration à Tunis* (Paris: s.n., 1853).

and new capitalist industries and monopolies (*fermier et fournisseur general*) as well as head of the newly founded Tunisian Bank (1847).[27] This position helped him to make a quick fortune and to become a close adviser of the minister of finance, Khasnadar.[28] He became so rich that a French journalist was able to say that he was 'le budget vivant du gouvernement de Tunis'.[29] During one of his visits to Paris where he was sent by the Tunis government to require a state loan, he asked the French government for naturalisation. From August 1850 onwards, he was the owner of various properties in France, such as a palace by the Seine near the later constructed Quai d'Orsay or the passage in Paris now called 'Ben Ayad'.[30]

His newly enacted status of resident helped him to obtain, on 13 September 1852, his naturalisation as a French citizen.[31] The French law of 1849 stipulated that a citizen had to live in France for at least ten years before being eligible for naturalisation, but this delay could be reduced to one year in some cases. Ben Ayad was able to benefit from very good relations with important people in order to obtain the French nationality.[32]

The fact that he was already a French citizen in 1852 was important for the case since Ben Ayad could therefore obtain a better protection from the French authorities.[33] It also made the dispute international as it opposed the Tunisian state to a French citizen for having neglected its public finance. After the refusal of Ben Ayad to come back to Tunis, the bey and the court lost their confidence in Ben Ayad and decided to seize all his Tunisian property and to imprison his wife and sons. After the arbitration, Ben Ayad settled in Istanbul and stayed there until his death in 1881, keeping away from state affairs. Since the award was never implemented, he spent the rest of his life lost between different jurisdictions in Europe and beyond.[34]

27 *Ibid.*

28 *Ibid.*

29 *Le monde illustré*, 14 August 1858.

30 Ben Ayad bought the 'Hotel Collot' (now Gallerie J. Kugel, 25 Quai Anatole France in Paris), the Galerie Mandar (today called Passage Ben-Aiäd in the 2th arrondissement of Paris), as well as the Castle of Bouges in the Loire Valley (owned by the mistress of Talleyrand, Dorothea of Courland from 1818 to 1826).

31 See AMAE, Contentieux 432, folder 1.

32 Loi du 3 décembre 1849. Naturalisation et séjour des étrangers en France. See also Sylvie Aprile, Delphine Diaz, 'L'Europe et ses réfugiés politiques au XIXe siècle', *La vie des idées* (15 mars 2016), http://www.laviedesidees.fr/L-Europe-et-ses-refugies-politiques-au-XIXe-siecle.html.

33 AMAE, Contentieux 432, folder 1; Brown, *The Tunisia of Ahmad Bey, 1837–1855*, 336.

34 See AMAE, Contentieux 432, folder 2. On 1 February 1860 the French minister of foreign affairs was asked for the execution of the decision but in a more favorable way. The affair went on in some Italian courts like Livorno see Mahmoud Ben Ayad, *Lettre du général Mahmoud Benaïad adressée au directeur du journal L'Italie* (Paris, s.n., 1875). See also

The case did not only involve Ben Ayad as it would have further ramifications. Nissim Samama (1805–1873), one of the closer advisers of Ben Ayad at the court of the Bey, was likewise accused of corruption. He too escaped from Tunisia to France in 1864 during the so-called great revolt, and bought various properties in France.[35] After the Franco-Prussian War, he went to Livorno and died in 1873. His succession provoked a dispute between his heirs and Ben Ayad's heir.[36] Also implicated in the affair was the minister of finance of that time, namely Mustapha Khaznadar (1837–1873), a highly corrupt Greek Mameluke, who managed to stay in power over thirty years before being replaced in 1873.[37]

On the side of the bey of Tunis, an enlightened monarch and a reformer like his successor Mohammed Bey, General Hayreddin was the main actor.[38] He originated from the Caucasus and was educated as a Mameluke in the palace of the bey in the 1840s before being sent on various diplomatic missions to Paris and Istanbul.[39] Between 1853 and 1857, he worked in Paris as an emissary of the bey and as his representative in the Ben Ayad case. Later on, he published a famous essay in Arabic with the tittle *The Surest Path to Knowledge regarding the Condition of Countries.*[40] This book would have great resonance, especially in the Arab world but also in Europe after the translation in French made by Hayreddin and published under the name *Réformes nécessaires aux états*

Affaire Benaïad contre le gouvernemement tunisien, Tribunal civil de la Seine, Première chambre, 23 June 1891.

35 Nissim ou Nessim Samama (aussi Scemama ou chemama) (1805–1873), see Jean Ganiage, *Les origines du protectorat français en Tunisie, 1861–1881* (Tunis: Maison tunisienne de l'édition, 1969), 88, 162–170, 197.

36 See for many documents: Tribunal civil de la Seine. *Mémoire en défense pour : 1 ° M. le commandeur Moïse Samama... 2 ° Mme Ziza Samama... 3 ° M. Joseph Samama, 4 ° M. Nathan Samama... contre M. le Général Mahmoud-ben-Aiad... Défense à demande en paiement de 41, 769, 125 piastres; Demande reconventionnelle en paiement de 1, 154, 509 piastres* (Paris: Imp. de Ve Renou, Maulde et Cock, 1874); Tribunal civil de la Seine. Première Chambre. *Compte présenté par les héritiers Samama et observations en réponse aux contestations soulevées par les héritiers Ben-Aïad*, (Paris: Imp. de Ve Renou et Maulde, 1885).

37 Mustapha Khaznadar or Giorgios Kalkias Stravelakis (1817–1878).

38 On Ahmet Bey see Brown, *The Tunisia of Ahmad Bey 1837–1855*, 336.

39 On Hayreddin or Khayr ed-Din see as well Ali Chenoufi (éd.), *Le ministre Khéreddine et ses contemporains* (Tunis: Beit alHikma, 1990); Gerard S. Van Krieken, *Khayral-dîn et la Tunisie (1850–1881)* (Leiden: Brill, 1976), 24–30; Mzali et alii, *Kheredine. Homme d'état*, 26.

40 See, Khayr al-Din, *The Surest Path. The Political Treatise of a Nineteenth-Century Muslim Statesman*, Leon Carl Brown (éd.) (Cambridge: Harvard University Press, 1967).

musulmans.[41] Hayreddin – who with a great sense of 'modesty' called himself the new Ibn Khaldun – became one of the reformist leaders during the liberal ages of Islamic thought.[42] He became the prime minister of Sadok Bey in the 1870s before spending the last years of his life in Istanbul.[43]

In the French archives concerning the arbitration, there is a folder called the 'other' actors.[44] Three of them were members of the Lesseps family. It concerns the famous founder of the Suez Canal, Ferdinand, but also Jules who spoke Arabic perfectly and who was another agent of the bey in Paris.[45] The third member was a cousin named Jean-Charles who happened to be the lawyer of Ben Ayad and who would later on become involved in a conflict with his client regarding his remuneration.[46]

Another group of individuals who were involved in business and trade with Tunisia and were mixed up in the case, included the French vice-consul, Gaspary.[47] The fact that French officials were probably very much involved in corruption matters was, as we can read from the archives, a serious concern for the members of the litigation committee.[48] This was especially the case for the main judge of the case who was none other than the famous diplomat and jurist Joseph-Marie Portalis (1778–1858).[49] Portalis started a diplomatic career under Napoleon Bonaparte, before becoming a judge. Portalis had already written an article entitled *Notions sur les Etats Barbaresques* while his father was responsible for the *Conseil des prises.* Moreover, Portalis son had been acquainted with the Oriental question as foreign minister of France

41 See Kayir ed din, *Essai sur les réformes nécessaires aux Etats Musulmans (1867)*, Magali Morsy (éd.), (Aix-en-Provence: Edisud, 1987), 22–23.

42 See Albert Hourani, *Arabic Thought in the Liberal Age, 1789–1939* (Cambridge: Cambridge University Press, 1983).

43 Van Krieken, *Khayral-dîn*, 24–30.

44 See AMAE, Contentieux 430, pochette 5 'dossiers des tiers intéressés'.

45 Ferdinand de Lesseps (1805–1894), see Ghislan de Diesbach, *Ferdinand de Lesseps* (Paris: Perrin, 1998) ; Jules de Lesseps (1809–1887), envoy of the Bey in Paris until 1881.

46 Upon Jean-Charles de Lesseps (1804–1880), see *Conclusions motivées pour ch. Lesseps (demandeur : Fouret) contre le général Ben Aiad (défendeur : Castaignet)*, Tribunal civil de la Seine, 1er chambre, 6 August 1858 and *Note pour M. Charles Lesseps de maîtres Nicolet et Deroulède*, Cour impériale de Paris, 16 May 1859.

47 AMAE, Contentieux 430, Folder 5, Dossier des tiers intéressés. See also a folder on Gaspary.

48 AMAE, Contentieux 430, Folder 5, Dossier des tiers intéressés and AMAE, Contentieux 430, Folder 6.

49 On Joseph-Marie Portalis (1778–1858), see Joel-Benoit d'Onorio, 'Les Portalis. Une famille au service de l'état et du droit', *Les cahiers Portalis* 1 (2014), 9–18; Jean-Francois Niort, 'Les Portalis et l'esprit du XIXe siècle', *Droits* 42 (2005/2), 93–118. Raphaël Cahen, 'Joseph Portalis (1778–1858) et la liberté de la Presse vers 1820', *Cahiers du CRHiDI*, vol. 41, 2018. https://popups.uliege.be/1370-2262/index.php?id=518.

(May–August 1829).[50] Later on, he became the president of the Court of Cassation for more than twenty years and managed to keep his position under three different political regimes. At the end of his life, in February 1854, Portalis' son was nominated chairman of the litigation committee of the Ministry of Foreign Affairs. He obtained this position for his long career as judge and as a diplomat. The appointment came in the way of a reward: 'l'éclat d'un nom qui représente une des sommités de la magistrature et qui a figuré avec tant d'honneur en bas de nos pièces diplomatiques'.[51]

3 The Case and Its Impact on the Transformation of International Law

The litigation section of the French Foreign Ministry was created on 25 December 1810.[52] A consultative committee was added in 1835 in order to deal with the growing amount of new cases.[53] The first president of that committee was – not incidentally – Edouard Mounier, brother in law of Joseph-Marie Portalis.[54]

After the reorganisation of the arbitration committee by Napoleon III, Gabriac and then Portalis were first nominated as its chairman.[55] The committee became independent and formed an important section inside the Quai d'Orsay, as Yves Bruley recently noticed:

> The litigation was again prestigious since the number of affairs were constantly growing at that time and a kind of professionalization took place, even though the members of the Committee were not paid.[56]

---

50 Joseph-Marie Portalis, *Notions sur les Etats barabaresques* (Paris: Mercure de France, 1801); Lucien Bély, Georges-Henri Soutou, Laurent Theis, Maurice Vaïsse (éds.), *Dictionnaire des ministres des affaires étrangères 1589–2004* (Paris: Fayard, 2005), 278–279.

51 See Fonds Portalis, 482 PAAP/16, dossier 2 AMAE, La Courneuve and Décret du 28 février 1854, dossier personnel Portalis, 1er série 3333 comte Portalis folder 261 AMAE. The position as 'président du comité consultatif du Contentieux' of the French Foreign Minister at the end of his life is an unknown aspect of his Biography.

52 AMAE, Contentieux 118.

53 Ibid.

54 Ibid. Edouard Mounier (1784–1843) had been appointed as the first president of the committee. He stayed two years before being replaced by Siméon (also a cousin of Portalis) and then Rossi until 1848. Gabriac became president before Portalis and Troplong (1795–1869) took over from Portalis from 1859 to 1869 at the head of the committee.

55 For the reorganisation see AMAE, Contentieux 118 and Yves Bruley, *Le quai d'Orsay impérial. Histoire du ministère des Affaires étrangères sous Napoléon III* (Paris: Pedone, 2012), 63.

56 Bruley, *Le quai d'Orsay impérial*, 63–68.

The committee increasingly counted jurists among its members, most of them drawn from the highest juridical courts of France. It included the occasional law professor such as Pellegrino Rossi.[57]

After the official letter from the bey was sent to Napoleon III asking him to arbitrate the conflict, the committee started its work on 15 May 1854 and spent almost two years on the case, until the end of November 1856.[58] The choice for arbitration, which entailed the submission of a dispute to the decision of a person (or persons) especially appointed to the case rather than its submission to the competent court, was not unusual for the nineteenth century or the Early Modern Age.[59] The case was not a typical international arbitration while French as well as Tunisian courts would be afterwards involved in the dispute. There was a significant increase of the use of arbitration during the second half of the nineteenth century.[60] It was prestigious for Napoleon III to serve as arbiter at the time of the Congress of Paris. Later, he would play the role at least one more time, namely in the Suez Canal Case in 1864.[61]

The committee was comprised of five members and a secretary – two lawyers, Marchand and Duvergier; two diplomats, Gabriac and Lefebvre; one judge-diplomat, Portalis; and Gaudin as secretary –, who would meet almost every two weeks.[62] It was a very long procedure since the committee had to deal with a lot of complicated and sometimes unprecedented legal issues, one of them stemming from the French citizenship of Ben Ayad, and more

57 On Pellegrino Rossi (1787–1848) see Luigi Lacché (ed.), *Un Liberale Europeo : Pelligrino Rossi (1787–1848)*, (Milan: Guiffrè editore, 2001).

58 See AMAE, Contentieux 431.

59 Cornelis G. Roelofsen. 'The Jay Treaty and all That', in A.H.A. Soons (ed.) *International Arbitration: Past and Prospects* (Dordrecht: Kluwer, 1990), 200–208; Lesaffer, 'Peace Through Law', 31–52.

60 See Cornelis G. Roelofsen, 'International Arbitration and Courts', in Bardo Fassbender and, Anne Peters (eds), *The Oxford Handbook of the History of International Law* (Oxford: Oxford University Press, 2012), 145–169, 163–167; Gaurier, *Histoire du droit international*, 657–658.

61 See AMAE, Contentieux 431. And on the Suez Canal see Lapradelle et alii, *Recueil des Arbitrages Internationaux* (Paris: Pedone, 1923), vol. 2, 344–386; La Fontaine, *Pasicrisie internationale 1794–1900. Histoire documentaire des arbitrages internationaux* (The Hague: Brill, 1997), 122–129.

62 Ernest de Cadoine de Gabriac (1792–1865), famous diplomat, ambassador in Stockholm, Rio de Janeiro, Mexico, Washington; Armand Lefebvre (1800–1864), diplomat and historian was an ambassador in Berlin (1851–1853) before being member of the committee; Jean-Baptiste Duvergier (1792–1877), famous lawyer and jurist, he became minister of justice at the end of the Second Empire. There is not much information to be found on A. Marchand. He was member of the Council of State as well as member of this committee for long time; Emile-François Gaudin (1825–1884), diplomat, lawyer and politician was the secretary of the Committee, AMAE, Contentieux 431.

precisely from the fact that the accusations against him concerned a period during which he was not French yet.[63]

Ben Ayad was very much aware of the importance of his new nationality and constantly insisted on it in all his memoirs and letters either to the French minister of Foreign Affairs or to the members of the committee.[64] Among the social and political highlights of this long process were the frequent confrontations between Hayreddin and Ben Ayad, which has been organised several times by the committee but with no results.[65] The representative of the bey and Ben Ayad came several times to defend their positions but they stood by their positions and the committee could not bring them to any compromise. They also both wrote and published dozens of memoirs, justifications, and official documents (often fake) which certainly helped to widely advertise the case.[66]

In concrete terms, the bey was claiming 47 million piasters for Ben Ayad's alleged mismanagement of the national Bank, the Cereals, the so called *Teskérés* (Treasury bills), the Olive Oil and finally the various State monopolies Ben Ayad held.[67] Ben Ayad himself was asking for 60 million piasters which he

63 See AMAE, Contentieux 430, folder 1, 3 and 6.

64 AMAE, Contentieux 430, folder 3. We find a note from Ben Ayad to Walewski asking for protection since he was now French and that was 'conforme au droit des gens et à l'équité naturelle' to help him.

65 AMAE, Contentieux 430, folder 2. On 6 September 1855, Hayreddin and Ben Ayad met without results; on 2 May 1856, they met with Marchand, Gabriac and Lesseps.

66 See for example, from Ben Ayad: *Note réfutative du général Mahmoud Benaïad sur le mémoire lithographié des agents du Gouvernement Tunisien intitulé 'Réponse aux réclamations de M. Benaïad'* (Paris: s.n., 1854); *Le gouvernement tunisien et le général Mahmoud Benaïad. Le dernier mot sur les comptes en blé du général Benaïad et le prétendu compte de Bahram* (Paris: s.n., 1855); *Les questions de la Commission et les réponses du général Mahmoud Benaïad : le gouvernement Tunisien et le général Mahmoud Benaïad* (Paris: s.n., 1855); *Le général Benaïad sur la onzième communication tunisienne : teskerés de sortie d'huile* (Paris: s.n., 1856); *Note du général Benaïad sur la sixième communication des agents tunisiens (Céréales)* (Paris: s.n., 1856) *Explications du général Benaïad aux dernières questions du Comité sur ses réclamations personnelles* (Paris: s.n., 1856). From Hayreddin : *État des pièces justificatives classées par chapitres avec les explications qui en déterminent la signification et la valeur* (Paris: s.n., 1855); *Réponse du général Khérédine aux observations de M. Benaïad sur la onzième communication tunisienne : teskérés de sortie d'huile* (Paris: s.n., 1855); He has also published a version of the decision with some additionnal documents from the Bey see : (Hayreddin), *Sentence arbitrale rendue par Sa Majesté l'empereur des Français sur les réclamations réciproques de Son Altesse le Bey de Tunis et du général Benaïad* (Paris: s.n., 1857).

67 See *Sentence arbitrale rendue par sa majesté l'empereur des français sur les reclamations réciproques de son altesse le Bey de Tunis et du general Benaïad* (Paris: s.n., 1856).

claimed on the basis of assets he held from his dealings with important French commercial houses and from personal assets.[68]

The final decision was taken on 30 November 1856 and the results were not so clear given that various official addresses about the outcomes were made to the two parties. The decision was accepted and all parties seemed to be happy with it, probably because the committee had left the calculation of the sums that the parties needed to pay to be done at Tunis. By consequence, both parties could interpret the decision in their own favour.[69]

Both parties were consequently claiming that they had won the case. Indeed, there are two printed copies of the final decision that have been published in 1857: one by the editor of the French Emperor and a *'résumé des comptes'* stating that the bey had to pay 26 million piasters to Ben Ayad.[70] But Hayreddin published the final decision with other documents as well, claiming that Ben Ayad had to pay 27 million piasters.[71] In 1868, Ben Ayad asked four famous jurists for a 'consultation' regarding the enforcement of the arbitration.[72] The four lawyers were in favour of the enforcement of the decision – so 26 million piasters for Ben Ayad – and one of them wrote that the case was 'à la fois du droit civil, du droit naturel et du droit des gens et obligent les parties en tous lieux, sans considération de frontières et de nationalités'.[73]

As a file in the French archives shows, the affair went on at least until the beginning of the French protectorate in Tunisia in 1881 before the parties agreed to drop the decision's enforcement.[74] In fact, the affair continued even until the beginning of the twentieth century with relation to Ben Ayad's inheritance – he had left a fortune of 300 million francs.[75] So the decision was

---

68 *Ibid.* and AMAE, Contentieux.

69 *Ibid.* and Contentieux. They (Ben Ayad and Hayreddin) both came to the Quai d'Orsay on the 3 February 1857 to take back all copies of the memoirs they had given during the arbitration. See also a letter from Ben Ayad to the bey.

70 *Sentence arbitrale rendue par sa majesté l'Empereur des français sur les réclamations réciproques de son altesse le Bey de Tunis et général Benaïad* (Paris: Henri Plon, 1857) ; *Résumé des comptes dressés pour l'exécution de la sentence arbitrale rendue le 30 novembre 1856 par sa majesté l'empereur Napoléon III entre son altesse le Bey de Tunis et le général Mahmoud Benaïad* (Paris: Henri Plon, 1857).

71 *Sentence arbitrale rendue par sa majesté l'Empereur des français sur les réclamations réciproques de son altesse le Bey de Tunis et du général Benaïad* (Paris: Eugène Penaud, 1857).

72 *Consultations pour le général Benaïad dans sa contestation avec son altesse le Bey* (Paris: s.n., 1868).

73 *Ibid.*

74 See Ahmed Ouerfelli, *L'arbitrage dans la jurisprudence tunisienne* (Tunis: LGDJ, 2010), 454. The Tribunal of Tunis (17 December 1884) and the Court of Appeal of Algiers (20 July 1887) both refused to give the *exaquatur* to the decision given by Napoleon III.

75 AMAE, Contentieux 432, folder 2. See Italian affair and other aspects of the case.

never implemented but the state finances of Tunis were irremediably damaged by the affair and enhanced the dependence of Tunis on France. Through the case, the French minister of Foreign Affairs and French diplomats at the court of the bey gained more influence over Tunis' state finances.

4 Conclusion: The Juridification of International Relations

The arbitration in the Ben Ayad case and the newly independent committee of litigation were signs of the professionalisation of international law. The case also marks the rise of private actors in the fields of international relations and law.[76] The role of individuals as well as lobbies and associations significantly increased at that time and this kind of experimentation formed the path to the later foundation of a scientific discipline of international law.[77]

The Ben Ayad case was also an important step towards the economic and political dependence of Tunis upon France, since in 1863 Tunis had finally obtained its state loan but went bankrupt in 1869. After, its finances were put under the control of a European commission. Ben Ayad was not the only actor involved given that others like Khaznadar had certainly contributed as much, if not more to the collapse of the Tunisian state finances.

The Ben Ayad case was a turning point in this respect, since the case had such an echo in France and in Europe through the press as well as in diplomatic circles. The fact that the Ben Ayad case and the arbitration of Napoleon III occurred at the same time as the first World Fair, with an independent space for Tunisia, and the Congress of Paris (February-March 1856), also aided in its publicity. The events also have to be considered as important moments in the long struggle of French diplomacy to renegotiate the 1815 agreements.[78] The Vienna Order was rejected by almost all French politicians from all political sides from Guizot to Napoleon III, as well as historians such as Frédéric Sirtema de Grovestins who wrote a book in 1856 about the Vienna Congress and the upcoming Parisian one.[79] In Paris, the Ottoman Empire had a representative at

76 See AMAE, Contentieux 118. It will be also interesting to see if the other main Foreign Affairs Ministries in Great-Britain, Prussia (later Germany), Austria and Russia had a committee of litigation as well.

77 See on the institut du droit international see also AMAE, Contentieux 95. Association pour la réforme du droit des gens founded in 1875 in The Hague.

78 Bruley, *Le Quai d'Orsay Impérial*, 160–190; Michel Kerautret, 'Quelques réflexions sur l'historiographie française du congrès de Vienne', *Napoleonica* 22/1 (2015), 87–103.

79 Charles Frédéric Sirtema de Grovestins, *Le congrès de Vienne en 1814 et 1815, et le congrès de Paris en 1856*, (Paris: Dentu, 1856).

the negotiation table unlike in Vienna and Article 7 of the Peace Treaty of Paris formally declared that the Ottoman Empire was an equal member of the concert of Europe, even though many legal restrictions remained which blocked the Ottoman Empire from full equality and sovereignty.[80]

Both the 1856 congress and the Ben Ayad case marked turning points in international law. The nationality principle and the concept of 'civilisation' were heavily involved in the Ben Ayad case. Many questions that had been raised at Vienna would eventually be settled at the Paris Congress. These included the right of neutrals and the abolition of privateering.[81] Furthermore, from a more political point of view, Napoleon III, 'the first modern dictator' to paraphrase an American historian, had succeeded in gaining new prestige and in changing the order of 1815 by helping new nation-states such as Tunisia or Romania – after the fusion of Walachia and Moldavia a few years later – to emerge.[82] He had managed to turn France into the world centre of diplomatic relations and international law. The new and sumptuous building of the Foreign Ministry at the Quay d'Orsay, where the Ben Ayad case was resolved, became the architectural symbol of that new era.[83]

As the French plenipotentiary to the 1878 Berlin Congress, Hyppolite Desprez, pointed out in 1856: 'La France exerçait une sorte d'arbitrage moral. On la consultait de toutes parts et on l'écoutait'.[84]

---

80 See Luigi Nuzzo, *Origini di una Scienza. Diritto internazionale e colonialismo nel XIX secolo* (Frankfurt: Klostermann, 2012), 4–6, 61–77 and Eliana Augusti, 'La Sublime Porta e il Trattato di Parigi del 1856. Le ragioni di una partecipazione', *Le Carte e la Storia* 1 (2008), 151–159.

81 See Jan Martin Lemnitzer, *Power, Law and the End of Privateering* (London: Palgrave Macmillan, 2014).

82 R.R. Palmer, *A history of the Modern World* (New York: Knopf, 1956), 502.

83 Bruley, *Le quai d'Orsay impérial*, 10–180.

84 *Ibid.*, 117.

CHAPTER 7

Public-Private Colonialism: Extraterritoriality in the Shanghai International Settlement

Stefan Kroll

1 Introduction[1]

During the second half of the nineteenth century, traditional Chinese principles of inter-power normativity were substituted by European international law.[2] Up to this point, East Asian international relations were organised by a hierarchical system in which China was acknowledged as hegemon.[3] This system was successively displaced by the normative order of European international law, which was based on the principle of sovereign equality but at the same time established unequal treaty relations between European and non-European powers. Against the background of a tradition of hierarchy, the first indignation of Chinese elites with international law was with regard to the principle of equality. It was not the lack of reciprocity of the regulations of the Treaty of Nanjing (1842) which was considered as a problem but the principle

1 Section 3 of this chapter quotes material which I have used also in the context of another article on the Shanghai International Settlement and which focused on the multi-normativity of the mixed court, see Stefan Kroll, 'Zooming in on Norm Research: Towards a Suitable Scale for the Shanghai Mixed Court', *Global Constitutionalism* 5 (2016), 383–404. The research on this chapter benefited from the support of the DFG *Exzellenzcluster The Formation of Normative Orders* at Goethe University Frankfurt. Finally, my special thanks go to Randall Lesaffer and Inge Van Hulle, as well as the participants of the conference 'International Law in the Long Nineteenth Century (c. 1775–1914): From the Public Law of Europe to Global International Law?', held at the University of Leuven in November 2016, for comments on earlier version of this chapter.

2 On the differentiation of 'international law' and 'law between political powers' in studies on the non-European history of international law, see Heinhard Steiger, 'From the International Law of Christianity to the International Law of the World Citizen. Reflections on the Formation of the Epochs of the History of International Law', *Journal of the History of International Law* 3 (2001), 180–193, 181.

3 David C Kang, *East Asia before the West. Five Centuries of Trade and Tribute* (New York: Columbia University Press, 2010), 54. On the use of the notion of hierarchy in this context, see Nianshen Song, '"Tributary" from a Multilateral and Multilayered Perspective', *The Chinese Journal of International Politics* 5 (2012) 155–182, 156.

 | DOI:10.1163/9789004412088_008

that the partners of this treaty were regarded as equals.[4] Of course, also the unequal regulations of the treaties became subject of political and legal debates in China in the following decades. However, the term 'unequal treaties' (*bupingdeng tiaoyue*) was not used in Chinese discourses before the 1920s.[5]

Against this background, it is not surprising that inequality is the most important aspect in studies of China's international and legal relations during the nineteenth- and early twentieth centuries. While studies on the construction and the content of the unequal treaties emphasise the aspect of power asymmetries, studies on the translation and adaptation of normative models, which the unequal treaties initiated as well, accentuate the agency of local elites. The adaptation of international law in China was not just a process of passive reception. On the contrary, international legal arguments were used to limit foreign influences and to terminate the unequal treaties as they represented a violation of sovereignty. More generally, unequal relations in China, but also in the context of other cases, led to creative processes of reinterpretation as well as hybridisation with local normative patterns. A paramount example for the latter is the case of the Shanghai Mixed Court which is discussed in this chapter.

Over the last two decades, there has been great scholarly interest in this history of international law as an instrument of empire. Within this context, the case of China was considered as representative as it illustrates the ambivalent role of international law in imperial projects, being both an instrument of domination and a language of resistance. As Martti Koskenniemi has recently observed, however, the research on international law and empire is largely focused on states and sovereignty, while 'much of Europe's expansion took place through private operators'.[6]

Taking this as a vantage point, the chapter aims at using the case of Shanghai to get beyond the usual dichotomy of Western and non-Western public authorities which characterises studies on extraterritoriality. Within the settlement, political and judicial authorities were fragmented between Chinese authorities, the Consular Body and the Shanghai Municipal Council (SMC). The SMC was founded in 1854. It was a group of foreign business representatives elected by the ratepayers of the settlement. During the second half of the

4 Harald Kleinschmidt, *Das europäische Völkerrecht und die ungleichen Verträge um die Mitte des 19. Jahrhunderts* (Tokyo: OAG, 2007), 19.

5 Dong Wang, 'The Discourse of Unequal Treaties in Modern China', *Pacific Affairs* 76 (2003), 399–425, 401.

6 Martti Koskenniemi, 'Introduction: International Law and Empire. Aspects and Approaches', in Martti Koskenniemi, Walter Rech and Manuel Jiménez Fonseca (eds.), *International Law and Empire: Historical Explorations* (Oxford: Oxford University Press, 2017), 1–18, 10.

nineteenth century, it turned into the de facto government of the settlement which claimed to be independent from the consular authorities. It represented a form of self-governance, which extended beyond the exercise of delegated authority in the context of extraterritoriality. This chapter is therefore not only interested in the differences between official foreign and Chinese authorities but also in the interactions between public and private foreign actors.

The chapter is divided, after the introduction, into three sections: the chapter introduces general thoughts on extraterritoriality and how it is described and conceptualised in recent research in legal and international relations literature (Section 2). Taking this as a vantage point, the case of Shanghai is presented as an important instance of nineteenth-century extraterritoriality while at the same time it stands for the emergence of distinctive political and judicial institutions within this context. As instruments of foreign influence and as impediments of Chinese sovereignty, the SMC and the mixed court inadvertently stimulated the construction of a local community which claimed to be autonomous of external influences (Section 3). In the finals section, a case of Chinese dissidence, which was tried at the mixed court at the turn of the century, is used to illustrate the tensions between the different authorities within the settlement (Section 4).

2 The Study of Extraterritoriality

China was a site of informal empire during the nineteenth- and early twentieth centuries.[7] Imperialism in China was informal as Western powers were not interested in colonising Chinese territories or in exercising direct rule. Western powers had different understandings of their imperial activities in China. Especially the United States was eager to distinguish itself from the British and their tendency to use force and even attempted to project an 'anti-colonial self-image'.[8] Despite differing interpretations, the instruments of informal empire were altogether very similar in their political effects among the Western powers. Unequal treaties were used to regulate the status of foreign diplomats,

7 Jürgen Osterhammel, 'Semi-Colonialism and Informal Empire in Twentieth-Century China: Towards a Framework of Analysis' in Wolfgang J. Mommsen and Jürgen Osterhammel (eds.), *Imperialism and After: Continuities and Discontinuities* (London: Allen & Unwin, 1986), 290–314.

8 Jedidiah J. Kroncke, *The Futility of Law and Development: China and the Dangers of Exporting American Law* (Oxford: Oxford University Press, 2016), 49–50.

missionaries and traders on Chinese territories.[9] These treaties, which had been used from 1842 until the 1940s, included extraterritoriality as a central feature of unequal relations.

Extraterritoriality in China generally implied two aspects. First, the immunity of Western foreigners from local jurisdiction. Second, the right of foreign consuls to exercise judicial authority over their nationals. This application of extraterritoriality was an extension of classical understandings of extraterritoriality, which meant the immunity of envoys from the jurisdiction of a host state. In the context of nineteenth-century imperialism, extraterritoriality referred to Europeans in the East in general and not exclusively to members of a foreign mission.[10] In the case of extraterritoriality, the law of a state or polity was not bound to a particular territory but to the person who belonged to this state or polity.[11] Extraterritoriality was thus not a means to diffuse Western concepts of normativity in non-Western world regions. On the contrary, the access to Western norms and Western legal proceedings were restricted to Western actors by the rules of extraterritoriality.[12]

Studies on the history of extraterritoriality showed, however, that it initiated the adaptation of foreign legal and political models. One motivation for adaptation that seems paradoxical at first glance is the adaptation that is motivated by the attempt to resist foreign influence. The termination of the regime of unequal treaties and extraterritoriality in China, as well as in other polities which had been suffering from it, was closely related to reform efforts through which adaptations of Western legal models and proceedings were introduced.[13] Intellectual elites in non-Western polities were convinced that the adaptation of foreign models would strengthen them. This process was captured aptly by Lauren Benton who concluded: 'We need not deny that extraterritoriality was imposed by force in order to see that it was also used strategically by local elite factions in representing and shaping state institutions'.[14] More generally,

9 Wang, Dong. *China's Unequal Treaties: Narrating National History* (Lanham: Lexington Books, 2005).

10 Johannes Berchtold, *Recht und Gerechtigkeit in der Konsulargerichtsbarkeit: Britische Exterritorialität im Osmanischen Reich 1825–1914* (München: R. Oldenbourg Verlag, 2009), 37–38.

11 Johannes Berchtold, 'Exterritorialität im Zeitalter der ungleichen Verträge' in Rainer Klump and Miloš Vec (eds.), *Völkerrecht und Weltwirtschaft im 19. Jahrhundert* (Baden-Baden: Nomos 2012), 221–243, 222.

12 Ibid, 225.

13 Turan Kayaoğlu, *Legal Imperialism: Sovereignty and Extraterritoriality in Japan, the Ottoman Empire, and China* (Cambridge: Cambridge University Press, 2010), 51.

14 Lauren Benton, *Law and Colonial Cultures: Legal Regimes in World History, 1400–1900* (Cambridge: Cambridge University Press, 2002), 252.

the introduction of legal reforms corresponded with the claims, uttered in the context of concepts of an international law of civilised nations, that extraterritoriality was a necessary means of civilisation, as the normative patterns in colonial areas were perceived as not meeting Western legal 'standards of civilisation'.[15] By providing Western powers with proof of normative patterns, which met the Western standards, the termination of extraterritoriality was pursued by non-Western polities.

Another strand of research on extraterritoriality reveals that the introduction of foreign normative patterns was less a matter of imitation than of re-interpretation and hybridisation of existing customs.[16] In cases of extraterritoriality, different normative expectations did not only coexist or compete, but were rather amalgamated in local judicial practice. This is one of the reasons why extraterritoriality is discussed in the context of legal pluralism and multi-normativity. Thomas Duve recently substantiated the concept of multi-normativity as an instrument for, especially, legal historical research.[17] According to him, the concept of multi-normativity has the advantage, that it does not, in contrast to the concept of legal pluralism, prioritise the law vis-à-vis other types of normativity.[18] Furthermore, it is an instrument of praxeological historiography, which strengthens the micro-perspective on making normative decisions.[19]

A third strand of research on extraterritoriality concerns the actors who were involved in these practices. Similar to the extension of extraterritoriality from envoys to foreigners in general, in China 'extraterritoriality came to mean more than a jurisdictional arrangement: it symbolised a panoply of practices establishing and protecting foreigners' prerogatives'.[20] As a consequence, extraterritoriality implied more than the agreement between two governments on extraterritoriality in an international treaty and a consul who decided judicial cases by means of consular jurisdiction. Extraterritoriality in practice meant the exercise of judicial and political authority in a broader sense. The actors who were involved in this process included not only official representatives of a foreign government but also private foreign actors. However,

15 Gerrit W. Gong, *The Standard of Civilization in International Society* (Oxford: Clarendon Press, 1984), 8.

16 See also Stefan Kroll, *Normgenese durch Re-Interpretation: China und das europäische Völkerrecht im 19. und 20. Jahrhundert* (Baden-Baden: Nomos, 2012).

17 Thomas Duve, 'Was ist Multinormativität? Einführende Bemerkungen', *Rechtsgeschichte-Legal History* 25 (2017), 88–101.

18 Ibid, 91.

19 Duve, 'Was ist Multinormativität', 93; Kroll, 'Zooming in on Norm Research', 389.

20 Benton, *Law and Colonial Cultures*, 251.

extraterritoriality, as a legal practice, was a state-centric enterprise in the sense that it 'transformed the non-Western unilateral grants of merchant legal self-governance into the extraterritorial rights of European states in non-Western states', as Kayaoğlu has put it.[21] Against this backdrop, this chapter will further discuss the role of municipal self-governance by private actors, which was established within the context of a regime of extraterritorial rights of states.

The case discussed in this chapter is the Shanghai International Settlement which was established in 1863 by the fusion of the British and the American settlements.[22] Within the settlement, various groups of foreigners, public and private, exercised political and judicial authority. Studies on extraterritoriality usually emphasise a dichotomy between foreign and domestic interests. As a consequence, extraterritoriality has classicaly been understood as an instrument of foreign interests. These interests are furthermore depicted as monolithic and undivided. However, this chapter illustrates that in Shanghai the interests of the foreign consuls and the SMC were not necessarily the same. On the contrary, the self-government of the SMC had the effect to reduce both the authority of the Chinese government as well as the authority of the foreign consuls. This highlights the authority exercised by private actors within the context of semi-colonialism and shows how it deviates from the authority as represented by foreign governments.

3 The Shanghai International Settlement

Shanghai was opened to foreign residence and trade by unequal treaties concluded between China and Western powers during the 1840s. The first was the Treaty of Nanjing (1842) between China and the United Kingdom. The treaty was supplemented by another treaty from 1843, which further outlined the conditions of extraterritoriality. These Sino-British treaties were followed by treaties between China and the United States (1844) and France (1844), following the same model. Often the treaty between the US and China is quoted to illustrate the regulation of extraterritoriality. Article 21 reads:

> Subjects of China, who may be guilty of any criminal act towards citizens of the United States, shall be arrested and punished by the Chinese authorities according to the laws of China; and citizens of the United States,

21 Kayaoğlu, *Legal Imperialism*, 42.

22 Isabella Jackson, *Shaping Modern Shanghai: Colonialism in China's Global City* (Cambridge: Cambridge University Press, 2018), 4.

> who may commit any crime in China, shall be subject to be tried and punished only by the Consul, or other public functionary of the United States, thereto authorized, according to the laws of the United States. And in order to the prevention of all controversy and disaffection, justice shall be equitably and impartially administered on both sides.[23]

The article confirmed the separation of a Chinese and a foreign legal sphere by emphasising that Chinese citizens were subject to Chinese authorities and US citizens were subject to public functionaries of the United States. Furthermore, it made clear that the exercise of judicial authority had to be the preserve of a public authority and was bound to US laws. Thus, the article reflected the state-centred approach of extraterritoriality as described above. However, the case of the International Settlement illustrates that both conditions, the separation of legal spheres and the exercise of public authority by the state, were not implemented in this strict sense.

Shanghai, as a treaty port, formed a distinctive type of 'colonial formation': 'The major treaty-ports, such as Shanghai and Tianjin, contained multiple foreign settlements with extraterritorial jurisdiction, formal enclaves of foreign residence and governance that facilitated imperialism without the costs or responsibilities of full colonialism'.[24] The foreign settlements were characterised by local administration in the hands of foreigners and financed by local taxes.[25] The Shanghai International Settlement was the result of the merger of the settlements of the US and the British in 1863. The population of the settlement was international, representing 45 different nationalities by the 1930s, while the huge majority of the population was Chinese.[26] As I have discussed elsewhere,[27] during the long existence of the settlement, its different groups of residents did not only conserve their national identities, Chinese or foreign, but also developed an identity as citizens of Shanghai as a distinctive

---

23 Treaty of Peace, Amity, and Commerce, between the United States of America and the Chinese Empire, 3 July 1844 (s.l. : s.n., 1846), https://catalog.hathitrust.org/Record/011554001, 6.

24 Bryna Goodman and David S.G. Goodman, 'Introduction: Colonialism and China' in Bryna Goodman and David S.G. Goodman (eds.) *Twentieth-Century Colonialism and China. Localities, the Everyday and the World* (London: Routledge 2012), 1–22, 2.

25 Albert Feuerwerker, 'The Foreign Presence in China' in John K Fairbank (ed.), *The Cambridge History of China: Republican China 1912–1949* (Cambridge: Cambridge University Press 1983), Part 1, vol. 12, 128–207, 129.

26 Isabella Jackson, 'Who Ran the Treaty Ports? A Study on the Shanghai Municipal Council' in Robert Bickers and Isabella Jackson (eds.), *Treaty Ports in Modern China. Law, Land and Power* (London and New York: Routledge 2016), 43–60, 44–45.

27 Kroll, 'Zooming in on Norm Research', 396.

community.[28] Robert Bickers has described this for the case of the British settler community who referred to themselves as 'Shanghailanders'.[29]

How was this particular kind of foreign dominance organised? Shanghai represented a case of extraterritoriality wherein both the classic separation of public and private spheres as well as of foreign and domestic spheres of legal and political authority became blurred. To indicate this, first, a narrow understanding of extraterritoriality will be applied which refers to the issue of jurisdiction and judicial decision-making. Second, a broader reading of extraterritoriality will be used to discuss wider practices of legal and political authority exercised by foreigners and those that were subject to foreign influence respectively.

The narrow understanding of extraterritoriality refers to the reading of the unequal treaties and concerns the legal immunity of foreign residents as well as the jurisdiction of foreign consuls. According to this, those residents who were represented by a treaty power were exempted from Chinese jurisdiction and subject to consular jurisdiction as provided by institutions such as the United States Court for China or the British Supreme Court for China.[30] However, these courts, while representing the regular pattern of extraterritorial jurisdiction, covered only a small amount of judicial disputes, which appeared in the International Settlement. As has been described above, the population of the settlement was highly multi-national. Thus a judicial body was needed which would exercise jurisdiction over the Chinese residents as well as those foreigners who were not represented by a treaty power.

This gap was filled by the Shanghai Mixed Court. The mixed court was initiated by the British authorities in 1864. The intention was to establish within the settlement a Chinese court with a Chinese judge and the authority to apply Chinese law.[31] In cases where foreign interests were concerned, a foreign assessor was to be involved in the process of decision-making. While the mixed court certainly was a subject of foreign control, it was at the same time an entity of local decision-making which made use of different kinds of procedural

28 Kelly Hammond, *The Shanghai Mixed Court 1863–1880. Colonial Institution Building and the Creation of Legal Knowledge as a Process of Interaction and Mediation between the Chinese and the British* (Simon Fraser University: Master Thesis, 2007), 24–25.

29 Robert Bickers, 'Shanghailanders: The Formation and Identity of the British Settler Community in Shanghai, 1843–1937', *Past and Present* 159 (1998), 161–211, 161.

30 For more information on these courts, see Pär Kristoffer Cassel, *Grounds of Judgment. Extraterritoriality and Imperial Power in Nineteenth-Century China and Japan* (Oxford: Oxford University Press, 2012), 63–84; Teemu Ruskola, *Legal Orientalism: China, the United States, and Modern Law* (Cambridge: Harvard University Press, 2013), 152–197.

31 Ruskola, *Legal Orientalism*, 27.

elements and of substantial norms, Chinese and foreign, as well as of local customs and regulations made by the municipal administration.[32] In this sense, the mixed court forms a paramount example of multi-normativity as described above. Both in contemporary accounts as well as in secondary literature, the court's decisions were being criticised for not meeting Western standards of jurisprudence. In contrast, the concept of multi-normativity is not meant to measure the legal quality of a normative institution such as the mixed court against some kind of Western model but allows to reflect on it as an institution of normative decision-making within a very specific context: 'the judges were not yet in a position to "enact" a particular set of norms and procedural mechanism but just to "act" in a situation where a conflict had to be regulated by its decisions'.[33]

There are two levels of authority or control, which should be considered with regard to the mixed court. The first is the authority of the Chinese judge who was impaired by the foreign assessor in cases were foreign interests were concerned. Nevertheless, against the background of the huge number of decisions made by the court, according to Lee 'about five and a half million cases during its seventy-eight years of operation',[34] as well as the influence of local customs and Qing legal procedural elements for its decisions, there obviously was room for making normative decisions that were not entirely controllable by foreign actors. The second level is the authority over the court by superior authorities or institutions. Also here it is important to state that local Chinese officials 'did have some control over the court' during its first decades of existence as for example by appointing '[t]he Mixed Court Magistrate [who] was the sole deliverer of case decisions'.[35]

Foreign control was exercised especially by the Consular Body, which was established by the consuls and other representatives of the consulates of those nations residing in the settlement, and the Shanghai Municipal Council. The relationship between the Consular Body and the mixed court was complex. On the one hand, the Consular Body was the highest governing authority for the court,[36] but on the other hand, the court reduced the judicial authority of the individual consuls and thereby threatened their authority.[37] Furthermore, as

32 Tahirih Victoria Lee, *Law and Local Autonomy at the International Mixed Court of Shanghai* (Yale University: unpublished thesis, 1990), 289.

33 Kroll, 'Zooming in on Norm Research', 402.

34 Tahirih Victoria Lee, 'Risky Business. Courts, Culture, and the Marketplace' *University of Miami Law Review* 47 (1993), 1335–1414, 1347.

35 Lee, *Law and Local Autonomy*, 216.

36 *Ibid.*, 229.

37 *Ibid.*, 233.

of the beginning of the twentieth century, the SMC was responsible for financing the court and, by doing so, it was able to isolate itself 'from any real direction by the Consular Body'.[38]

Altogether, the mixed court was characterised by a shared or even fragmented authority on two levels. On the level of decision-making, the Chinese judge was controlled by a foreign assessor in some cases but in many others was flexible to apply a multiple set of different local, Chinese and foreign norms and procedural elements. This flexibility grew spontaneously and was not grounded in the rules of the court. While the mixed court was one variety of extraterritoriality, it also stands as an example of limited foreign control.

Furthermore, the separation of foreign and domestic legal spheres, which was an element of extraterritorial approaches, was not upheld in the practice of the court as it applied domestic and foreign norms and procedures. However, with regard to criminal matters, historical sources describe the court as essentially Chinese.[39] Eventually, also the role of public authorities was made relative, as is visible in the important role of the SMC in controlling the activities of the court. Taking this latter point as a vantage point, a broader understanding of extraterritoriality must also be applied, which should, having Benton in mind,[40] not only focus on consular jurisdiction but also on forms of foreign and political authority in the International Settlement more generally.

In the 1950s, Thomson described the strange political character of the international settlement as 'a city on Chinese soil, governed by foreigners representing not their governments but the foreign residents of the city'.[41] More recently, Jackson has described the unique character of the SMC as a colonial institution, which should be understood as a transnational form of colonialism representing a case of 'colonial governance by non-state actors'.[42] This form of colonial governance by non-state actors is closely related to debates on 'company sovereigns'[43] or 'corporate sovereignty'[44] in colonial contexts.

38 *Ibid.*, 236.

39 Kroll, 'Zooming in on Norm Research', 395.

40 Benton, *Law and Colonial Cultures*, 251.

41 John Seabury Thomson, 'The Government of the International Settlement at Shanghai. A Study in the Politics of an International Area' (Columbia University: unpublished thesis, 1954), 22.

42 Jackson, *Shaping Modern Shanghai*, 8.

43 Andrew Phillips, 'Company Sovereigns, Private Violence, and Colonialism' in Rita Abrahamsen and Anna Leander (eds.), *The Routledge Handbook of Private Security Studies* (London: Routledge, 2016), 39–48, 39.

44 Philip J. Stern, '"Bundles of Hyphens": Corporations as Legal Communities in the Early Modern British Empire' in Lauren Benton and Richard J. Ross (eds.), *Legal Pluralism and Empires, 1500–1850* (New York: New York University Press, 2013), 21–47.

This literature deals with the role of private corporations which exercise public functions, such as law-making, collecting taxes and providing security, and which 'were far more than intermediary bodies or outsourced, privatized extensions of the state'.[45]

The activities of the SMC were more than an extension of the Consular Body. As Jackson emphasises, the SMC was a central political authority in the settlement, which, in some cases, 'secured for itself a degree of autonomy that proved highly frustrating to these authorities [consuls and diplomats, SK]'. Furthermore, as the council was elected, it was 'accountable to its electorate, rather than the consular body which represented diplomatic authority'.[46] The SMC was elected by the ratepayers and landowners of the settlement. Thus, the council was not representative for all the people who lived in the settlement but only for a minority of wealthy foreigners.[47] The case of the SMC makes clear that the standard dichotomy in studies on extraterritoriality, which is the dichotomy between foreign and domestic interests, requires further differentiation. The interests of the consular authorities were not necessarily the same as the interests of the community of foreign merchants who built the SMC.

Altogether, the Shanghai International Settlement was a case of extraterritoriality in which political and legal authority was fragmented between foreign and local as well as between state and non-state actors. Thus, the Shanghai International Settlement belongs to the universe of cases of what has been described as 'layered sovereignty' in colonial contexts.[48] According to this '[a] variety of individuals and corporate groups could carry delegated legal authority into empire in ways that helped to shape the contours of imperial territories [...]'.[49]

The authority which was exercised by the SMC as well as the mixed court was not only bound to the individual but also had territorial elements as, in many cases, it applied to the settlement as a territory and not just to one particular group of its residents. Furthermore, with regard to the aspect of delegation, the chapter showed that the authority of these entities was not just delegated, but at the same time expanded to a degree that it confronted the interests of the actual principal. This shall be further explained by a case which

45 Ibid, 21.

46 Jackson, 'Who Ran the Treaty Ports?', 44.

47 Ibid, 45.

48 Elizabeth Dale, 'The Su Bao Case and the Layers of Everyday Citizenship in China, 1894–1904' in Willem Maas (ed.) *Multilevel Citizenship* (Philadelphia: University of Pennsylvania Press, 2013), 110–126, 120.

49 Lauren Benton, *A Search for Sovereignty: Law and Geography in European Empires, 1400–1900* (Cambridge: Cambridge University Press, 2010), 31.

was tried at the mixed court and which, due to its political background, led to controversies not only among the Chinese and foreign authorities but at the same time illustrates tensions between the foreign envoys and the SMC.

4 The Su Bao Case

The complex relationship of overlap and tension between the interests of the different authorities within the international settlement is clearly visible in the *Su Bao* case of 1903–1904.[50] The factual background to this case was a series of dissident articles, which were published in the Shanghai based newspaper *Su Bao*. The authors of these articles were Chinese citizens who resided in the settlement. According to the treaties, these citizens were subject to the Chinese judiciary and Chinese laws. However, the consular authorities rejected to extradite the dissidents to the Chinese authorities and only accepted to arrest them under the condition that they would be tried before the mixed court. Both the dispute over extradition as well as the trial before the mixed court were not only cases were Chinese and foreign interests clashed but examples in which the differing views of the SMC and the Consular Body in Shanghai and the Diplomatic Body in Beijing became tangible. In the end, it was especially the SMC that pushed the case into a direction where the municipal autonomy was strengthened and extraterritoriality was extended to Chinese citizens within China.

At the turn of the century, Shanghai was an important centre for revolutionary ideas and the international settlement served as a refuge for political dissidents.[51] Many of the Chinese dissidents had been politicised while students in Japan. In 1896, a programme was initiated by the Chinese government to send students to Japan to learn from the experience of the Meiji Restauration. This program, however, resulted in the 'political awakening' of a generation of students who began to press for political reform and revolutionary change.[52]

It was this very path that also the initiators of the articles in *Su Bao* had taken. Zou Rong and Zhang Binglin, who were the two principal defendants in this case, had just returned from Japan when they published the articles in *Su Bao*.[53] The articles were motivated by nationalist views and claimed to

50 Dale, 'The *Su Bao* Case', 116–120.

51 Mary B. Rankin, *Early Chinese Revolutionaries: Radical Intellectuals in Shanghai and Chekiang, 1902–1911* (Cambridge: Harvard University Press, 1971), 48.

52 Paula S. Harrell, *Sowing the Seeds of Change: Chinese Students, Japanese Teachers, 1895–1905* (Stanford: Stanford University Press, 1992) 183.

53 Dale 'The *Su Bao* Case', 112.

strive for the removal of the dynasty and the introduction of a 'constitutional government'.[54] When the trial opened on 15 July 1903, the general charge against the two defendants was that they 'did maliciously write, print and publish or cause to be printed and published seditious libels'.[55] After this first hearing, however, the trial was interrupted until December.

The reason for this interruption was that the Chinese government still tried to compel the extradition of the defendants. On the side of the consular and the diplomatic bodies, there were voices that supported this claim. Within the settlement it was especially the SMC which advocated that the defendants should be tried and probably punished within the settlement. This position of the SMC also raised worries within the foreign community of Shanghai as expressed in a comment in the *North China Herald* of 10 July 1903: 'There has seemed of late, however, some disposition on the part of the Council to antagonise the Consular Body, and to take a line of its own in opposition to the Chinese authorities'.[56]

While the Consular Body in Shanghai and even more the Diplomatic Body in Beijing focused on the rules of extraterritoriality as expressed in the treaties, which required the Chinese defendants to be extradited, the SMC as well as the English-language media in the settlement mobilised political rights and humanitarian principles. Within the settlement, the right of free press and free speech were protected. The rendition of the defendants would place Chinese sovereignty 'above the claims of humanity, the dictates of reason, and the first principles of civilisation'.[57] Against the background of the status of the settlement as an autonomous place, where the principles of free press were to be protected, the *Su Bao* case was considered as 'probably the most important one that has ever been tried within our limits'.[58]

While at the end of July a majority within the Diplomatic Body at Beijing supported extradition,[59] the British House of Commons eventually decided that the prisoners would not be extradited.[60] As Wang emphasised, the British played a key role in this conflict because of their close relationship with the

54 *North China Herald*, 17 July 1903, 144–145.

55 *Ibid.*, 17 July 1903, 144.

56 *Ibid.*, 10 July 1903, 63.

57 *Ibid.*, 31. July 1903, 225.

58 *Ibid.*, 14. August 1903, 424.

59 John Lust, 'The Su-Pao Case. An episode in the Early Chinese Nationalist Movement'. *Bulletin of the School of Oriental and African Studies* 27 (2) (1964), 408–429, 423.

60 *North China Herald*, 7 August 1903, 315.

SMC.[61] The SMC had the power simply to release the defendants from custody, in case there would be a decision that they should be extradited.[62] According to Wang, the risk that the dissidents could be released and thus escape, as well as the public indignation over the execution of another journalist in Beijing in July, contributed to the decision of the government to follow the position of the SMC and to refuse extradition.[63]

What followed until December was a period during which the issue was disputed in Beijing between the Chinese government and the Diplomatic Body. The *North China Herald* reprinted a letter from a *Times* correspondent in which he observed: 'The Consular Body, realizing the strength of public opinion in the matter, says it will insist on the man being punished in the Settlement'.[64] Meanwhile the SMC kept on trying to influence the Consular Body in this matter. When the ratepayers met for their annual meeting in early 1904, they recalled events of the previous year and concluded: 'It is unnecessary to refer to the "Supao" case, [...], further than to say that it is a source of gratification to the Council that its action in that matter, in conformity with civilised usage and the dictates of humanity, has since been endorsed even by those who in the first instance opposed it'.[65] Altogether, all this illustrates how the merchant community in Shanghai pushed the consular and diplomatic authorities to strengthen the autonomy of the settlement at the cost of Chinese sovereignty beyond the original framework of the unequal treaties.[66]

When the trial re-opened at the mixed court in December, the prosecutor on behalf of the Chinese government, A.S.P. White-Cooper explained that it was the duty of the court to come to a decision on ground of Chinese laws and customs.[67] During the proceedings, however, the persons involved in the trial repeatedly made analogies to European legal principles and proceedings.[68] The disputes over the norms which were to be applied as well as the rules of the proceedings culminated in a bizarre sequence of exclamations, wherein the prosecutor claimed, '[t]his is a Chinese court', whereas the British Assessor

61 C.Y. Wang, 'The Su-Pao Case. A study of Foreign Pressure, Intellectual Fermentation, and Dynastic Decline'. *Monumenta Serica* 24 (1965), 84–129, 113.

62 Ibid. 114–115.

63 Ibid. 115–116.

64 *North China Herald*, 25 September 1903, 654.

65 *Ibid.*, 18 March 1904, 545.

66 Wang, *The Su-Pao Case*, 128–129.

67 *North China Herald*, 4 December 1903, 1210.

68 *Ibid.*, 11 December 1903, 1245–1252.

replied, '[t]his is a Mixed Court' and the counsel added, '[a] Chinese Mixed Court'.[69]

There can be no doubt, however, that the legal questions were of minor importance in this political case. When one of the Chinese judges rendered a first judgement in which the defendants were sentenced to life imprisonment, the British assessor declared the judgement 'null and void' and stated that there could be no judgement without his consent.[70] It was not until May 1904 that a final decision was made with the consent of the assessor that imposed only light sentences of two and three years of imprisonment for the defendants.[71]

Altogether, the case illustrates how the SMC managed to strengthen the autonomy of the settlement with the support of the consular and diplomatic authorities, even though these had different opinions when the controversy started. This occurred at the cost of Chinese sovereignty and extended the framework of extraterritoriality. Even though the political case of the *Su Bao* might not be representative for the overall practice of the mixed court, it shows how different kinds of normativity were applied and the separation of the Chinese and foreign normative spheres became blurred.

5 Conclusion

Taking recent debates on extraterritoriality as a starting point, this chapter discussed the role of private actors within the context of semi-colonialism. While the extraterritorial rights, as included in the unequal treaties, could be understood as turning extraterritorial practices into rights of states, the chapter illustrated that this did not meet the reality of transnational forms of self-government as practiced in the Shanghai International Settlement. Within the settlement, the SMC, which first of all represented the foreign business elite, formed the de facto government which competed with the authority of the Consular Body.

The chapter referred to the *Su Bao* case to illustrate the tensions between different foreign authorities within the settlement. The *Su Bao* case was a case of Chinese dissidents who published a series of revolutionary pamphlets in the Shanghai based newspaper *Su Bao*. In contradiction to the treaties, their case was heard at the Shanghai Mixed Court and not at a Chinese court. It was

69 *Ibid.*, 1247.
70 *Ibid.*, 1246.
71 *Ibid.*, 27 May 1904, 1121.

first of all the SMC that pushed for a trial within the settlement in order to strengthen its municipal autonomy.

Above all, the chapter illustrates that the practice of extraterritoriality in the Shanghai International Settlement was extended beyond the framework of state rights and the clear separation of foreign and domestic legal spheres. During the more than eighty years of its existence, the settlement developed an autonomous character. Different kinds of normativity intermingled in its political and judicial institutions, and both Chinese sovereignty and foreign public authorities were deeply challenged.

PART 3

The Rise of Modern International Law

CHAPTER 8

Permanent Neutrality or Permanent Insecurity? Obligation and Self-Interest in the Defence of Belgian Neutrality, 1830–1870

Frederik Dhondt

1 Introduction

Neutrality is one of the most controversial issues in public international law[1] and international relations history.[2] Recent scholarship considers neutrality as a general narrative within nineteenth-century international relations: between the Congress of Vienna and the Great War, neutrality was the rule, rather than the exception.[3] In intellectual history, Belgium's neutral status is seen as linked to the rise of international law as the 'Gentle Civilizer of Nations' at the end of the nineteenth century.[4] Belgian International lawyers' and politicians' activism brought three Noble Peace Prizes (August Beernaert, the *International Law Institute*, Henri La Fontaine) to the country. The present contribution focuses on the permanent or compulsory nature of Belgian neutrality in nineteenth-century diplomacy, from the country's inception (1830–1839)[5] to the Franco-Prussian War (1870).[6]

1 Michael Bothe, 'Neutrality, Concept and General Rules', in Rüdiger Wolfrum (ed.), *Max Planck Encyclopedia of Public International Law* (2012), available at http://opil.ouplaw.com/home/epil.

2 Jukka Nevakivi and Commission of History of International Relations, *Neutrality in History: Proceedings of the Conference on the History of Neutrality, Organized in Helsinki, 9–12 September 1992* (Helsinki: SHS, 1993).

3 Maartje Abbenhuis, *An Age of Neutrals: Great Power Politics, 1815–1914* (Cambridge: Cambridge University Press, 2014).

4 Martti Koskenniemi, *The Gentle Civilizer of Nations: The Rise and Fall of International Law, 1870–1960* (Cambridge: Cambridge University Press, 2001).

5 Albert Goblet d'Alviella, *Des cinq grandes puissances de l'Europe dans leurs rapports politiques et militaires avec la Belgique* (Bruxelles/Leipzig: Lacroix, Verbroeckhoven & C°, 1863).

6 Geoffrey Wawro, *The Franco-Prussian War: The German Conquest of France in 1870–1871* (Cambridge: Cambridge University Press, 2003).

 | DOI:10.1163/9789004412088_009

The subject has generally been left to political or diplomatic historians.[7] Three aspects impede an unprejudiced appreciation of the period treated here. First, the Great War has distorted our reading of the nineteenth century. The German invasion of Belgium in August 1914 amounted to a violation of the country's status of permanent neutrality.[8] The ensuing debate between German and Belgian – and allied – scholars has focused on this sole episode, namely the end of permanent neutrality in the Treaty of Versailles and the famous Article 231 of the same treaty, blaming Germany as the sole responsible for the war. 'Poor Little Belgium' used the image of the ruthless Hun to gather food supplies and sympathy in Britain – which activated its obligation to intervene as a guarantor – and the United States. During the conflict, 'Soldier-King' Albert I (1875–1934) clung to neutrality as a tool of statecraft.[9] Neutrality allowed for the preservation of Belgian armed forces from senseless slaughter in large-scale attacks, and permitted bilateral negotiations with Germany.

Second, nationalist historiography has used neutrality as a sign of moral elevation above traditional monarchical or great-power politics. If Belgium escaped the Franco-Prussian confrontation of 1870,[10] its neutrality status must have had the effect of a 'miracle drug'.[11]

Finally, traditional law of nations theory had a greater impact than a prima facie reading of sources would suggest. The vocabulary of diplomatic reasoning is that of generic early nineteenth-century law of nations doctrine. Vulgarised legal terms such as 'constitution', 'sovereignty', 'public law of Europe', abundantly present in parliamentary exchanges, diplomatic dispatches or private correspondence, refer to the common legal culture of the 'diplomatic mind'.[12] The works of Johann Klüber or Frédéric de Martens lean heavily on eighteenth-century authors such as Emer de Vattel and Gaspard Réal de Curban.[13]

---

7 Emile Banning, *Les origines & les phases de la neutralité belge* (Bruxelles: Albert Dewit, 1927); Horst Lademacher, *Die belgische Neutralität als Problem der europäischen Politik 1830–1914* (Bonn: Röhrscheid, 1971); Brison Dowling Gooch, *Belgium and the February Revolution* (The Hague: Nijhoff, 1963).

8 Albert De Lapradelle, 'The Neutrality of Belgium', *North American Review* 200 (1914), 847–857.

9 Jan Velaers, *Albert: Koning in tijden van oorlog en crisis, 1909–1934* (Tielt: Lannoo, 2009).

10 Emile Vandewoude, 'In het raam van de neutraliteit. Leopold II en de ambulance van Ciergnon (1870)', *Revue Belge d'histoire militaire* 19 (1971), 227–251.

11 Rik Coolsaet, *België en zijn buitenlandse politiek, 1830–2015* (Leuven: Van Haelewijck, 2015), 132, 137.

12 Thomas G. Otte, *The Foreign Office Mind: The Making of British Foreign Policy, 1865–1914* (Cambridge: Cambridge University Press, 2011).

13 Jean Matthieu Mattei, *Histoire du droit de la guerre, 1700–1819: introduction à l'histoire du droit international : avec une biographie des principaux auteurs de la doctrine internationaliste*

The mainly political and diplomatic scholarship on the subject would suggest a lack of conceptual primary-source material. I argue, on the contrary, that political and diplomatic exchanges were steeped in international law-discourse. As the discursive arena of international politics, international law was impossible to evade. Hence, Belgian nineteenth-century neutrality cannot be properly understood without having recourse to legal sources.

First, from the legal historian's point of view, neutrality cannot be approached without a conceptual legal definition. This question might sound less convoluted than it turns out to be. 'Permanent' neutrality was an invention of the Congress of Vienna and was connected to the specific status imposed on the Swiss Confederation, the City of Cracow and the territory of Moresnet.[14] Previously, the law of nations only recognised voluntary – self-imposed, temporary – neutrality.[15] This distinction is essential for our understanding of the 'permanent' neutrality imposed on Belgium by Article VII of the Treaty of London, signed at the British Foreign Office.[16] Scholars and diplomats alike understood that state practice would clarify the nature and extent of Belgium's obligations under a radically novel legal status. If 'neutrality' was the standard of nineteenth-century international politics, we should only understand this as voluntary neutrality: the freedom to abstain from a conflict between two other nations.[17] The 'hermaphrodite' regime of permanent neutrality was therefore an enigma.[18]

Second, the issues of international recognition and the imposition of permanent neutrality were intimately linked. Was Belgium's sovereignty conditional upon the observance of its obligations under the status of permanent neutrality? The eternal controversy in international doctrine on the constitutive or declaratory effect of international recognition surfaced in practical politics.

---

de l'Antiquité à nos jours (Aix-en-Provence: PUAM, 2006); Frederik Dhondt, 'Balance of Power, Neutrality and the Vienna Congress: Conceptual Innovation or Practical Continuity ?', in Mathias Schmoeckel and Miloš Vec (eds.), *The Vienna Congress and its Legacy for International Law* (forthcoming).

14 Gaétan de Raxis de Flassan, *Histoire du congrès de Vienne* (Paris: Treuttel et Würtz, 1829).

15 Eric Schnakenbourg, *Entre la guerre et la paix : neutralité et relations internationales, XVIIe–XVIIIe siècles* (Rennes: Presses Universitaires de Rennes, 2013). For the Prince-Bishopric of Liège: Paul Harsin, *Les Relations extérieures de la principauté de Liége sous Jean Louis d'Elderen et Joseph Clément de Bavière (1688–1718)* (Paris: Champion, 1927).

16 Treaty between Austria, France, Great Britain, Prussia and Russia, and Belgium, London, 19 April 1839, in Clie Parry (ed.), *The Consolidated Treaty Series* (231 vols., Dobbs Ferry: Oceana, 1969–1981), vol. 88, 421 [hereinafter CTS].

17 Dominique Gaurier, *Histoire du droit international* (Rennes: Presses Universitaires de Rennes, 2014), 310.

18 Speech by Charles de Brouckère (Henri's brother, mayor of Brussels, 1848–1860) in the National Congress, the 1830–1831 constituent assembly; Banning, *Les origines*, 48.

To whom did Belgium owe gratitude for the success of the 1830–1831 revolution? Were the young state's hands tied? Would permanent neutrality mean 'permanent intervention'?[19] Belle Époque scholarship tended to discard the question entirely. The most elaborate treatise on Belgian neutrality, written by Edouard Descamps, professor of international law in Leuven, stated that from 9 July 1831 on – the date on which the constituent assembly consented to the proposed Peace Treaty of XVIII Articles – 'permanent neutrality became constitutional among us and contractual towards the London Conference, signing on behalf of Europe'.[20] This conformed to the scepticism among revolutionaries concerning the law of nations in general, seen as a vector of conservative Great Power diplomacy.[21] I will demonstrate in this contribution that this discourse overestimated the autonomy of Belgium, regarded by its guarantors as an object they had created, and underestimated the constraints of the laws of neutrality.

Finally, Belgium's internal constitutional order pops up regularly in diplomatic quarrels. Sovereignty and neutrality were intermingled. The 1831 constitution was seen as the most liberal in Europe.[22] This generated British sympathy, but French condescendence at the same time. The priority given to free enterprise and to a reduced role of the state could even count as an excuse to deflect diplomatic invectives.

2 Nineteenth-Century Neutrality in Its Own Terms: 'A right and a duty at the same time'[23]

The appropriate yardstick to determine the extent of obligations imposed by Article VII of the Treaty of London consists of a combination of the classical sources of international law. The 1839 treaty was not elaborate in its wording and stated nothing more than that 'Belgium will be an independent and perpetually neutral state. She will be obliged to observe this very neutrality

19 Speech by Van Meenen in the National Congress, *Ibid.*

20 Edouard Eugène François Descamps, *La neutralité de la Belgique au point de vue historique, diplomatique, juridique et politique: étude sur la Constitution des Etats pacifiques à titre permanent* (Bruxelles: Larcier, 1902), 202.

21 Speech by Joseph Lebeau in the National Congress, quoted in *Ibid.*, 195.

22 Els Witte, *Le Royaume perdu – Les orangistes belges contre la révolution (1828–1850)* (Bruxelles: Éditions Samsa, 2016).

23 John Russell in Van de Weyer to de Vrière, London, 24 June 1859 (copy), Brussels, Belgian Ministry of Foreign Affairs Classement B, Indépendance-Neutralité-Défense Nationale (IND), vol. 1A [hereinafter BMFA].

towards all other states'.[24] Neither were the Protocol of 20 December 1830, or the ensuing proposals of XVIII and XXIV articles of peace any more elaborate.[25] However, we do have at our disposal the 1870 bilateral treaties in which Britain affirmed its intention to act as guarantor, concluded with France and Prussia.[26] As I will illustrate further on, these documents raise questions, and do not clarify the legal regime Belgium was supposed to be subject to. Doctrine, as always a supplementary source of the law of nations, mainly used as an argumentative treasure trove,[27] left considerable leeway to states.

3 Origins of Permanent Neutrality and Its Consequences: 'A Government that owes everything to France and England'[28]

If permanent neutrality is to be distinguished from voluntary neutrality, we should not take this conceptual distinction too literally in assessing the prehistory of Belgium's status. At the Congress of Vienna, the United Kingdom of the Netherlands obtained international recognition. This new state was a British creation.[29] William VI of Orange (1772–1843)[30] obtained compensation for the loss of his ancestral dominions in Germany, and of the Cape Colony. Acclaimed by the Dutch nation at the end of 1813, William ruled first as sovereign prince, obtained next an extension of his sovereignty in the former French departments of Belgium[31] and, ultimately, could call himself king.[32] William's

24 'La Belgique formera un Etat indépendant et perpétuellement neutre. Elle sera tenue d'observer cette même neutralité envers tous les autres Etats'.

25 Banning, *Les origines*, 39.

26 Treaty between Great Britain and Prussia relative to the Independence and Neutrality of Belgium, London, 9 August 1870, 141 CTS 435; Treaty between France and Great Britain relative to the Independence and Neutrality of Belgium, London, 11 August 1870, 141 CTS 441.

27 Amnon Lev, 'The Transformation of International Law in the 19th Century', in Alexander Orakhelashvili (ed.), *Research Handbook on the Theory and History of International Law* (Cheltenham: Edward Elgar, 2011), 111–142.

28 Barrot to Drouyn de Lhuys, Brussels, 10 April 1854, Paris, Ministère des Affaires Étrangères et Européennes, Archives Diplomatiques, Correspondance Politique (CP), Belgique, 35, f. 216v° [hereinafter AMAE].

29 N.C.F. (Niek) Van Sas, *Onze natuurlijkste bondgenoot : Nederland, Engeland en Europa 1813–1831* (Groningen: Wolters-Noordhoff, 1985).

30 Jeroen Koch, *Koning Willem I, 1772–1843* (Amsterdam: Boom, 2013).

31 Ernest Nys, 'Notes sur la neutralité (premier article)', *Revue de droit international et de législation comparée* 2 (1900), 588.

32 Frederik Dhondt, 'Inaugurating a Dutch Napoleon? Conservative Criticism of the 1815 Constitution of the United Kingdom of the Netherlands', in Ulrike Müßig (ed.), *Reconsidering*

centralised rule was rejected by the liberal bourgeoisie and the Catholic Church in the Belgian Revolution. The United Kingdom of the Netherlands failed to install a genuine national identity, as two centuries of religious, political and economic separation had driven North and South apart.

However, the international position of the United Kingdom was one of the more solid reasons for unification. The Netherlands counted as a buffer state against future French expansionism. William's kingdom had to tolerate the fortresses of the Wellington Barrier. Apart from this limitation, William could opt for neutrality, not established by treaty, 'but by policy'.[33] 'Permanent' neutrality was devised at the London Conference (1830–1832) to prevent Belgium from becoming a cause of strife between the great powers.[34] Yet, at the same time, the status fitted the maintenance of the Wellington Barrier, cut in half, conformably to Talleyrand's wishes.[35] Analogies with the status of Switzerland in 1815 are inappropriate, as both the geographical and political context was fundamentally different.[36]

The Belgian provisional government declared independence on 4 October 1830. This decision was far from decisive in establishing national sovereignty. Dutch troops had retreated at their own initiative. Moreover, in August 1831, a Dutch invasion almost undid the new state altogether. French military intervention forced the retreat. The Antwerp citadel was only liberated in December 1832, due to – again – French intervention.

In the ensuing succession of European crises, Belgium had to fear for its independence at several instances. In 1839, Marshal Soult, a former Napoleonic general, proposed a throttling customs union: the French Court of Cassation

---

Constitutional Formation II: Decisive Constitutional Normativity. From Old Liberties to New Precedence (Heidelberg: Springer, forthcoming).

33 J.E. Kaufmann and H.W. Kaufmann, *The Forts and Fortifications of Europe 1815–1945: The Neutral States: The Netherlands, Belgium and Switzerland* (Barnsley: Pen and Sword, 2014), xi.

34 AMAE, CP, Angleterre, v. 631–641; Foreign Office Great Britain, *Papers Relative to the Affairs of Belgium* (London: J. Harrison & Son, 1833).

35 Belgium was allowed to raze five fortresses (Menin, Ath, Mons, Philippeville, Mariembourg), but had to tolerate the fifteen others: Convention relative to the Belgian fortresses between Austria, Great Britain, Prussia, Russia and Belgium, London, 14 December 1831, 82 CTS 299. The Barrier was abandoned in 1847, to the profit of more elaborate fortifications around the main strategic points of Antwerp, Liège and Namur. Banning, *Les origines*), 63; Descamps, *La neutralité*, 262.

36 André Holenstein, *Mitten in Europa: Verflechtung und Abgrenzung in der Schweizer Geschichte* (Baden: hier + jetzt, 2014).

would claim competence over all matters belonging to export and import duties. French officials would take over operations at the border.[37]

The structural position of the country, caught between the Romanic and the Germanic worlds, caused uproar in 1840, when the President of the French Council of Ministers, Adolphe Thiers (1797–1877), threatened to invade the Rhineland in reaction to Britain, Prussia, Russia and Austria's exclusion of the July Monarchy in the Egyptian crisis. On 10 November 1840, the Belgian King Leopold I (1790–1865) affirmed before both houses of parliament that 'neutrality [...] inscribed in our public law [...] is the true basis of our policy; its maintenance in a sincere, loyal and strong way should be our constant goal'.[38] The sovereign commissioned Wilhelm Arendt's 'Essai sur la neutralité de la Belgique' to palliate the lack of a comprehensive international law treatise covering Belgium's sui generis legal position.[39] For Leopold I it was essential that Belgium showed its hybrid national character, belonging to the Germanic-speaking as well as to the French-speaking world. Giving in excessively to the latter would depict the country as a French protectorate.[40]

Arendt's treatise made a prudent synthesis of the available doctrine and law of nations precedents and concluded that Belgium would need to invest in national defence, abstain from conflicts between third states, and enter into as many commercial conventions as possible, in order to draw sufficient profit from its geographical position at the heart of the continent.[41] For Arendt, the centralised and representative internal constitutional order of Belgium could count as a guarantee that the country would defend its borders and abstain

37 Max Suetens, *Histoire de la politique commerciale de la Belgique depuis 1830 jusqu'à nos jours* (Brussels: Librairie encyclopédique, 1955); Helmut Sydow, *Die Handelsbeziehungen zwischen Belgien und dem Zollverein 1830–1885* (Köln: Böhlau, 1979), vol. 2, 53.

38 Banning, *Les origines*, 69. *L'Indépendance Belge*, 11 November 1840; *Messager de Gand*, 12 November 1840.

39 Lademacher, *Die belgische Neutralität*, 122. Guillaume Arendt, *Essai sur la neutralité de la Belgique* (Bruxelles/Leipzig: Muquardt, 1845). Wilhelm (Guillaume) Arendt was educated in Lutheran theology in Berlin, but converted to Catholicism while teaching in Bonn. He lost this position due to his new confession, but was recruited by de Ram, first rector of the newly founded Catholic University of Malines (1834), which moved to Leuven in 1835. Arendt taught mainly philology and archaeology, but turned to history and – at the king's request – legal issues. Arendt acted as the king's special envoy at the Frankfurter Nationalversammlung (1848–1849), hoping Leopold would be elected emperor. His son Léon (1834–1924) became director of political affairs at the Foreign Affairs department.

40 Gita Deneckere, *Leopold I. De eerste koning van Europa* (Antwerpen: Bezige Bij, 2011).

41 Frederik Dhondt, 'Neutralité permanente, interprétations mutantes: la neutralité belge à travers trois traités de juristes', *Tijdschrift voor Rechtsgeschiedenis/Revue d'Histoire du Droit/The Legal History Review* 86 (2018), forthcoming.

from bellicose behaviour.[42] However, the restrictions imposed at the Treaty of London were real: *volenti non fit iniuria*. If Belgium had accepted recognition by the great powers, it had to suffer the limitations of the countervailing obligations of neutrality as well.[43]

The February Revolution in France (1848) was a challenge to Belgium's first single party-liberal government under Walthère Frère-Orban (1812–1896) and Charles Rogier (1800–1885).[44] Belgium had to please the more conservative central powers and could thus not recognise the new French government in too precipitated a manner. The Revolutionary February government saw borders, and thus equally the legal order of the Vienna Congress, as a purely factual starting point in discussions, and not as a legally binding situation.[45] The revolutionary faction eagerly awaited a spontaneous merger with Belgium, driven by Belgian public opinion.[46] Frère and Rogier astutely managed the wishes of the guarantors and recognised the Second French Republic on 28 May 1848.[47]

The 1860s brought on the American Civil War (1861–1865)[48] and the Mexican Crisis (1862–1867), during which Frère-Orban hoped that Belgian neutrality could be seen as limited to the European continent, allowing Belgium to act more forcefully and trade in contraband outside Europe.[49] Belgium dismissed soldiers from the army with the permission to enlist as volunteers to defend the cause of Archduke Maximilian (1832–1867), who had wed Leopold I's daughter Charlotte.[50] Enlisting for foreign service was only forbidden in cases

42 The country did not suffer the vicissitudes of federal states or loose confederations. Guillaume Arendt, *Essai sur la neutralité de la Belgique*, 75.

43 *Ibid.*, 95.

44 Gooch, *Belgium and the February Revolution.*

45 *Ibid.*, 39.

46 *Ibid.*, 80. See also 83, footnote 3: Ledru-Rollin was thought to have instigated the Belgian Legion's failed invasion of Belgium and the battle of Risquons-Tout. AMAE, CP, Belgique, 30.

47 Gooch, *Belgium and the February Revolution*, 100. Descamps, *La neutralité*, 470; Alphonse Rivier, *Principes du droit des gens* (Paris: Rousseau, 1896), vol. 1, 59. For Rivier, permanently neutral states had to await the approval of their guarantors before proceeding to the recognition of a new state. In view of the different political systems between the more authoritarian Northern courts in 1848, this was untenable for the French February and May–June regime changes.

48 Declaration regarding the Observance of Neutrality in the American Civil War, 22 June 1861, in Francis Deák and Philip C. Jessup (eds.), *A Collection of Neutrality Laws, Regulations and Treaties of Various Countries* (Washington; Carnegie Endowment, 1939), 58 nr. 10a.

49 Descamps, *La neutralité*, 489. See also Ernest Nys, 'Notes sur la neutralité (troisième article)', *Revue de droit international et de législation comparée* 3 (1901), 24.

50 Deneckere, *Leopold I*, 619–635.

of interstate conflicts, not for civil wars.[51] This rather remarkable line of political argumentation was in overt contradiction with the Department of Justice's advice, which stated that 'Belgium would fall short of its duties by tolerating that help would be given on its territory to a belligerent, and, even more so, when a nation without political existence would be helped in its separatist insurrection against its mother state'.[52] Yet, in practice only France and Britain determined what was admissible or not with regards to the laws of neutrality.[53]

4 'Notre redoutable voisin'[54]

Napoleon III's arrival to power modified the political configuration dramatically. The 'Emperor' sought to annex Belgium,[55] and repeatedly bullied the country into submission. Napoleon demanded and obtained the conclusion of a convention for the protection of intellectual property.[56] This treaty brought down the profitable and active Belgian typographical industry, which plagiarised books published in France. Second, France dictated the introduction of a criminal offence of insults against a foreign head of state, to muzzle 'the bad press'.[57]

51 Banning, *Les origines*, 169; Nys, 'Notes sur la neutralité (troisième article)', 33. This did not withhold Britain from recruiting an 'English legion' in Belgium during the Crimean War. Department of Justice to Department of Foreign Affairs, 27 July 1864, BMFA, IND, vol. 1A.

52 Department of Justice to Department of Foreign Affairs, 27 July 1864, Ibid.

53 Lademacher, *Die belgische Neutralität*, 169.

54 Expression used in the note 'Délits de presse', BMFA, Délits de Presse.

55 Henri de Brouckère to Leopold I, 8 June 1853 (n. 52).

56 Commercial Convention between Belgium and France, Paris, 22 August 1852, 108 CTS 421.

57 Barrot to Drouyn de Lhuys, 16 March 1854, AMAE, CP, Belgique, 35, f. 138v°. Belgium's popular juries had rejected the application of a 1816 law stemming from the United Kingdom of the Netherlands. The first measure of Minister of Justice Charles Faider in de Brouckère's government was the introduction of a Belgian law to lift all ambiguity. See Belgium, Law on the Punishment of Insults to Foreign Heads of State, 20 December 1852, *Moniteur Belge*, 21 December 1852; Bram Delbecke, *De lange schaduw van de grondwetgever : perswetgeving en persmisdrijven in België (1831–1914)* (Ghent: Academia Press, 2012). Under Belgium's first liberal government (1847–1852), French dissidents d'Haussonville and Thomas had been acquitted before the Court of Assises, just like the radical opposition newspapers 'Le Bulletin Français' and 'La Nation'. French pressure resulted in unrest with the voters and thus electoral losses for the liberal party. See Theo Luykx, *De Belgische kamerverkiezingen van 8 juni 1852: cijnskiezers onder Franse politieke druk* (Louvain: Nauwelaerts, 1966), 96: 'votez pour les Cléricaux, ou vos intérêts matériels seront sacrifiés, vous n'aurez plus de relations commerciales avec la France'. See also d'Anethan's 1871 statement, according to which the Belgian press had a responsibility to abstain from reports angering a big power: Descamps, *La neutralité*, 455.

At the height of French pressure, Belgium lived under a 'unionist' cabinet since 31 October 1852.[58] Foreign Affairs minister, Henri de Brouckère (1801–1891), was its de facto leader.[59] He preached a cautious policy of submissive deference towards France: 'In our political acts, we should not show partiality to any Power; yet, in our intimate relations, in our most private acts, if I am allowed to use this language, we are free – I would even go further – it belongs to every Belgian stateman's duties, to show France our natural inclination for her, and the sympathy uniting us to our powerful neighbour'.[60] Sympathy and officious pro-French preferences ought to convince Napoleon III that Belgium would not remain indifferent to his countless whims.[61] Counterbalancing France through a royal multilateral network across Europe failed.[62] Belgian officials feared that, notwithstanding Leopold's firm insistence on an even-handed approach, Belgium's neutrality would become 'coûteuse en cas de conflit entre la France et la Prusse'.[63] If Napoleon III's expansionism was to be feared, he could also be seen as a guarantor of internal stability after the revolution of 1848.[64]

5 Belgium as an Object: The 1870 Treaties of London

International relations histories can draw an active or a passive image of a state in its interactions with others. Belgium's role as a diplomatic hub at the heart of Europe should not be underestimated.[65] Yet, in the eyes of its guarantors, the country was an object first, and an actor only in second place. The confirmation of Belgian neutrality in 1870 was illustrative of this essentially double dimension of diplomacy.

---

58 Theo Luykx, *Politieke geschiedenis van België*, (Amsterdam: Elsevier, 1978), 109.

59 The institution of prime minister was only introduced after World War I: Els Witte, Alain Meynen and Dirk Luyten, *Politieke geschiedenis van België van 1830 tot heden* (Antwerp: Manteau/WPG, 2016), 182. De Brouckère, lawyer, magistrate and professor at the Université Libre de Bruxelles, was a member of the House of Representatives until 1870, as well as governor of the provinces of Antwerp (1840–1844) and Liège (1844–1846).

60 Barrot to Drouyn de Lhuys, 16 March 1854 (n. 58), f. 124v°.

61 E.g. '[le nom] de l'Empereur Napoléon retentit aujourd'hui dans le monde comme l'expression de toutes [v°] les idées de droit et de justice': de Brouckère in Barrot to Drouyn de Lhuys, 19 March 1854 (n. 58), f. 129v°.

62 Coolsaet, *Buitenlandse politiek*, 116.

63 De Brouckère in Barrot to Drouyn de Lhuys, 6 April 1854 (n. 58), f. 202r°.

64 Yves Bruley, *La diplomatie du sphinx* (Tours: CLD, 2015), 31–32.

65 Coolsaet, *Buitenlandse politiek*.

The 1870 Franco-Prussian War was declared on 19 July 1870. Barely a week later, the so-called Benedetti Treaty appeared in the 'Times' (25 July 1870). Chancellor Bismarck leaked confidential proposals made by French ambassador de Benedetti to the British press.[66] France would have offered to annex Belgium and Luxemburg,[67] in return for the accession of the Southern German Confederation to Bismarck's North German Confederation.[68]

In view of the state of war between France and Prussia, the British cabinet emphasised the need to safeguard the port of Antwerp and Belgium in general. On 4 August 1870, Edward Gladstone (1868–1874) addressed the House of Commons emphasising that the 'public right in Europe' would become extinct in case of a violation of Belgium's neutrality. This was in accordance with his predecessor Palmerston's intervention during the trouble days of 1848,[69] and equally contradicted French expectations according to which 'experience and industrial egoism' would force Britain to tolerate the annexation of Belgium and Luxemburg, as it had in 1860 with respect to Nice and Savoy.[70] 'La vieille Angleterre' would intervene, as it had done in the days of Marlborough and Wellington.[71]

The correspondence of French ambassador in London, Charles de la Valette (1806–1881), reveals the composite mind set of imperial diplomats. French arguments against the Hohenzollern claim to the Spanish throne were phrased as 'nothing that would not be conformable to the best established precedents of European public law. Our principles are those that the Great Powers had made prevail in 1831 in Belgium against the Duke of Nemours as King of the

66 *Ibid.*, 132.

67 The Grand-Duchy of Luxemburg became independent pursuant to the dissolution of the German Confederation and Bismarck's refusal to have this state enter the North German Confederation. In analogy with Belgium, Luxemburg became perpetually neutral. Jules Garsou, *Le Grand-Duché de Luxembourg entre la Belgique, la France et la Prusse (1867–1871)* (Luxembourg: Editions des cahiers Luxembourgeois, 1936); Michael Richard Daniel Foot, 'Great Britain and Luxemburg 1867', *English Historical Review* 47 (1952), 352–379.

68 The Prussian garrison in the fortification of Luxemburg was part of the German Confederation's system of defence. Consequently, William I had continued to reign as a prince of the German Confederation, in a personal union with the Netherlands (Sebastiani to Talleyrand, 22 December 1830 (n. 35), 631bis, f. 158v°). The dissolution of the Confederation created an independent Luxemburg.

69 Banning, *Les origines*, 88: 'The Great Powers do not have the right, but the obligation to intervene on Belgium's behalf. We should however replace this affirmation into its context: Palmerston meant an intervention against revolutionary France. Prussia – as defender of the legitimacy principle – eagerly supported this thesis, since this intervention would repress revolution', Gooch, *Belgium and the February Revolution*, 91.

70 Van de Weyer to de Vrière, London, 18 May 1860 (n. 52) (copy).

71 Ibid.

Belgians'.[72] France based its claims on 'that great law of ponderation of forces between states, the basis of the European system',[73] or 'the salutary rule of international modern jurisprudence forbidding any Great Power to move the balance of forces by looking for a foreign crown for one of its princes'.[74] Gladstone's proposal to conclude a treaty of guarantee was eyed with suspicion: 'this [Belgian] territory will be inviolable as long as it will be the case for Prussia as well (...). The French government has always considered with defiance the compromising conventions offering her advantages that could not have been disposed of'.

According to Foreign Secretary, Earl Granville (1815–1891),[75] the use of the reiteration of 1839 was that 'both the Emperor [Napoleon III] and the King [Wilhelm I] subject their respective assurance to the condition that it is observed by the other, which seems to preclude an opinion on their part that the declaration is not complete'. Moreover, a British assurance 'in a solemn Act, either Treaty of Protocol' would serve to quell potential French unrest as well, and state that safeguarding Belgium's neutrality was a 'common determination'.

French ambassador La Valette, in turn, questioned the utility of a reiteration: 'why and to what point would it be convenient to sign a new protocol, to affirm the clauses of an international act of which all parties have solemnly acknowledged the value? Wouldn't this second affirmation entail the inconvenience to believe that time can invalidate treaties, and that they lose their mandatory force as the date of signature becomes more remote?'[76]

These fundamental objections haunted European diplomacy in the ensuing decades. Would every new casus belli between belligerents require the reiteration of their initial obligation to guarantee Belgian neutrality? Descamps tried to refute them in his landmark essay on Belgian neutrality: Britain had mediated as 'neutral guarantor' between two 'belligerent guarantors'.[77] However delicate and subtle this answer was, Belgium had been left out of this agreement. The confirmation of the 1839 treaty was dependent on the political

72 Antoine de Gramont (minister of Foreign Affairs) to embassies London, St Petersburg, Vienna, Florence, Madrid, Munich, Stuttgart and Dresden, 9 July 1870 (n.35), 752, f. 207r°.

73 Gramont to la Valette, 21 July 1870, Ibid., f. 301v°.

74 Gramont to la Valette, 14 July 1870, Ibid., f. 247r°.

75 Muriel E. Chamberlain, 'Gower, Granville George Leveson-, second Earl Granville (1815–1891)', in Leslie Stephen (ed.), *Oxford Dictionary of National Biography* (*Online Edn.*) (Oxford: Oxford University Press, 2008).

76 This affirmation is all the more relevant in light of Napoleon III's exhortation to organise a European congress in 1862–1863. According to the French Emperor, the treaties of 1815 had 'ceased to exist'. Banning, *Les origines*, 134.

77 Descamps, *La neutralité*, 327.

and arbitrary decision of France, Britain and Prussia. To equate this with the 'forces of law and the eternal interests of the European equilibrium', as formulated in the address by the Chamber to Leopold II (1835–1909), was merely a demonstration of the indeterminacy and flexibility of balance-of-power-discourse.[78] Foreign Affairs minister, Jules d'Anethan (1803–1888),[79] could rejoice at the upholding of neutrality, but the legal execution of the guarantee was questionable.[80] Moreover, when Leopold II hoped to obtain a renewed British commitment to neutrality in 1887 against the background of Boulangist agitation in the French Third Republic, the Catholic cabinet of August Beernaert (1884–1894) blocked his tentative.[81]

Finally, Britain explicitly stipulated that its recognition would only concern Belgium's continental borders as established in 1839. Potential acquisitions in other continents were left out of the guarantee. This argument was used later on, when Belgium annexed the Congo Free State in 1908. In 1870, this reinforced Frère-Orban's view that permanent neutrality was an institution of European public law, and did not concern relations with states outside the continent, let alone barbarous or savage political entities.[82]

6 'L'étrange doctrine de neutralité du gouvernement belge': Belgium and the Arms Trade:[83] 'Les Moyens Constitutionnels'

In theory, the Belgian constitution imposed parliamentary participation for the conclusion of treaties entailing obligations for its citizens or the country (Article 68).[84] In practice, the monarchy monitored political activity.[85] King

78 Chamber of Representatives, 16 August 1870, Proceedings on www.plenum.be [last accessed 14 July 2017].
79 Alexandre Cosemans, 'ANETHAN (Jules-Joseph baron d')', in Académie royale de Belgique (ed.), *Biographie nationale de Belgique* (Brussels: Bruylant, 1956), 93–96.
80 Chamber of Representatives, 16 August 1870, Proceedings on www.plenum.be [last accessed 14 July 2017].
81 Alfred De Ridder, 'La crise de la neutralité belge de 1887', *Revue catholique des idées et des faits* 41 (1927), 14–18.
82 Descamps, *La neutralité*, 488.
83 Expression drawn from Barrot to Drouyn de Lhuys, 24 March 1854 (n. 58), f. 112v°.
84 See Catholic MP Charles Woeste refuting rumours of a secret Belgo-German Treaty of Alliance, arguing that without parliamentary participation, no international treaty can be binding on the Belgian nation: Charles Woeste, *La neutralité belge. La Belgique et la France* (Bruxelles/Paris: Société belge de librairie/Nouvelle librairie parisienne, 1891), 73.
85 Christophe Chevalier, 'La mission de Jean-Baptiste Nothomb à Paris d'août 1856. Jeux de pouvoir et diplomatie officielle au sein du Gouvernement belge', *Revue d'histoire diplomatique* 129 (2015), 5–20.

Leopold I was described by the French ambassador Adolphe Barrot (1801–1870) as 'doing nothing but what he desires, and when he desires'. Leopold's secretary, Jules Van Praet (1806–1887),[86] his officious Parisian envoy, Firmin Rogier(1791–1875),[87] the Prince of Chimay or, later on, baron Lambermont (1819–1905),[88] were agents of this para-governmental and extra-parliamentary policy: the king's men of confidence were primary actors of foreign policy, without a formal mandate.[89]

The Belgian government actively used the liberal nature of its constitution to implore British sympathy, or to avoid regulating the arms trade. Sylvain Van de Weyer (1802–1874), long-standing Belgian ambassador in London, pleaded passionately in the national representation contrasting authoritarian or revolutionary France to steadfast and freedom-inspired Belgium.[90] Yet, in practice, the implication of the national representation was thus rather restricted.

Napoleon III put pressure on Belgium, as well as on Switzerland,[91] to expel political refugees and cease to be a hub of political trouble on the borders of the great powers. If any 'enemy plots' originated in Belgium, they had to be proactively monitored by police and prosecuting authorities. Individual liberties prevented repressive action against the press. The national representation acted as a true legislator, and not as a mere ratification body.[92] To avoid an invasion, the Belgian government had already made parliament swallow restrictions on civil liberties. Napoleon III would have wished the Belgian authorities to prosecute his opponents *motu proprio*.[93]

86 Barrot to Drouyn de Lhuys, 4 August 1853, AMAE, CP, Belgique, 34, f. 31r°.

87 Lademacher, *Die belgische Neutralität*, 165.

88 Lambermont obtained the diploma of candidate (Bachelor) in law. He was appointed as civil servant in the Department of Foreign Affairs in 1842, rising fast to head of unit (1848) and director at interim (1852). Lambermont played a key role in the acquittal of the Scheldt toll and the acquisition of Congo. He died at the eve of the festivities for the 75th anniversary of the country. For Lambermont's personal involvement in negotiations with Napoleon III, see Barrot to Drouyn de Lhuys, 28 February 1854 (n. 58), f. 89v°.

89 Coolsaet, *Buitenlandse politiek*, 134.

90 Herman Van der Linden, 'WEYER (Jean-Sylvain, VAN DE)', *Biographie nationale de Belgique* 17 (1938), 245–274; Mario Hoste, *Leopold I, S. Van de Weyer en het Ministerie van Buitenlandse Zaken. Een bijdrage tot de politieke en diplomatieke geschiedenis van België (1831–1845)* (Ghent: unpublished thesis, 1991).

91 Edgar Bonjour and Charles Oser, *La Neutralité suisse* (Neuchâtel/Paris: À la Baconnière/Payot, 1979).

92 Marcel Morabito, *Histoire constitutionnelle de la France (1789–1958)* (Paris: LGDJ, 2008), 264–269.

93 This rendered the law on insults against a foreign head of state de facto inapplicable. Its Article 3 foresaw in a written official complaint and precluded spontaneous public prosecution. See: Réclamations adresssées au Gouvernement belge par des Gouvernements

7 'A merchant's calculation!'

France and Britain were indignant of the Belgian attitude in the Crimean War (1854–1856). Starting 23 October 1853 onwards, this conflict pitted Russia against the Ottoman Empire.[94] France, Britain (31 March 1854), Austria (2 December 1854) and Piemonte-Sardinia (26 January 1855) chose to 'protect Turkey by arms' against a possible Russian preponderance in the East, in case Czar Nicolas I (1796–1855) would have managed to absorb parts of the Ottoman Empire.[95]

Classical law of nations forbade neutral states to aggrieve the situation of a belligerent in particular. Pursuant to this logic, neutral states could not let contraband pass their borders.[96] The Belgian government interpreted these provisions broadly. It followed Vattel,[97] according to whom states with a historical arms industry could export to all belligerents, if the latter received equal-handed treatment: 'the duty imposed on Belgium [...] is that of complete impartiality, of an absolutely identical treatment of both belligerents [...] to furnish arms to both parties equally'.[98] Neutrality does not mean complete abstention, but 'equal friendship towards both parties'.[99] This completely disregarded the prolongation of hostilities caused by the arms trade.[100]

étrangers en matière de presse, après la promulgation de la loi du 20 décembre 1852, BMFA, Classement B, 'Délits de presse'.

94 Russia had aggressed the Ottoman navy at the battle of Sinopel, whereas multilateral negotiations were still going on: Saint-René Taillandier, 'Frédéric-Guillaume IV et le baron de Bunsen – IV', *Revue des deux mondes* 44/3 (1874), 143.

95 Ibid., 147. On the notion of hegemonic peace and balance of power, see: Bruno Arcidiacono, *Cinq types de paix : une histoire des plans de pacification perpétuelle, XVIIe–XXe siècles* (Paris: Presses Universitaires de France, 2011).

96 Arendt, *Essai sur la neutralité de la Belgique*, 184; Schnakenbourg, *Entre la guerre et la paix*, 31.

97 'Si une nation commerce [...] en munitions de guerre, je ne puis trouver mauvais qu'elle vende tout cela à mon ennemi, pourvu qu'elle ne refuse pas de m'en vendre aussi à un prix raisonnable. Elle exerce son trafic sans dessein de me nuire et en le continuant comme qi je n'avais point de guerre, elle ne me donne aucun sujet de plainte'.: De la neutralité maritime et commerciale de la Belgique, 1862 (n. 52) and Emer de Vattel, *Le droit des gens ou princes de la loi naturelle* (London: s.n., 1758), 3.7.110. In the same vein: Giovanni Maria Lampredi, *Du commerce des neutres in tems de guerre: Ouvrage élémentaire, destiné à fixer les principes des conventions maritimes et commerciales entre les nations* (Paris: Chez H. Agasse, 1802), 60.

98 De Brouckère to Barrot, 18 March 1854 (n. 58), f. 147r°.

99 Gaurier, *Histoire du droit international*, 308–309.

100 Henri Brocher, 'Les principes naturels du droit des gens', *Revue de droit international et de législation comparée* 5 (1873), 567.

The bloody conflict in Crimea would cost France 95,000 soldiers, and Britain 21,900. Full-scale battles and cholera devastated the guarantors' armies.[101] The Belgian attitude was vexing. The Netherlands, the Hanse, Hanover, the Two Sicilies, Portugal and Spain issued declarations of neutrality. The United States adhered to a manifesto issued by Denmark and Sweden on 15 November 1853, listing the rights of neutral vessels during the conflict.[102] The Northern courts would not sell any arms or munitions to the belligerents.[103] Henri de Brouckère proclaimed before the Senate on 12 May 1854 that Belgium would adhere to these principles, and remind its citizens.

The situation was more complex. The commercial road to Russia ran either overseas, through Antwerp to Gdansk[104] and Greece,[105] or by land, through the Prussian possessions by the Rhine.[106] Russian agents bought up all military material they could get their hands on in Liège.[107] Only when Prussia declared its neutrality in the conflict, were export possibilities truly limited.[108] Pressure mounted on Frederick William IV (1795–1861).[109] Prussian abstinence in the common fight against Russia was portrayed as immoral.[110] Bilateral Franco-British pressure was needed to cut off the land road to Russia.[111]

Russia established full diplomatic relations with Belgium as late as 1853. The French ambassador astutely reminded that this had only happened 'at the

101 Sylvie Aprile, *La révolution inachevée 1815–1870* (Paris: Belin, 2014), 416–417.

102 Henry De Brouckère to O'Sullivan, 4 February 1854, MFB, DA, IND, vol. 1A; Lademacher, *Die belgische Neutralität*, 163.

103 Barrot to Drouyn de Lhuys, 7 March 1854 (n. 58), f. 98r°–v°.

104 Barrot to Drouyn de Lhuys, 7 March 1854, Ibid., f. 103r°.

105 Barrot to Drouyn de Lhuys, 14 March 1854, Ibid., f. 115v°.

106 Barrot to Drouyn de Lhuys, 14 March 1854, Ibid., f. 112r°.

107 Barrot to Drouyn de Lhuys, 14 March 1854, Ibid., f. 115r°.

108 At least in theory. Westlake, quoting correspondence between Granville (Foreign Secretary) and Bernstorff (Prussian ambassador) regarding the Franco-Prussian War, reports numerous violations of Prussian exports restrictions and an almost continuous stream of land transports from Belgium to Russia. John Westlake, 'Est-il désirable de prohiber l'exportation de la contrebande de guerre ?', *Revue de droit international et de législation comparée* 2 (1870), 617, 621. See also Jan Martin Lemnitzer, *Power, Law and the End of Privateering* (New York: Palgrave Macmillan, 2014), 30–33. Westlake further argues (633) that Britain would not have exerted pressure on Prussia to execute its internal regulations. The same cannot be said for Belgium, as Howard de Walden was on the same line as Barrot.

109 Taillandier, 'Frédéric-Guillaume IV', 137.

110 Roger Marlin, *L'opinion franc-comtoise devant la guerre de Crimée* (Paris: les Belles lettres, 1957), 43; Barrot to Drouyn de Lhuys, 16 March 1854 (n. 58), f. 132v°: 'la Prusse [...] ne pourrait faire autrement sans se mettre au ban de l'Europe'.

111 Barrot to Drouyn de Lhuys, 14 March 1854 (n. 106), f. 117v°: 'un acte peu amical' [...] 'une violation presque aussi flagrante de la neutralité prussienne que si la Prusse ouvrait son territoire au passage de troupes ennemies'.

very last moment, […] when it was in line with its current policy to make this sacrifice of governmental and dynastic antipathies'.[112] Why would the Belgian government then take the risk to tolerate the fabrication and transit of arms to Russia, 'meant to be used against our soldiers'?[113] If all the major interests in Europe coalesced against the Russian boar, why would Belgium mobilise all of its industrial resources to serve a malicious cause? Belgium's neutrality should be 'agreeable to a cause recognised by the whole of Europe as just'.[114]

The Belgian government replied that the all too well-known 'revolutionary dispositions' of the Province of Liège forbade any intervention in the arms export. Only God knew the consequences of a revolution against the king's government in this turbulent province![115] Ruin and desolation would come to the whole region, which drew its living from this sole industry for centuries. Liège had even sold more arms to the Turks – in this case France and Britain's ally – than to the Russians![116] The Russian *chargé d'affaires* in Brussels had even approved of Belgian sales to the Ottomans.[117] Moreover, the constitution forbade intervention against 'private arms factories', 'as independent from the Government as cloth or cigar factories', or banks.[118] Liège held a royal canon foundry, a weapons factory and a pyrotechnical establishment. If France insisted on action against private enterprises, a law would be necessary, implying a long – and public – discussion in both Chamber and Senate.[119] The government, entrusted with a mission to protect its industry, could not consent in committing an act of cruelty by issuing a decree that would close forever all iron casting plants, coal plants or workshops.[120] Especially not with parliamentary elections coming up on 13 June 1854!

French anger at Belgian official refuge behind 'constitutional neutrality' was expressed in harsh threats. Would de Brouckère have forgotten British arms deliveries, even before Belgium had been recognised officially by Whitehall? How could 'petty money concerns' justify governmental inaction and thus keep in place an industry 'wanting to draw profits from the adversities of war'? Why should Belgium be allowed to produce arms on a wholly disproportionate scale

112 Barrot to Drouyn de Lhuys, Brussels, 7 March 1854 (n. 104), f. 95r°.
113 Barrot to Drouyn de Lhuys, Brussels, 28 February 1854 (n. 58), f. 92r°.
114 Barrot to Drouyn de Lhuys, 14 March 1854 (n. 106), f. 113v°.
115 Barrot to Drouyn de Lhuys, 7 March 1854 (n. 104), f. 96r°.
116 Ibid., f. 95v°; Barrot to Drouyn de Lhuys, 16 March 1854 (n. 58) f. 136v°.
117 Barrot to Drouyn de Lhuys, 7 March 1854 (n. 104), f. 97v°.
118 See Lademacher, *Die belgische Neutralität*, 176 on de Brouckère's refusal to intervene against Belgian banks giving loans to Russia.
119 *Ibid.*, 173.
120 Barrot to Drouyn de Lhuys, Brussels, 7 March 1854 (n. 104), f. 97r°.

to its own needs? Cruisers would be sent out to Belgian ports, to stop vessels carrying arms and apply the normal rules of contraband.[121]

De Brouckère implicitly recycled Arendt's arguments: 'if neutrality imposed duties, it also has generated rights [...] why would we renounce these, if we stick to its obligations?'[122] How on earth could the Belgian government be understood to patrol the borders of Russia, to ensure an effective check on arms exports?[123] This discourse was conformable to the line held by Foreign Minister Joseph Lebeau (1794–1865) in 1840, stating that 'neutrality does not mean impotence'.[124] Yet, de Brouckère was caught in his own contradictions. Refuting the French ambassador's example of Denmark and Sweden, the Foreign Affairs minister stated that the latter countries were voluntary neutral, and had settled their affairs 'comme bon leur a semblé'. Belgium, on the contrary, lived under neutrality as an 'existential condition'. Consequently, limitations on arms and ammunition trade should not create the effect of extinguishing Belgian sovereignty.[125]

De Brouckère returned to the French example of British arms deliveries in 1831 to state that 'no rule of international law' could oblige a state to close its arms industry.[126] Belgium had behaved in an exemplary way during the Carlist Revolt in Spain (1833–1839). At that time, all exports had been communicated to the great powers. Why would the Crimean War be any different? If the Belgian government informed France and Britain on arms exports to Russia, they could be intercepted 'very easily'.[127] Producers only needed to inform intermediaries of this risk, and the arms industry would be safeguarded. Adopting this procedure, Belgium would even go beyond the normal expectations of the

121 Van de Weyer feared the British cabinet was even more determinate to block the port of Ostend if necessary as a means of pressure. Lademacher, *Die belgische Neutralität*, 172. Lemnitzer, *Power, Law*, 28.

122 De Brouckère to Barrot, 18 March 1854 (n. 99), f. 147v°: 'pourquoi renoncerions-nous aux droits puisque nous observons les devoirs?'.

123 De Brouckère to Barrot, 18 March 1854 (n. 99), f. 146v°. In August 1870, Granville (Foreign Secretary) developed a similar argument to answer Prussian complaints on deliveries to the French. The inspection of all vessels would require setting up an expensive and complex customs system, of an inquisitorial nature, opening and examining every potentially suspect package. Westlake, 'Est-il désirable', 631. British public opinion would have been allergic to inquisitorial powers, more than any other nation in the world. Moreover, restricting exports would scare off states to stick to neutrality, and would encourage them to declare them for one of the belligerents. Ibid., 634.

124 Joseph Lebeau to all Belgian legations abroad, 4 August 1840 (n. 52).

125 Barrot to Drouyn de Lhuys, 7 March 1854 (n. 104), f. 99r°.

126 Barrot to Drouyn de Lhuys, 8 March 1854 (n. 58), f. 104v°; de Brouckère to Barrot, 18 March 1854 (n. 99), f. 144v°: 5 000 rifles.

127 Barrot to Drouyn de Lhuys, 8 March 1854 (n. 127), f. 105v°.

great powers, who did not bother to be informed of transactions with Italian, German and Hungarian agents in 1848![128]

This reasoning, according to the French ambassador, was 'plus spécieux que fondé'.[129] If any link at all existed between the fundamental nature of Belgian perpetual neutrality and the interpretation of the country's obligations, it should reside in respect for the 'two powers that are your most sincere friends'. De Brouckère defended himself against measures that had not been demanded by France and Britain to begin with. The Belgian head of cabinet presented the guarantors' claims as a request to close private companies, contrary to the freedom of industry and commerce enshrined in the constitution. Yet, not the arms factories themselves, but the transport to Russia were problematic. Irrespective of the liberal and free-trade oriented constitution, the Belgian state could not close its eyes to its responsibility to oversee exports. Were exports not submitted to customs officers as state organs?[130]

On 20 March 1854, the French ambassador could report good news to Paris. De Brouckère had ordered the governor of Liège to advise manufacturers only to conclude new deals with the utmost prudence. He had also used personal governmental links to the entrepreneurs to dissuade them.[131] Deliveries from state workshops and factories would cease immediately.[132] Transporting arms on vessels in Antwerp had been rendered almost impossible: they were sent back to Liège.[133] Customs officers were told to share all necessary information with French and British consuls.[134] Clandestine maritime transports would be intercepted by French and British cruisers at the start of the war. To render victory complete, Frederik William IV published a decree on 18 March,

---

128 De Brouckère to Barrot, 18 March 1854 (n. 99), f. 144v°. This is supported in Montague Bernard's analysis of the American Civil War, wherein he states that 'it has not hitherto been judged reasonable or expedient that neutral Governments should be held bound to restrain their subjects from trafficking with belligerents in munitions of war [...] The usage of nations leaves the belligerent free to take advantage of these enterprizes [sic] so far as they serve his turn, and to repress them as well as he can so far as they assist his enemy'. Montague Bernard, *A historical account of the neutrality of Great Britain during the American Civil war* (London: s.n., 1870), 391.

129 Barrot to Drouyn de Lhuys, 7 March 1854 (n. 104), f. 99v°.

130 Ibid., f. 100v°.

131 Barrot to Drouyn de Lhuys, Brussels, 20 March 1854 (n. 58), f. 155v°–156r°.

132 Barrot to Drouyn de Lhuys, Brussels, 22 March 1854 (n. 58), f. 161v°.

133 Ibid., f. 164r°. See also ff. 185v°–186r° for a full list of weapons sent out from the port of Antwerp (New Orleans, Valparaiso, Bahia, Hamburg...).

134 Howard de Walden to Clarendon, 14 March 1854, National Archives (NA), Foreign Office (FO), 10/181. Hereafter NA; Lademacher, *Die belgische Neutralität*, 174.

prohibiting land transport of arms in the most absolute manner, conformable to the general laws of neutrality.[135]

The *Moniteur Belge* of 25 April 1854 listed the measures of the Belgian government concerning corsairs and letters of marque.[136] Aligning itself with the conduct of the Northern courts was the wisest option, after thinly veiled French menaces that Belgian vessels carrying enemy goods would be seized and confiscated if necessary.[137] Similarly, the British ambassador in Brussels, had demanded compulsory special licences for arms exports.[138] British Foreign Secretary, Lord Clarendon (1800–1870),[139] entirely supported the French demand to end the furnishing of arms.[140] Interestingly, and contrary to the next example discussed, Van de Weyer advised de Brouckère to cut off deliveries to Russia. For the Belgian ambassador in London, it was clear that Belgium should support the cause of France and Britain against the Czar, who could not sustain a lengthy conflict with the limited Russian arms industry alone.[141] Van de Weyer's correspondence shows a genuine worry: he considered Clarendon's answer to de Brouckère's call to respect the 'rights' of neutrals that respected their 'obligations' as cynical, remarking that 'if neutrality has its rights, self-preservation has its duties…'.[142]

135 Barrot to Drouyn de Lhuys, 22 March 1854, (n. 133), f. 163r°; Notice issued by the Minister of Finance prohibiting the Transit of Arms, Berlin, 20 March 1854, Deák and Jessup, *A Collection*, 655, nr. 17; Extension to ammunition, 1 June 1854, *Ibid.*, 656–657, nr. 17d. See also Ordinance of the Bremen Senate concerning Commerce and Navigation with the Belligerents, Bremen, 13 April 1854, *Ibid.*, 631–632, nr. 3; Hamburg, Proclamation of the Senate prohibiting the Exportation of Contraband of War and concerning Blockade, 10 April 1854, *Ibid.*, 636–637, nr. 6; Hanover, Act concerning the Maintenance of Neutrality in the Present War, 5 May 1854, *Ibid.*, 639–640, nr. 8; Lübeck, Ordinance of the Senate concerning the Export of Contraband of War, 11 April 1854, *Ibid.*, 644, nr. 13; Mecklenburg-Schwerin and Oldenburg, see *Ibid.*, 644–646, nr. 13 and 15.

136 Declaration regarding the Observation of Neutrality in the Crimean War, Brussels, 25 April 1854, in Deák and Jessup, *A Collection*, 57, nr. 9. See also circular instructions by Minister of Justice Faider to Government Attorneys, 29 April 1854, *Ibid.*, 65, nr. 16.

137 Barrot to Drouyn de Lhuys, 7 March 1854 (n. 104), f. 101v°.

138 Barrot to Drouyn de Lhuys, 7 March 1854 (n. 103), f. 101v°; Lademacher, *Die belgische Neutralität*, 170–171. Howard de Walden used thinly veiled threats according to which the British public would not understand Belgian inflexibility, Howard de Walden to de Brouckère, 10 March 1854, NA, FO 10/180. Britain would even have threatened to search vessels under the Belgian flag or calling in Belgian ports: Lemnitzer, *Power, Law*, 32.

139 David Steele, 'Villiers, George William Frederick, fourth earl of Clarendon (1800–1870)', *Oxford Dictionary of National Biography* (*Online Edn.*) (2009).

140 Barrot to Drouyn de Lhuys, 8 March 1854 (n. 127), f. 104r°.

141 Lademacher, *Die belgische Neutralität*, 172.

142 Clarendon to Howard de Walden, NA, FO, 10/179. Ibid., 173.

8 Latin-America: Another World, a Different Doctrine?

Ten years later, under the long 'doctrinal' liberal ministry Rogier/Frère-Orban (1857–1870), Belgium had managed to participate in the general upswing in international trade and the Franco-British commitment to free trade and the respect of neutral vessels.[143] Its industry produced abundant quantities of goods, available at competitive prices. Unfortunately, the internal market was insufficient to satisfy this output. In 1860, 'L'Indépendance' suggested to participate in British gunboat-diplomacy in China, as part of 'commercial and civilised Europe', in order to convince the Empire of the Middle to abandon its 'stupid policy to isolate three hundred sixty million humans from the rest of the world'.[144] In 1863, the Belgian government bought off the mandatory duties on the river Scheldt, definitively opening access to the port of Antwerp.[145]

The Liège arms manufacturers participated again in a conflict, but this time on another continent. Between 1864 and 1870, Paraguay faced a coalition of Brazil, Argentina and Uruguay in a bitter and bloody conflict.[146] On 13 April 1865, the Belgian ambassador in Berlin, alerted Charles Rogier, minister of Foreign Affairs. Fifteen thousand rifles were said to be waiting in Antwerp for export to Brazil.[147] Alfred de Graty, a Belgian-born adventurer acting as *chargé d'affaires* for Paraguay in Berlin,[148] sent several letters from Liège. Moracs, a Brazilian

143 Lemnitzer, *Power, Law,* 109. See also 'De la neutralité maritime et commerciale de la Belgique', 1862 (n. 52). The Paris Conference (1856) which ended the Crimean War, established the following principles: abolition of privateering; free ship, free good, except for contraband; neutral goods cannot be seized on board of enemy vessels; blockades need to be effective in order be binding.

144 *L'Indépéndance*, 2 January 1860.

145 The Treaty of London (1839) had revived the Dutch practice since the separation of the Netherlands in 1585 to impose duties on vessels descending the Scheldt estuary to Antwerp, *L'Indépendance*, 22 April 1839. Although the Belgian state had taken up these payments itself from 1831 on, lifting this burden was seen as a sign of national regeneration. Coolsaet, *Buitenlandse politiek*, 114–115. See: Treaties of Commerce and Navigation, for the Regulations of Drawings of Water from the Meuse, and for the Extinction of the Scheldt Tolls between Belgium and the Netherlands, The Hague, 12 May 1863, 127 CTS 453; Convention between Belgium and the Netherlands for the Redemption of the Scheldt Pilotage Dues, The Hague, 29 September 1863, 128 CTS 209; Treaty between Austria, Belgium, Brazil, Chile, Denmark, France, Great Britain, the Hanse Towns, Italy, Oldenburg, Peru, Portugal, Prussia, Russia, Spain, Sweden-Norway and Turkey, Brussels, 15 July 1863, 128 CTS 95.

146 Luc Capdevila, *Une guerre totale Paraguay, 1864–1870* (Rennes: Presses Universitaires de Rennes, 2007).

147 Nothomb to Rogier, 13 April 1865 (n. 52).

148 Jacques Robert Lecomte, 'MARBAIS DE GRATY (Alfred)', *Biographie nationale de Belgique* (1965), 470–473; Alfred Louis Hubert Ghislain Marbais du Graty, *La République du Paraguay* (Brussels: C. Muquardt, 1865).

captain presenting himself as delegate of the Brazilian imperial government, had met several arms manufacturers at the Hôtel de l'Europe. Brazil requested in total 10,000 infantry rifles with bayonets, 5,000 carbines and 5,000 muskets. The orders had been distributed among the factories of Malherbe, Lemille, Ancion, Mordan and Denster. All had to be finished within six to eight months, the arms leaving Liège as soon as possible, transported *franco* – at the Brazilian government's expense – via Antwerp. Payments were to be made in London after delivery. According to de Graty, the big arms order was of public notoriety in Liège, including the customer's identity. He asked the Belgian government to prevent the transport from leaving Antwerp, since there was no doubt as to the nature of the transaction or the identity of the parties.

Rogier's answer to his ambassador in Berlin was laconic and clear: 'The Belgian government will observe the most complete impartiality by refusing neither of the two belligerents the faculty to order or buy arms in Belgium. No privilege or private facility will be granted to either party'.[149] De Graty, of course, insisted on the 'principles of neutrality admitted by all Nations regarding the export and transport of war material to belligerents'.[150] Why would the Belgian government publicly proclaim its neutrality in the conflict between Brazil and Paraguay and discount the circumstances of the conflict, which rendered an even-handed approach of the belligerents impossible?

De Graty referred to the blockade at the confluence of the Paraguay and Panama rivers by a Brazilian squadron. This de facto deprived Paraguay of its access to maritime arms transports.[151] Neutral third states had to abstain from trading with Paraguay, pursuant to the general characteristics of their status.[152] France and Britain had already called an embargo on arms trade. If permanently neutral Belgium had to appreciate the Paraguayan case, it could not ignore the assessment of these powers. Moreover, if Belgium persisted in its attitude, irrespective of the 'lois prohibitives' upheld by all Great Powers, the country would become the military and maritime arsenal of all belligerents. In other words, Belgian harbours would be the intermediaries for all clandestine trade of all neutral states.

If Belgium, a permanently neutral state, would tackle questions of international law by reasoning through exceptions, and not the general rules of

149 Rogier to Nothomb (draft), 28 April 1865 (n. 52).

150 De Graty to Rogier, 30 April 1865, Ibid.

151 Ibid. De Graty also invoked a 1853 treaty on the free navigation on the Rio de la Plata, forbidding the transit of arms. De Graty to Nothomb, 15 May 1865, Ibid.

152 Gaurier, *Histoire du droit international*, 794.

prohibition, it would violate the very nature of its permanent neutrality. The latter had been conceived of in 1830–1839 as a restriction, and not as a licence to sell anything to anybody. The laws of neutrality applied more strictly than to any other neutral state, 'since neutrality is a condition of Belgium's political existence as an independent state'.[153] A mere three days after de Graty's admonition, the first cargo of arms was loaded on the *Caesar* in Antwerp.[154]

A month later, in June 1865, Sylvain Van de Weyer communicated British Foreign Secretary, Sir John Russell's, scepticism on the Paraguayan point of view, disavowing de Graty's arguments. Britain adhered to the same principles as its protégé Belgium. The elder statesman claimed to have been the first to come up with the idea of permanent neutrality, and was treated by Van de Weyer as an authority.[155] The Belgian ambassador consulted with Layard, undersecretary of state.[156] During the Crimean War, Britain itself had placed 'considerable commands' of carbines in Belgium, to pre-empt possible Russian claims on them.[157] In any case, he argued that Belgium had no 'paternal lessons' to receive from the British. The Paraguayan reasoning would imply the death of its arms industry, which was exactly what de Brouckère had sought to prevent in 1854. How could a decent arms industry exist under a prohibition to sell to any warring state? Moreover, Brazilian harbours were not under blockade and could thus receive Belgian arms.[158] The Belgian ambassador in London, Van de Weyer, ignored de Graty's arguments, and reproduced Vattel's basic reasoning. Pereiro, the Paraguayan chargé d'affaires in London, had completely misinterpreted the question. Belgium applied the same principles as Britain did and did not 'officially encourage the sale of arms'.[159] Layard and Van de Weyer agreed that the Belgian government could only warn private entrepreneurs of the risks taken in such contracts.[160] Finally, Lord Russell addressed

153 De Graty to Nothomb, 15 May 1865 (n. 52).

154 Nothomb to Rogier, 4 May 1865, Ibid.

155 Van de Weyer to de Vrière, 24 June 1859 (copy), Ibid.; Rolin-Jaequemyns, 'Chronique du droit international', *Revue de droit international et de législation comparée* 2 (1870), 698.

156 Austen Henry Layard (1817–1894), archaeologist (Iraq, Persia), trustee of the British Museum and undersecretary of state from 1861–1866, MP from 1852 to 1869, envoy extraordinary in Madrid (1869), ambassador in Constantinople (1877).

157 Van de Weyer to Rogier, 9 June 1865, (n. 52).

158 Van de Weyer to Rogier, 12 June 1865, Ibid.

159 Ibid.

160 Ibid. See also congratulatory note transmitted on behalf of John Russell by Charles Ellis Howard de Walden, British ambassador, 20 June 1865 (n. 52). This is not surprising, in view of Britain's position as a main arms producer and seller. Stephen C. Neff, *The Rights and Duties of Neutrals* (Manchester: Manchester University Press, 2000), 106.

a hand-written note to Pereiro to confirm that 'the Belgian government may freely sell and export arms from Belgium, who is not called upon to provide against the accidental circumstances which render it easier for one party than another to acquire such arms'.[161] Of course, this did not alter the French or Italian embargo.[162]

Back in Berlin, de Graty tried to bring the affair to the attention of the public. Russell's point of view had been very clear. The five guarantors of Belgian independence and neutrality would not take a common position against Rogier and Van de Weyer's point of view.[163] O'Sullivan de Grass, Belgian ambassador in Vienna,[164] reported that Franz Joseph's government supported the Belgian arms doctrine.[165] De Graty had counted on them as inspectors of the law of nations, rather than as mere safeguards of geopolitical stability. The German press (*Journal de l'Europe*, Frankfurt) attacked the selfish Belgian attitude, and suspected a community of interests with Britain in altering the balance of power in the Rio de la Plata region.[166] However, the Belgian government was informed by the Brazilian diplomatic services of a dark cloud over de Graty's arguments. It appeared from an intercepted letter from de Graty to President Francisco Solano Lopez of Paraguay (1827–1870), that the former had commanded rifles in Liège himself, at the workshop of Malherbe & Cie![167] De Graty had taken precuationary measures to smuggle these arms out of Belgium, in case the government would decree a ban on arms exports.[168]

---

161 Russell to Pereiro, 1 July 1865, (n. 52) (copy).

162 De Graty to Nothomb, 8 August 1865, Ibid.

163 De Graty pretended to have had a conversation with Bismarck concerning the matter, as Prussia forbade arms exports to the region. De Graty to Nothomb, 9 May 1865, Ibid.

164 Emile de Borchgrave, 'O'SULLIVAN DE GRASS (Alphonse-Albert-Henri comte)', *Biographie nationale de Belgique* 16 (1901), 351–355. Served as a diplomat under the United Kingdom of the Netherlands. From 1836 on resident and then envoy extraordinary and plenipotentiary in Vienna.

165 O'Sullivan de Grass to Rogier, Vienna, 28 October 1865 (n. 52). The Paraguayan chargé d'affaires had not been accredited to Vienna. Foreign Minister Count Alexander Mensdorff-Pouilly (1813–1871) informed the Prussian and Belgian ambassador directly of his support.

166 Rogier to Van de Weyer, Brussels, 28 June 1865, Ibid.

167 Miguel Maria Lisboa to Charles Rogier, Rio de Janeiro, 19 June 1865, Ibid. De Graty, a native Belgian, could easily move from Berlin to Belgium for the Summer.

168 Rogier to Van de Weyer, 28 July 1865, Ibid. (copy). This would not have been incompatible with Westlake's opinion. According to the British lawyer, continuing an established arms trade during the conflict was not incompatible with neutrality. Only the start of a new trade relationship was. John Westlake, 'Est-il désirable', 627.

9 Conclusion

By 1860, bold and proud Belgian patriotism could have formed a solid de facto obstacle to foreign annexation.[169] Any foreign occupier would have found it difficult to obtain the support of the Belgian population. Yet, the rhetorical intermingling of neutrality and sovereignty should not lead to a juridical assimilation of external and internal factors. The international context in which Belgian sovereignty originated heavily influenced diplomatic debates and material power relations in the ensuing decades. The ambiguous guarantee given by France and Prussia in 1870 was essentially a result of British commitment to Belgian independence, but raised questions by its very existence.

We should not limit our analysis to the self-confident ex post affirmations of Belle Époque doctrine nor to the debate on the Great War to dismiss these interrogations.[170] History of international law, just as any other field of historiography, has an open-ended past as its object, wherein the context of legal discourse is one of the 'possibilities'[171] perceived by contemporaries and is therefore not the result of fixed outcomes or determinist evolutions.

The unequal march of European states towards liberal and parliamentary constitutions is reflected in the Belgian government's argumentative strategy towards Britain and France. Neutrality is not only presented as a – restrictively interpreted – limitation on the country's freedom of action, but also as an endemic characteristic, preventing state intervention in sectors the French ambassador would naturally see within its power. The scarce doctrinal references in diplomatic exchanges do not preclude a legal analysis. Quite the contrary, diplomatic actors deliberately have recourse to the classical concepts of *jus inter gentes* as a vector of consensus (freedom, equality and external sovereignty), established in a long tradition of scholarship and state practice. Foremost because of the conflicting Belgian and French Imperial conceptions of internal sovereignty, but equally to frame the ill-defined permanent neutrality as a restriction, but never as a negation of Belgium's internal and external freedom[172]

If the country's external conduct was subject to the traditional limits of neutrality, commercial opportunities might balance the damage incurred. Yet,

---

169 Jean Stengers et Eliane Gubin, *Le grand siècle de la nationalité belge: de 1830 à 1918* (Brussels: Racine, 2002), 43. Stengers and Gubin quote Frère-Orban on 16 July 1860, distinguishing the Belgian case from Nice and Savoy, annexed by Napoleon III in the process of Italian unification.

170 Nys, 'Notes sur la neutralité (troisième article)', 42–43.

171 Quentin Deluermoz and Pierre Singaravélou, *Pour une histoire des possibles* (Paris: Seuil, 2016).

172 Nys, 'Notes sur la neutralité (troisième article)', 20: 'in dubio pro libertate'.

French and British pressure during the Crimean War made clear that a blended prism of 'legality, moral obligation and requests of European interest'[173] offered sufficient opportunities to stretch Belgium's freedom of action according to circumstances. The German historian Lademacher argues that Henri de Brouckère was desperate to prevent a possible precedent that would ensure the ruin of the Belgian arms trade.[174] Belgium furnished arms to its most important guarantors, and (officially, at least) cut off sales to Russia.

The Brazilian-Paraguayan conflict gave ample possibility to justify such a diplomatic course of action. As soon as France and Britain were not directly implied, the Belgian government could uphold its doctrine of even-handed arms trade with all belligerents. Even if this turned out to be practically impossible. In the contrary case, wherein the transport of arms to Russia would have been possible, but subject to Franco-British searches and seizures, Belgium was not officially asked to break its obligations as a neutral, but to render marks of sympathy to the states present at its cradle in 1830.[175] Hence the tendency to narrowly interpret the status in case of extra-European conflicts, and to lift the obligations where possible, even if they were tied to a status congenital to the nation's very existence.[176] The guarantors could always decide to come back on their pledge towards the Belgian state. Paraguay held far less leverage.

From a more remote perspective, the Belgian government could hide behind the lack of codification of the laws of neutrality. There was no international consensus with regards to the internal measures necessary to respect the state's obligation of impartiality and abstention towards belligerents.[177] Consequently, adopting stringent export interdictions would have harmed Belgium's position, since neutrality was a permanent and not a voluntary, temporary status. In the Paraguayan case, arm trade could continue, irrespective of the state of war between the belligerents. In the Crimean case, French and British pressure caused the government to give in. How firm was the doctrinal

173 Lademacher, *Die belgische Neutralität*, 170.

174 *Ibid.*, 173.

175 *Ibid.*, 175.

176 A similar argument is given by Bernstorff to defend Prussia's attitude in 1854: the conflict in Crimea between Russia and the Ottoman Empire was too remote for Prussian interest to have been directly involved. If Britain wanted to discard criticism of its furnishing contraband (munitions) to France, this was inconsequential with respects to the pressure exerted on Frederick William IV in 1854 to forbid transport of contraband towards Russia. Westlake, 'Est-il désirable', 621.

177 Hence suggestions by Joseph Thonissen, Catholic member of the House of Representatives, to proceed to an international uniform code of rights and duties. Gustave Rolin-Jaequemyns, 'Chronique du droit international', *Revue de droit international et de législation comparée* 4 (1872), 358.

Anglo-American position that neutrals could carry contraband, just as belligerents could seize their vessels, 'with equal legal rights'?[178] The Belgian example suggests that politics, and not abstract principle, decided on a case per case basis.

Acknowledgements

My thanks to Stephanie Plasschaert (Free University of Brussels) and Matthias Van Der Haeghen (University of Ghent/FWO) for their remarks on an earlier version of this text.

178 Neff, *The Rights and Duties of Neutrals*, 92, 106.

CHAPTER 9

The Role of Comparative Law in the Development of Modern Private International Law (1750–1914)

Ana Delic

1 Introduction

In 1899, the board of directors of the *Société de Législation Comparé* (founded in 1869) took a resolution to hold an international comparative law congress to mark the world fair in Paris of 1900. In the historiography of comparative law, the congress has been referred to as the birth of modern comparative law.[1] The congress was the first legal conference dealing with comparative law with participants from continental European nations. During the session of 2 August 1900, François Eugène Gaudemet (1872–1933), professor of the University of Aix-Marseilles, asked about the usefulness of comparative law for private international law.[2] Franz Michael Kahn (1861–1904), a bailiwick judge from Mannheim, saw comparative law as constituting an international competition of ideas and as a foundational method to achieve harmonised rules in private international law. Kahn highlighted that comparative law was the future method of private international law as comparative studies would influence this legal field. Furthermore, comparative law was to be utilised for the interpretation and application of foreign laws. Armand Lainé (1841–1908), professor at the University of Paris, disagreed somewhat, asserting that comparative law was more so a useful accessory to private international law for the jurisconsult, the legislator and the judge. The importance that Lainé attached to these three roles revealed three distinct interactions between private international law and comparative law. Firstly, comparative private international law was a scholarly endeavour and, secondly, this scholarship was an important source

1 Marc Ancel, 'Deux dates mémorables dans le développement du droit comparé en France', *Revue Internationale de droit comparé* 34 (1982), 131–144, 132; Walter Hug, 'The History of Comparative Law', *Harvard Law Review Association* 45 (1932), 1027–1070.

2 Société de Législation Comparé, *Congrès international de droit comparé tenu à Paris du 31 Juillet au 4 août 1900: procès verbale* (Paris: Librairie Générale de Droit et de Jurisprudence, 1905), 88–90.

 | DOI:10.1163/9789004412088_010

for the drafting of legislation. Thirdly, comparative private law was used by lawyers in defending clients and judges when interpreting, applying and enforcing foreign law.[3] The debate between Kahn and Lainé brings forth some essential questions. Was comparative law, as Kahn suggested, a competition of legal ideas driving the evolution of modern private international law or was it, as Lainé suggested, a helpful accessory for scholars, legislators, lawyers, and judgesin applying foreign law? The central thesis of this paper is that Kahn and Lainé were both correct: comparative law was both foundational and accessorial to modern private international law. After a short explanation of the early-modern origins of private international law, three separate yet connected spheres of private international law will be considered: the common law tradition, the civil law tradition and the international law tradition.

In common law systems, continental conflict of laws authors were key resources for the establishment of American and English precedent (1750s–1850s). The American author, Joseph Story (1779–1845), wrote the first comparative study of private international law that considered both continental and common law traditions (1823). Comparative private law treatises became important legal aids in the application of foreign law in English courts (1830s–1860s). Finally, the common law conflicts tradition began a phase of national insularisation, going as far as a denial of continental European roots (1850s–1910s).

In the civil law tradition, French courts and authors avoided comparisons by clinging to the universality of statutist principles (1800s–1850s). In Germany, comparative legal science was born (1740s–1860s). It highlighted a comparison of national legal systems in order to weed out a shared legal spirit among European nations as the result of a common Roman and Christian legal history. Friedrich Carl von Savigny (1779–1861) presupposed a historically contingent Christian community of European nations and a shared private law tradition as the basis for a state's neutral application of the law of the transaction's 'real seat' (1849).

Lastly, Savigny's approach compelled statesmen in both Italy and the Netherlands to convene an international congress devoted to private international

3 *Ibid*, 92; Bénédicte Fauvarque-Cosson, 'Comparative Law and Conflict of Laws: Allies or Enemies? New Perspectives on an Old Couple', *American Journal of Comparative Law* 49 (2001), 407–727, 407; Mathias Reimann, 'Comparative Law and Private International Law', in Mathias Reimann and Reinhard Zimmerman (eds.), *Oxford Handbook of Comparative Law* (Oxford: Oxford University Press 2006), 1363–1396, 1364.

law (1860s–1890s). This was finally achieved by the Montevideo Congress (1888–1889) among Latin American states and the first four sessions of the Hague Conference on Private International Law (1893, 1894, 1900, 1904) among continental European nations. Both congresses utilised comparative legal methods during the drafting of the first private international multilateral conventions.

2 Comparative Conflict of Laws at the Eve of the Modern Period

From the Middle Ages (c. 500–1500) to the Early Modern Age (c. 1500–1750), the tradition of conflict of laws scholarship was comparative in the sense that it was unconfined to one legal tradition. Medieval scholars such as the Italian Bartolus de Saxoferrato (1313–1357) and the French Jacques de Révigny (1270–1296) examined Roman law and built on the discipline. In the early modern period, two schools moulded the discipline: the French school of Bertrand D'Argentré (1519–1590) and Charles Dumoulin (1500–1566) and the Dutch School with Ulrik Huber (1636–1694). At the eve of the modern period (c. 1750–1914), conflict of laws theory was the amalgam of Roman law, Italian, French and Dutch scholarship. Authors advocated a tripartite system to delineate the reach of local statutes. Firstly, immovable property was within the ambit of the territorial statute where it was located. Secondly, personal statutes meant that the personal law of the individual governed status, capacity and (according to some thinkers) movables regardless of where this individual or his property were territorially situated. Thirdly, a transaction be it a contract, a marriage, or testament would fall within the ambit of the statute of the location where it was concluded. In the seventeenth century, Huber propagated the application of the territorial statute to all subjects be they temporarily or permanently situated thereby diminishing the applicability of the personal statute. He also introduced the idea of comity or 'from convenience and tacit consent of nations' as the reason why a local court would recognise and enforce a contract, a will or a marriage executed according to the law of another state albeit this sovereign nation's legal tradition had to be intrinsically Christian and Roman.[4]

4 Ernest G. Lorenzen, 'Huber's De Conflictu Legum', *Illinois Law Review* 375 (1919), 375–418, 403.

3 The Common Law Tradition: Continental Traditions Bolster the Common Law Conflict of Laws Tradition (1750s–1850s)

Before the seventeenth century, the nature of the case determined the court and the applicable law.[5] Transnational mercantile cases were governed by the *jus gentium* or *lex mercatoria*, which were transnational substantive legal norms as defined by the admiralty courts where the cases were heard. On the other hand, common law courts applied the common law exclusively and accepted jurisdiction for domestic cases only. By the early seventeenth century, *lex mercatoria* began to be applied by the common law courts as fact and not as law. After the Restoration (1660), common law courts seized almost exclusive jurisdiction over the application of *lex mercatoria*.[6] Admiralty courts could only claim jurisdiction for cases if the entire matter took place on the sea and in no way involved matters on land. This did not solve the issue of jurisdiction and applicable law for cases connected to foreign municipal law. Foreign municipal law was not part of *jus gentium* or *lex mercatoria* and not an English custom discernible to a jury. At the end of the seventeenth century, a lack of clarity prevailed on this point, particularly, as admiralty courts were denied from taking jurisdiction of cases involving foreign municipal law and as the common law courts hesitated to assume jurisdiction on these cases as well.

The mid-eighteenth century witnessed a flourish of English precedent, which at last found solutions to conflicts of laws and opened the doors for the application of foreign municipal law in domestic courts. Since the common law tradition had no conflict of laws, judges began to refer to continental authors, particularly Huber, in order to grapple with the novel application of foreign law in the common law court.[7] In *Scrimshire v Scrimshire* (1752) Judge Sir Edward Simpson affirmed that marriage in conflicts of laws was to be guided by the *lex loci celebratis* (the place of the celebration of the marriage), a doctrine which was 'conformable to what is laid down in our books, and what is practised in all civilized countries, and what is agreeable to the law of nations, which is the law of every particular country'.[8] Simpson's approach was to find a universally accepted conflict of laws rule through a comparative analysis of

5 Alexander N. Sack, 'Conflicts of Law in the History of the English Law', in Allison Reppy (ed.), *Law, A Century of Progress*, vol. 3 (New York: William A. Reppy 1937), 342–447.

6 *Ibid.*, 376–377.

7 Mansfield and Simpson were certainly influenced by civilian writers from the sixteenth and seventeenth centuries: Brian Levrack, *The Civil Lawyers in England 1693–1641: A Political Study* (Oxford: Oxford University Press, 1972).

8 Consistory Court of London, *Scrimshire v Scrimshire*, 2 Hagg Con. 395, 161 Eng. Rep. 782 (1752).

books, customs, the *jus gentium* and national law. He decided that French law was to determine the marriage contract because the Scrimshires had married there, referencing the seventeenth century Dutch author Johannes Voet (1647–1714).[9] In *Robinson v Bland* (1760), Judge William Murray, Earl of Mansfield (1705–1793), concluded the law governing the contract was where the contract was made unless 'the parties (at the time of making the contract) had a view to a different kingdom'.[10] Mansfield's conflict of laws rule for contracts echoed a section from Huber on marriage, which emphasised that the place where the contract was entered into should not be considered absolutely if the parties had in mind another place at the time of contracting. It was also reflective of the statutist *locus regit actum* (location rules act) for personal and mixed statutues. A section from Hugo Grotius' (1583–1645) *The Laws of War and Peace* (1625) was referenced in the English Report, which stipulated that an individual who makes a contract in any place was under the laws of the place as a temporary subject.[11] In *Holman v Johnson* (1775),[12] Mansfield extrapolated from Huber to establish that a contract was void if the merchandise was sold and delivered in a place where it was illegal.[13] However, if the suit was brought where the merchandise was illegal but was to be sold and delivered in a jurisdiction where it was legal, then the contract was valid. Mansfield said that he was 'very glad the old books have looked into it. The doctrine Huberus lays down, is founded in good sense upon general principles of justice. I entirely agree with him'.[14]

The influence of Huber and 'old books' spread to American conflict of laws in large part via English precedent. In the Supreme Court case *Banks v Greenleaf* (1799), the question was raised whether a bankruptcy discharge under the laws of one state could be invoked as a defence against the creditor of another state.[15] Judge Washington said territorial sovereignty and comity were 'principles laid down by Huberus [and] universally acknowledged'.[16] In the New York Supreme Court's *Holmes v Remsen* (1820), Chancellor Kent handed down a decision in which he allowed English bankruptcy law to govern property situated in New York.[17] In establishing that a will of personal property was to be made

9 *Ibid*, 789
10 Court of Exchequer, *Robinson v* Bland, 2 Burr 1077, Eng. Rep. 717 (1760); Also in London, The National Archives (TNA), inv.nr C 12/2030/20.
11 Hugo Grotius, *The Laws of War and Peace The Rights of War and* Peace, (1625, Indianapolis: Liberty Fund, 2005), 11.5.
12 Court of King's Bench, *Holman v* Johnson, Cowp 341, Rep. 1120 (1775).
13 Ibid., 1121; Lorenzen, 'Huber's de Conflictu Legum', 406.
14 *Ibid.*
15 US Supreme Court, *Banks v Greenleaf*, 2 Fed. Cas. 756, No. 959 (CC. D. Va. 1799).
16 *Ibid.*
17 New York Supreme Court, *Holmes v Remsen*, 4 John. Ch. Rep. 460 (1820), 469.

according to the testator's domicile, he mentioned how Huber's essay was 'everywhere received as containing a doctrine of universal law'.[18] Judge Porter, who presided over the Louisiana Supreme Court decision *Saul v Creditors* (1827), decided that in the case of succession the local law of the place where the property was acquired (Louisiana) prevailed even if the marriage was contracted in another place (Virginia), thus siding with the children of the deceased over creditors.[19] Judge Porter, in delivering the opinion of the court, pinpointed the contradictions in the theories of real and personal statutes: 'by the continental writers of Europe, a subject more intricate and perplexed of any that has occupied the attention of lawyers and courts; one on which scarcely any writers are found entirely to agree'.[20] While the Supreme Court determined that capacity was to be governed by personal law, the losing party's attorney, Samuel Livermore (1732–1803), was so aghast at the Supreme Court's understanding of continental statutist theory that he published an eighty-page brief with copious continental sources, including the likes of Bartolus and D'Argentré, to argue that capacity should be governed by domicile. Even the application of local law proved to be an exercise in foreign law. Since Article 2370 of the Louisiana Civil Code (1825) or even Louisiana state case law would not be applied retroactively, Judge Porter established the rule by examining pre-Code Spanish Law, citing Spanish commentators such as Gregorio Lopez de Tovar (1496–1560).[21]

All in all, early English and American cases of the late eighteenth and early nineteenth centuries built upon the already existing Italian, French and Dutch foundations of private international law discourse in order to determine the chief conflict of rules in both the American and English legal systems. In particular, Huber's maxims advocating territorial sovereignty and comity found great traction amongst common law judges. European sources were also used to determine foreign substantive law, as was the case in *Scrimshire v Scrimshire* when Judge Simpson referred to the German author Andrew Gaill. Foreign sources were even accustomed to apply local law like in *Saul v Creditors* when Spanish law was used in order to avoid a retroactive application of the newly codified Louisiana state law.

The inspiration from continental traditions witnessed in case law was also reflected in scholarship. Story's *Commentaries on the Conflict of Laws: Foreign and Domestic* (1834) was a work outlining the major conflicts of laws

18 *Ibid*, 757.

19 Louisiana Supreme Court, *Saul v Creditors*, 17 Martin, R. 569 (1827), 569.

20 *Ibid*, 588.

21 G. Lopez, *Las Siete Partidas Glosadas* (Lyon: Al. Gomez de Henr. Toti, 1550), Part 4, xi, ley 24.

approaches in continental Europe, England and the United States.[22] This was the most systemic treatise on conflict of laws in English to date.[23] Story's was not the first American treatise on the subject. Six years earlier, the disgruntled losing attorney in *Saul v Creditors*, Livermore, published *Dissertations on the Questions which Arise from the Contrariety of the Positive Laws of Different States and Nations* (1828).[24] Livermore's treatise was overshadowed by Story's, which rose to prominence as the most important modern common law treatise on the subject. This was because Livermore's work was only a synopsis of the continental European conflict of laws, particularly the Dutch school, while Story compared civil law and common law traditions. Story even took a jab at the works of civil law jurists who he claimed 'abound with theoretical distinctions, which serve little other purpose than to provoke idle discussions'.[25] Despite the fact that Story dismissed continental legal traditions, he was highly indebted to the Dutch tradition. Story took the term 'conflict of laws', and the emphasis on territorial sovereignty and recognition of foreign rights by way of comity from Huber.[26] In a footnote, Story rejected the idea that the object of his work was a critical examination of the comparative merits or mistakes of the continental commentators 'but rather to gather from each what seemed most entitled to respect and confidence'.[27]

4 English Comparative Legal Studies Aid in the Application of Foreign Law (1830s–1860s)

Towards the middle of the nineteenth century, there was a need for comparative private law because common law courts had to administer many different legal systems due to British colonialism and increased international trade and travel. William Burge's *Commentaries on Colonial and Foreign Laws* (1837) was a comparative work, which not only summarised Story's doctrinal findings but

22 Kurt Nadelmann, 'Joseph Story's Contribution to American Conflict of Laws: A Comment', *American Journal of Legal History* 5 (1961), 230–253.

23 John Fonblanque, *Treatise of Equity* (London: Clark & Sons, 1831), 658–670; James Kent, *Commentaries on American Law* (New York: E.B. Clayton, 1840), 91, 106, 118, 393, 405, 428, 453; Henri Kames, *Principles of Equity* (Edinburgh: Bell & Bradfute, 1767), viii.

24 Samuel Livermore, *Dissertations on the Questions which Arise from the Contrariety of the Positive Laws of Different States and Nations* (New Orleans: Benjamin Levy, 1828).

25 Joseph Story, *Commentaries on the Conflict of Laws Foreign and Domestic* (Boston: Charles C. Little and James Brown, 1846), 10.

26 *Ibid.*, 19.

27 *Ibid.*, 11.

also included a glance at the substantive colonial and foreign laws.[28] In the dedication, Burge praised the work of Story but criticised his lack of consideration of foreign substantive law that the judicial tribunal might have to apply.[29] Since the Judicial Committee of the Privy Council, the highest appellate tribunal of the British Empire, had to apply the law of foreign legal systems because of the rise of the conflict of laws tradition, imperial expansion and international travel and trade, Burge hoped his work provided 'a more ready access to the sources from whence an acquaintance might be derived with these systems of foreign jurisprudence'.[30] Burge's treatise had a threefold purpose: (1) survey legal systems and legal sources in force in the British Empire; (2) study the law of persons and domestic relations, property and successions comparatively; and (3) determine principles of conflict in various legal fields. Burge's work became the most influential study of comparative law in Britain and America. The treatise was organised according to private law headings and the comparative scope included legal systems both foreign – for instance, Netherlands, Spain, France, Scotland, England, America – and colonial – for example, legal systems in the West Indies and North America.

The application of foreign law in admiralty court from the late nineteenth century onwards manifested itself because of the nationalisation of commercial maritime law and incurred the need for a similar treatise of commercial comparative law. In the eighteenth century, the admiralty court claimed jurisdiction over contracts made on or to be executed on the high seas, torts on the high seas, proceedings in rem on bottomry bonds executed in foreign lands, suits for wages for mariners, and enforcement of the decisions of foreign admiralty courts.[31] During the first half of the nineteenth century, *lex mercatoria* or customary commercial maritime norms were interpreted by the admiralty court.[32] As the result of legislation and accumulated judicial precedent, the law administered by the admiralty court became a branch of the municipal law. In *Cammwell v Sewell* (1858), a common law court judged in favour of an application of foreign – Norwegian – municipal law because there was no applicable maritime law and the international codes brought forth indicated a lack of uniformity at the level of international law.[33] This case marked an important step in phasing out the admiralty courts and the application of *lex mercatoria* in favour of foreign municipal law.

28 William Burge, *Commentaries on Colonial and Foreign Laws* (London: Saunder and Benning Law Booksellers, 1838).

29 *Ibid.*, xi.

30 *Ibid.*, xix.

31 Sack, 'Conflicts of Law in the History of the English Law', 398.

32 Court of King's Bench, *Freeman v The East India Co.* 5 B. & Old. 106, Eng. Rep. 1316 (1822).

33 Exchequer Chamber, *Cammwell v Sewell*, 5 H & N 728 (1760).

Since foreign commercial law was now being applied by common law courts, there was a need to know the substance of these laws. Leone Levi's (1821–1888) *Commercial Law: Its Principles and Administration* (1850–1851) was a mercantile manual enabling the English lawyer to be versed in foreign commercial laws. In the preface, Levi set out key conflict of laws figures who have inspired him, referring to Story as 'one of the brightest ornaments of American jurisprudence', Mansfield as the bringer of the 'Golden Age of Law' and Huber's maxims as chief 'principles of the law of nations'.[34] Each section of Levi's work delineated 'the Mercantile Law of Great Britain, and followed by the laws of all countries on the same subject'.[35] In the first chapter, 'Present state of commercial law' over fifty legal systems from all around the world passed the review. This was the most extensive comparative scope discernible in modern common law scholarship. The work was organised with private law headings like Burge's treatise but subheadings were also organised according to legal systems. For Levi, comparison had the goal of improving national legislation through foreign legal inspiration. Apart from the comparative legal study, the first few pages included the correspondence between the author and British royalty. Levi had written to Prince Albert hoping to garner support for an ambition of his: an international code of commerce among civilised nations discussed by deputies during an exhibition. Prince Albert's reply was laudable with regards to the treatise on comparative mercantile laws but less so on the proposal for the harmonisation of mercantile law since this would entrench upon the powers of the executive and the legislative branches.

5 The Denial of Foreign Influence in the Common Law Conflict of Laws Tradition (1850s–1910s)

As common law precedent involving conflict of laws evolved and multiplied, later nineteenth-century scholarship, notably, the English John Westlake's (1828–1913) *Treatise on Private International Law, or, the Conflict of Laws* (1858) and the American Francis Wharton's (1820–1889) *A Treatise on the Conflict of Laws, or Private International Law* (1872) increasingly concentrated on the domestic traditions of conflict of laws and referred less and less to foreign

34 Leon Levi, *Commercial Law, Its Principles and Administration* (London: A. and R. Stevens and Haynes, 1850), vi, ix.

35 *Ibid.*, vi.

private international legal traditions.[36] Albert's Dicey's (1835–1922) *A Digest of the Laws of England with Reference to Conflicts of Law* (1896) represented a new stage in an insular approach to conflict of laws.[37] For Dicey, the chief aim of conflict of laws was to discover the jurisdiction whose laws governed the set of facts and where the legal rights related to the case were vested.[38] Joseph Beale's (1861–1943) *Treatise on Conflicts of Law* (1916) paved the way for the supremacy of Dicey's vested right approach in America during the first half of the twentieth century.[39] Beale was the guiding force behind the *Restatement of Conflict of Laws* (1934), the treatise on the general principles of American conflicts of laws created by the American Law Institute (founded in 1923). Beale's vested rights theory was territorial in that the applicable law was determined by the location of a significant territorial factor or occurrence. He advocated that '[n]o law is administered as such by the courts except [its] territorial law'[40] but the forum court could enforce foreign vested rights (not foreign law) unless it went against public policy. Beale was already a fan of Dicey's work from the first year of its publication. In a review of Dicey's book published the same year, Beale wrote: '[T]he crowning quality of a book on this branch of the common law, [is the] ability to keep clear of the Continental writers'.[41] Like the mainstream common law approach, Beale – and Dicey to a limited extent – emphasised a territorial system of conflict of laws but posited that the reasoning behind this was the territorial character of legal authority.[42] Furthermore, they argued that the legal authority needed to pay heed to the legal traditions embedded in a territorial landscape. Beale emphasised a preservation of the correctness and parity of the common law, rejecting the approaches of judges such as Mansfield and American scholars

36 John Westlake, *A Treatise on Private International Law or the Conflicts of Law* (London: W. Maxwell, 1858); Francis Wharton, *A Treatise on the Conflict of Laws, or Private International Law* (Rochester: The Lawyer's Cooperative Publishing, 1872).

37 Alfred V. Dicey, *A Digest of the Law of England with Reference to the Conflict of Laws* (London: Steve and Sons, 1908).

38 *Ibid.*, 23–27, 58–59.

39 Joseph Henry Beale, *A Treatise on the Conflict of Laws or Private International Law* (Cambridge: Harvard University Press, 1916).

40 *Ibid.*, 52.

41 Joseph Beale, 'Dicey's 'Conflict of Laws', *Harvard Law Review* 10 (1896), 168.

42 Perry Dane, 'Vested Rights, Vestedness and Choice of Law', *Yale Law Journal* 96 (1987), 1191–1275, 1195.

such as Livermore and Story who turned to the civil law tradition.[43] However, the very definition of conflict of laws, which Beale set forth, dealt primarily with the application of laws in space and harkened back to the German jurist Savigny.[44] Also, Beale's section on the generality and continuity of legal principles were reminiscent of the work of the French Albert Pillet (1857–1926) in his *Principes du Droit International* (1903).[45] Despite Beale's outcries against foreign legal contamination, the history of common law conflicts of laws could not be entangled from its foreign influences.

6 The Civil Law Tradition: The Universality of Statutism in France (1800s–1850s)

French private international law of the early nineteenth century continued to be statutist and thereby, ignorant or negligent of theoretical developments by Huber in particular. Statutism was evident in provisions of the Napoleanic Code (1804) and case law. In 1814, the Cour de Paris decided that capacity was governed by personal law.[46] This decision was an extrapolation of a statutist conflict of laws rule from Article 3 of the Napoleonic Code (1804). Article 3 had a distinct statutist bend stipulating that the law of immovables even if possessed by a foreigner was governed by French law (real statute), and that the French laws on status and capacity governed all French citizens even those abroad (personal statute). The judgment stated that an individual was 'perpetually enchained by the laws of his country'. In the hands of the Court of Paris judges, this provision detailing how French citizens were enchained by French law regardless of the territorial jurisdiction they were situated in, became a general doctrine applicable to foreigners in France as well. Similarly, in a case of 1837, the Court of Cassation, also on the basis of Article 3, said that not only immovable property (as stipulated by the provision) but also immovable property located on French soil was governed by French law. The court said that this approach 'conformed to ancient principles', which

43 Joseph Beale, 'What Law Governs the Validity of a Contract', *Harvard Law Review* 2 (1909), 79–103; Yessel E. Yntema, 'The Hornbook Method and the Conflict of Laws', *Yale Law Journal* 37 (1928), 468–483, 475.

44 Beale, *A Treatise on the Conflict of Laws*, 1–2.

45 Albert Pillet, *Principes de Droit International Privé* (Paris: Pedone, 1903).

46 Cour de Paris, 14 June 1814, S. 1814. 2. 393, in Bertrand Ancel and Yves Lequette (eds.), *Les grands arrêts de la jurisprudence française de droit international privé* (Paris: Dalloz, 2006), 1.

was an indirect reference to the real statute.[47] Unlike other provisions of the code,[48] reciprocity of the relevant foreign state was not a requirement for the application of Article 3.

Jean Jacques Gaspard Foelix's (1791–1853) *Droit International Privé du Conflict des Lois de Différentes Nations en Matière de Droit Privé* (1843) utilised the statutist tradition and French legislation as the starting point and subsequently referred to common law traditions when the subject required.[49] Foelix critiqued the vague notion of comity in Story, positing instead that mutual reliance between nations was the realm of public international law aided by the universality of the statutist approach and harmonised private law (*jus gentium privatum*).[50] All in all, the French conflict of laws approach advocated that the statutist tradition was universal, thereby there was no need to consider private international legal systems comparatively or look any further than the French Civil Code which emanated with statutist influence.

7 The Development of Comparative Legal Science in Germany and France (1740s–1860s)

Charles de Montesquieu's (1689–1755) *The Spirit of the Law* (1748) foreshadowed the German comparative legal movement of the early nineteenth century. For Montesquieu, human reason governed all. National divergences in the law were expositions of the manner in which human reason was influenced by local particularities, such as government, civil institutions, climate, quality of soil and the principal occupation of subjects.[51] Subsequently, German legal thinkers such as Immanuel Kant (1724–1804), Johann Gottfried Herder (1744–1803) and Georg Wilhelm Friedrich Hegel (1771–1831) established the theoretical groundwork that would enable comparative legal science to flourish in the

47 Cour de Cassation, 14 March 1837, S. 1837. 1. 95. DP 1837. 1. 275, in Ancel, Laquette, *Les grands arrêts* 2006, 22.

48 Articles 11 and 13 of the French Civil Code gave civil rights to foreign domiciles and sojourners if there was reciprocity.

49 Jean-Jacques Gaspard Foelix, *Droit International Privé Du Conflict des Lois de Différentes Nations en Matière de droit Privé* (Paris: Joubert 1843), vi, 2.

50 Ibid., 27; Ernst G. Lorenzen, 'French Rules of the Conflict of Laws', *Yale Law Journal* 36 (1927), 731.

51 Charles Louis de Secondat, Baron de Montesquieu, *The Complete Works of M. de Montesquieu*, trans. W. Watson (London: T. Evans, 1777), vol. 1, iii.

writings of Paul Johann Anselm von Feuerbach (1775–1833) and Eduard Gans (1797–1839).

Kant emphasised law to be the systemic science of what he called pure right. Nineteenth-century German writers searched for a new legal science, which was called *Rechtswissenschaft* or a systematic science of positive law.[52] For the previous generation of intellectuals of the natural law period, *Wissenschaft* meant the individual exercise of the mind rationally to deduce a system. The system was revealed in the general organisation of a piece of jurisprudence. Towards the end of the eighteenth century, *Wissenschaft* came to mean the whole body of knowledge. The systemic quality became a structural matrix that could be objectively deduced. This turn from a subjective to an objective pursuit of legal science was influenced by Kant. In *Groundwork for the Metaphysics of Morals* (1785), Kant conceptualised moral law as something pure and genuine discovered by 'a pure philosophy'.[53] In *The Science of Right* (1790), he separated the jurisconsult who was versed in positive external laws and whose knowledge belonged to jurisprudence from the jurisconsult who had a 'theoretical knowledge of right and law in principle' and thus belonged to the pure science of right.[54] Kant privileged the legal theorist who knew principles of right and law over the legal practitioner who knew the law.

Herder conceptualised the *Volksgeist* or the nation's spirit as the product of national history. He emphasised that different national European groups had unique spirits despite a connected history marked by Roman law and Christianity.[55] Herder believed that a single language buttressed the formation of the *Volksgeist*.[56] The historical process was not observable at the universal level but among different national branches of the law.

Hegel claimed that the different national spirits of the European community emanated with a universal spirit evidenced by history.[57] For Hegel, there was no praetor to judge the contractual relations between autonomous states.

52 Mathias Reimann, 'Nineteenth Century German Legal Science', *Boston College Law Review* 31 (1990), 838–897, 838.

53 Immanuel Kant, *Groundwork for the Metaphysics of Morals*, trans. Allen W. Wood (New Haven: Yale University Press, 2002), 4.

54 Immanuel Kant, *The Philosophy of Law: An Exposition of the Fundamental Principles of Jurisprudence as the Science of Right*, trans. W. Hastie (Edinburgh: Clark, 1887), Introduction, B.

55 Johann Gottfried Herder, *Another Philosophy of History and Selected Writings*, trans. Ioannis D. Evrigenis, Daniel Pellerin (Indianapolis: Hackett Publishing, 2004), 45.

56 *Ibid.*, 115–116.

57 Friedrich Hegel, *The Philosophy of Right*, trans. S.W. Dyde (Kitchener: Batoche Books, 2001), § 340.

Furthermore, a federation of states would always be tainted with the individual wills of the nations involved. European nations formed a family tied by universal principles. It was the history of the world which was 'the world's court of judgment'.[58] The history of the world as Hegel presented it in his *Philosophy of History* (1837) was a civilising process to attain rational freedom as the relation of the autonomous individual to the state.[59] The three stages of human freedom included the public freedom of the Greek polis and the Roman republican citizenship of Antiquity, individual freedom of the Protestant reformation, and civil freedom of the modern state. China and India were explicitly rejected from this historical scheme because there was no relation of the individual to the state[60] and, as such, these legal cultures were in perpetually 'vegetative' state, while Europe alone manifested a historical condition.[61] Persia was the first example of a continuous history which had passed away. According to Hegel, the history of rational freedom was dominated by the West since Antiquity and it was this history which was the universal spirit, the closest thing to a praetor adjudicating between sovereign European states.

Feuerbach and Gans took on the Kantian task of systematising a science of comparative law set against Hegel's insistence on history and a universal legal spirit. Feuerbach was the first to discuss comparative legal science. He stressed the empirical methodology based on the observation of the law and legal institutions of different nations in different historical periods. In *Unterholzner Juristische Abhandlung* (1810), Feuerbach questioned why legal scholars had not yet turned to the comparative method. In 1823, Feuerbach, then a student at the University of Heidelberg, became so interested in Hegel's philosophy that he transferred in 1824 to the University of Berlin where Hegel became the professor of philosophy in 1820.[62] In *Kleine Schriften Vermischten Inhaltes* (1833),[63] Feuerbach reiterated Hegel's philosophy but with a focalisation on the law. Feuerbach noted that comparing national legal systems unearthed a

58 *Ibid.*, § 269–270.

59 *Ibid.*, § 9.

60 *Ibid.*, 179.

61 *Ibid.*, 191.

62 See Eugene Kamenka, *The Philosophy of Ludwig Feuerbach* (New York: Praeger Publishers, 1969).

63 Paul Anslem Feuerbach, *Kleine Schriften Vermischten Inhaltes* (Rurnberg: Berlag von Theodor Otto, 1833), 163; Paul Anslem Feuerbach, 'Idee und Notwendigkeit einer Universaljurisprudens', in Ludwig Feuerbach, (ed.), *Biographischer Nachlaß, veröffentlicht von seinem Sohne Ludwig Feuerbach* (Leipzig: Ausgabe, 1853), 378; Hug, 'History of Comparative Law', 1054.

'universal legal system' that could in turn enrich the national legal systems individually. Although Feuerbach conceptualised an empirical and comparative universal legal science, he did not truly complete the task but for a short essay on the *Code Napoléon* in relation to the legislative and constitutional German states of Bavaria.[64] Gans actually took the comparative legal methodology to task with his *Universal-Historical Development of the Law of Successions* (1824, 1825, 1829, and 1835).[65] Gans like Feuerbach had met Hegel in Heidelberg and had followed him to the University of Berlin.[66] Gans' examination looked for the history of succession in many of the places and historical periods indicated by Hegel's conception of world history. For example, in the first volume, he examined Indian, Chinese, Mosaic, Muslim, Attic and Roman inheritance laws. In October 1823, Gans wrote to Hegel and sent him a first volume of his comparative study of the law of succession. In the letter, Gans wrote how indebted he was to Hegel's ideas.[67]

The 1820s to the 1860s was a period of institutionalisation of comparative law in legal academic circles in both Germany and France.[68] In Heidelberg, Carl Joseph Anton Mittermaier (1787–1867), a disciple of Feuerbach, analysed criminal law and criminal procedure in a comparative framework. The German periodical *Kritische Zeitschrift für Rechtswissenschaft und Gesetzgebung des Auslandes* (1829) ran for twenty-eight years. Each issue included a number of articles pertaining to foreign legal systems. This periodical was discontinued in 1856 and Mittermaier's death signalled the temporary abandonment of the comparative law approach at Heidelberg. Eugène Lerminier's (1803–1857) *Introduction Général à l'Histoire de Droit* (1829) brought the comparative methodology of Gans to France. Following in the steps of Mittermaier, Foelix founded the *Revue étrangère de Législation* (1834) with the aim to present foreign law to the domestic lawyer wishing to expand legal horizons and to improve French law.

64 Paul Anslem Feuerbach, 'Betrachtungen ueber den Geist des Code Napoleon und dessen Verhaeltnis zur Gesetzgebung und Verfassung deutscher Staaten ueberhaupt und Baierns insbesondere', in *Themis oder Beitraege zur Gesezbung* (Landshut: Philipp Krüll, 1812), 3–73.

65 Eduard Gans, *Erbrecht in weltgeschichtlicher Entwicklung* (4 vols., Berlin: Mauer, 1824–1835).

66 Michael H. Hoffheimer, *Eduard Gans and the Hegelian Philosophy of Law* (Dordrecht: Springer, 1995), x.

67 Johannes Hoddmeister (ed.), *Briefe von und an Hegel* (Hamburg: Felix Meiner, 1969), 3:32.

68 Hug, 'History of Comparative Law', 1056.

8 Savigny's Christian and European Private International Law and its Widespread Influence (1840s–1900s)

In the 1840s, German thinkers Carl Georg von Wächter (1797–1880) and Savigny presented versions of modern private international law, which reflected tenants of the budding methodology of German comparative legal science. Carl Georg von Wächter wrote a treatise on the private law of Württemburg in which he examined the sources of laws, leading him to the issue of conflict of laws. Wächter's essay on *The Collision of Private Laws of Different States* (1841) saw comity as an obligation of the state legislator.[69] There was no place for the judge to create law or fill in gaps of the written law through recourse to natural law, equity, utility, state interest, security of transactions or other general considerations.[70] The role of the judge was to investigate whether local law demanded an unconditional application to the dispute irrespective of whether the action or the parties were foreign. In Wächter's system, if local law could not be applied because of a lack of relevant provisions, the systematised Roman law – *das gemeine Recht* – was applicable as a last resort.

Wächter's idea of the systematised Roman law was influenced by Kant's idea of law as a discernible system, Hegel's conception of the universal spirit hovering over the nations of the European family and Savigny's emphasis on the Roman law as the historical foundation of the German legal spirit. Savigny's essay *Of the Vocation of our Age for Legislation and Jurisprudence* (1814)[71] put Kant's insistence on legal science and Herder's emphasis on the *Volksgeist* at the forefront for his solution to the German codification problem. The work was a critique on Anton Friedrich Justus Thibault's (1772–1840) recent call for a German codification by claiming that certain theoretical preliminaries had to be undertaken. Savigny deemed that German legal science was in a dismal state. The common law was Roman law but each state or region had its own particular interpretation of it. Savigny proposed that a new methodology was needed previous to codification, which took into account Herder's conception of the *Volksgeist* or 'a common conviction of the people, the kindred consciousness

69 Carl Georg von Wächter, 'Ueber die Collision der Privatrechtsgesetze verschiedener Staaten', *Archiv für die civilistische Praxis* 24 (1841), 230–311; idem, 'Ueber die Collision der Privatrechtsgesetze verschiedener Staaten', *Archiv für die civilistische Praxis* 25 (1842), 1–60, 161–200, 361–419.

70 Kurt Nadelmann, 'Wächter's Essay on Collision of Private Laws of Different States', *American Journal of Comparative Law* 13 (1964), 417.

71 Friedrich Carl von Savigny, *Of the Vocation of our Age for Legislation and Jurisprudence*, trans. Abraham Hayward (London: Littlewood, 1831).

of an inward necessity' manifested in nobler races, particularly in Germany.[72] For Savigny, this conception of the common law of Germany was based on the law books of Justinian and their interpretation by German jurists.

Savigny would explore this Roman legal foundation of Christian European nations in an eight-volume series entitled *System des heutigen romischen Rechts* (separately published from 1840 to 1849). The last volume (1849) covered conflict of laws.[73] According to Savigny, international law was the expression of a community of legal consciousness, resulting from a common European race but more importantly founded on Christian convictions.[74] In all but the 8th volume, Savigny consulted Roman law to base his system on. Roman law was less conspicuous in conflict of laws. The result was that the last volume on conflict of laws was the most comparative. since it was reliant, as the references reveal, on conflict of laws treatises hailing from the earlier Italian, French and Dutch traditions, as well as nineteenth-century authors such as Story and Foelix.

Savigny began the work with a conceptualisation of how the individual acquired rights from the state, entering into the territory of the state's rule of law. Two persons who belonged to two legal territories signified a collision. The applicable law could be determined by domicile, location of the thing as the object of the legal relation, place of the juridical act or the place of the tribunal where the lawsuit was brought.[75] Savigny separated these collisions into two fundamental categories: (1) personal relations or rights and capacities that attach to the individual and (2) legal relations, which as Kant first proclaimed, could be construed as either the right to things, succession, or family relations (including marriage, paternal power and guardianship).[76] For personal relations, and directly against the statutist tradition, Savigny posited that territorial domicile should prevail over personal nationality. Savigny's innovative theory of voluntary submission conceptually reflected Kant's conception of free will of the rational individual or autonomous choice adhering to principles of universal law.[77] Savigny conceptualised that the individual who wished

72 *Ibid.*, 24.

73 Friedrich Carl von Savigny, *A Treatise on the Conflict of Laws and the Limits of their Operation in Respect of Time and Place,* trans. W. Gunthrie (Edinburgh: T. & T. Clark, 1880), 53.

74 *Ibid.*, 26–27.

75 *Ibid.*, 27–28.

76 Kant, *The Philosophy of Law*, 67–78.

77 Kant, *Groundwork for the Metaphysics of Morals*, 58.

to live (domicile), contract (*lex loci contractus*), marry (*lex loci celebrationis*) or inherit property (*lex situs*) within the geographic territory of a state, voluntarily submitted to this state's legal system. The place of submission was the real seat of the legal transaction. In terms of legal relations, the point was to ascertain to which law 'in its proper nature it belongs or is subject'.[78] The idea of comity only arose as the preliminary phase of a friendly concession among states.

Savigny revolutionised private international law approaches at the national level in theory, in the courts and in codification. Savigny's theoretical influence spread to with late nineteenth-century treatises by the Belgian François Laurent (1810–1887), the Italian Pasquale Mancini (1817–1888) and the French Albert Pillet (1842–1928). Laurent's *Droit Civil International* in eight volumes (1880–1881) discussed Savigny at length.[79] Laurent re-imagined Savigny's Christian European legal community[80] as an evangelical fraternity.[81] Men were brothers in God and could not be strangers and enemies in civil relations. The only differences that existed between these brothers were political in nature. Laurent's work inaugurated a systemic comparative legal approach to private international law and was certainly influenced by the German tradition of comparative legal science. Laurent's first volume included sections on the national private international legal systems in France, England, America, the German states and Italy. This was the first private international law work that organised the different national systems into separate and clearly delineated sections, much like the trend witnessed in Gans.

Laurent wrote that the basis of private international law as an evangelical fraternity was witnessed in the Italian Civil Code (1865) and the result of the influence of Mancini who served as draftsman of the Committee on Legislation. Mancini would inaugurate an approach to private international law that would rival that of Savigny in both European and Latin American national systems as well as in international law. In Mancini's system, in the Italian Code, nationality – and not domicile as promoted by Savigny – governed capacity and status. Nationality also governed family relations and succession (Italian Code I, Articles 6 and 8). To alleviate the disparities in equal treatment for

78 Savigny, *Treatise on the Conflict of Laws*, 27.

79 François Laurent, *Droit Civil International* (Paris: Bruyant-Christophe Librairie, 1880).

80 *Ibid.*, vol. 1, § 25, § 39, § 132 f., § 147 f., § 413.

81 *Ibid.*, § 15.

those domiciled in a foreign land where they did not have citizenship, he advocated equal civil rights and liberties for all (Article 3). The basis for the equality in treatment of national and foreigner alike was the idea of the community of nations, but Mancini added that in this community each nation would respect a foreigner's national law. For contracts, Mancini stipulated that liberty with regard to choice of law should prevail as opposed to Savigny's idea that parties voluntarily submit their legal relation to a territorial jurisdiction. In 1874, the Italian Mancini, the French Édouard Clunet (1845–1922) and Charles Demangeat (1820–1896) founded the *Journal du Droit International Privé*. Demangeat, a scholar and member of the Court of Cassation, began the introductory article with a quotation from Savigny.[82]

Pillet affirmed the influence of Savigny for the civil law tradition when in 1893 he wrote that the nineteenth century signalled the gradual substitution of the old statutist universal system of private international law with the new science of Savigny.[83] Savigny's method reigned in the courts. Savigny's approach influenced a case in front of the Court of Appeal at Algiers (1889).[84] The decision affirmed that matrimonial property was governed by the law of France as the place where the immovables were located over the law of Malta as the place where the marriage was contracted. The court posited its decision not on precepts of positive law of either nation but on universal precepts of natural law, namely the conjugal link between the spouses in marriage. The court took a Savignyian approach in preferring territoriality of the property and the unity of principles of a universal juridical community above the application of French law. Savigny's approach even reached English courts. Justice Willes in *Phillips v Eyre* (1870) was inspired by Savigny when he established the leading precedent on torts.[85] In determining the application of local law, Justice Willes said the obligation 'derives its birth from the law of the place [of the wrong] and its character is determined by that law'.[86] Unlike earlier tort cases involving agents of the Crown that had established the application of English law, Justice

82 Charles Demangeat, 'Introduction', *Journal du Droit International Privé*, 1:1 (1874), 716, 7.

83 Albert Pillet, 'Le droit international privé: Sa définition, son origine rationnelle, son domaine, ses conditions générales et son but', *Journal de Droit International Privé et de Jurisprudence Comparée* 5 (1893), 5–24, 22–23.

84 Court of Appeal of Algiers, 24 December 1889, Clunet, 1891. 1171, in Ancel, Laquette, *Les grands arrêts*, 70–78.

85 *Phillips v Eyre*, LR 6 QB 1 (1870).

86 Ibid.; Peter Nygh, 'The Rule in Phillips v Eyre' in Petar Šarčević and Paul Volken (eds.), *Yearbook of Private International Law* (Sellier: European Law Publishers, 2000), vol. 2, 55–74, 56.

Willes applied the real seat doctrine set forth by Savigny that emphasised the application of the *lex loci delicti*.

Lastly, Savigny's private international law greatly influenced German codification of private international law. In 1874, the representative of Baden, Dr. Gebhard put forth conflict of laws rules to the First Commission for the drafting of a German Civil Code. The Second Commission wished to incorporate them into the Sixth Book of the Civil Code.[87] The Federal Council eliminated rules on property law and obligations, and limited the operation of the rules to German subjects or German territory. In the end, the conflicts rules were placed in the Introductory Law of the German Civil Code (Articles 7–31), and outside imperial legislation, they were housed in the Bills of Exchange Act (Articles 84 to 86), the Code of Civil Procedure, and in the law related to voluntary jurisdiction. The shining example of Savigny's influence was the codification's insistence on domicile. Section 7 of the Civil Code described domicile as a habitual residence which can occur simultaneously in several places and can be lost 'if, with the intention of abandoning it, residence is discontinued'. This reference to the intention of the individual to abandon their domicile evoked Savigny's conception of voluntary submission.[88] German legal science of the last decades of the nineteenth century and first decade of the twentieth century was dogmatic and obsessed in its detailed attention to German statute law. This was specifically the case for the Civil Code as the basis for the private international legal system.[89]

9 The International Law Tradition: Mancini's Attempts to Inaugurate an International Congress for Private International Law on the Basis of Legal Affinities (1860s–1880s)

While Savigny's real seat method slowly became incorporated at the national legal levels, his insistence on the Christian and European legal community whose legal traditions were founded in Roman law would set the tone for the organisation of international congresses to ratify multilateral conventions. The mid-nineteenth century triggered various attempts by statesmen to convene an international congress on private international law in order to achieve multilateral conventions. The first attempt was by Mancini. In 1867, Mancini,

87 Ernest G. Lorenzen, 'The Conflict of Laws in Germany', *Yale Law Review* 39 (1930), 804–836, 804.

88 Ibid., 805.

89 Reimann, 'Nineteenth-Century German Legal Science', 232.

then Italian Minister of Public Instruction, was charged with compiling an official negotiation to multiple governments with the view to define the status of foreigners, the extension and guarantee of foreigners' rights, and the facility of their participation in the legislative process.[90] The aim was to finalise a private international law accord.[91] A mild reception led to the eventual demise of this first attempt.[92] On 16 September 1881, Mancini, then the Italian Minister of Foreign Affairs, provided an advice accompanied by a memorandum to Italian diplomats abroad, which he eventually sent to the governments of foreign nations as well.[93] The cabinet of Rome was not seduced by the promise of a general agreement by all principal nations in all areas of law. Instead, Mancini proposed to begin with legislative affinities. These legislative affinities were best demonstrated by bilateral legal instruments. Mancini was very aware that the existing treaties on private international law did not constitute a rational or complete system. On the other hand, they gave an indication as to the success of future conventions. Mancini hoped to eradicate the fragmentary nature of treaties but he was hesitant about the possibility of conventions and highlighted that the basis for future co-operation needed to consist of principles of justice giving all citizens of contracting states the greatest benefits. Mancini's 1881 proposal was well received by European states.[94] The conference was to be held in Rome in 1885. An outbreak of cholera meant that the conference was first postponed and then forgotten after Mancini's death in 1885.

10 The First Multilateral Treaties and the Study of Legal Affinities at International Congresses among Latin American States (1870s–1900s)

The Congress of Montevideo (1888–1889) would be the first successful congress on private international law worldwide after the failure of the Congress

90 Kurt Lipstein, 'One hundred years of Hague Conferences on Private International Law', *International and Comparative Law Quarterly* 42 (1993), 553–653, 554; P. S. Mancini, 'De l'utilité de rendre obligatoire pour tous Les Etats, sous la forme d'un on de plusieurs traités internationaux, un certain nombre de règles générales du droit international privé pour assurer la decision uniforme des conflits entre les differentes législations civiles et commerciales', *Journal Du Droit International Privé* 1 (1874), 285–304, 285.

91 Pasquale S. Mancini, Négotiations Diplomatiques du Government Italien pour un Codification du Droit International Privé, 1882, London, The National Archive, Papers. Codification of Private International Law, inv.nr FO 881/5092, 1–9, 40.

92 Ibid., 40.

93 P.S. Mancini, 'Négotiations Diplomatique du Gouvernement Italien: Correspondance Diplomatiques et Mémoires', *Journal de Droit International Privé* 13 (1886), 35–56, 36.

94 Ibid, 45–52.

of Lima (1873) initiated by Peru.[95] On 14 February 1888, the Argentinian Foreign Affairs Minister, Noberto Quirno Costa (1844–1914), and the Uruguayan Envoy Extraordinary and Minister Plenipotentiary, Gonzalo Ramirèz (1846–1911), met to organise a South American congress to codify private international law. Ramirèz compiled a draft code of private international law. Delegates from Argentina, Bolivia, Brazil, Paraguay, Peru and Uruguay attended. The aim was not to harmonise legislation. As highlighted by the Argentine representative, and later the sixteenth Argentinian president, Roque Saens Peña (1814–1911), the work of the Congress of Montevideo demonstrated a respect for national sovereignty. The purpose was a study of convergences in private international law in order to strengthen ties between contracting nations.[96] This was very much a replication of Mancini's rhetoric for harmonisation since the emphasis was on already existing similarities in national conflict of laws rules.

The Montevideo Treaties – eight in all – covered an impressive breadth of topics including commercial law, civil law, penal law, procedural law, exercise of liberal professions (mutual recognition of professional accreditation), commercial and industrial trademarks and patents. These treaties were ratified by Argentina, Bolivia, Paraguay, Peru and Uruguay, and at times Colombia. The discussions were punctuated with references to the rich heritage of the continental European and common law traditions of conflict of laws and the growing array of positive law dealing with private international law in continental Europe and Latin America.[97] If the eight treaties themselves would point to any kind of study in convergences, the common thread between the nations that ratified the treaties was that their pre-existing national private international legal systems were largely based on Savigny. This is most obvious in the centrality of domicile to determine capacity, status and family relations in the treaties. The concept of domicile was even extended in the treaty on commercial matters in which the novel term 'commercial domicile' was introduced as the law applicable to a company's real seat. Multilateral treaties were achieved without the trouble of having to debate between intrinsically different approaches. Brazil and Chile did not ratify the treaties since their

95 The Treaty of Lima of 1 January 1879 was only ratified by Peru and never came into effect.

96 Margarita Argúas, 'The Montevideo Treaties of 1889 and 1940 and their Influence on the Unification of Private International Law in South America', in Maarten Bos (ed.), *The Present State of International Law and Other Essays* (Deventer: Kluwer Press, 1973), 345–360; Wyndham A. Bewes, 'The Treaties of Montevideo (1889)', *Transactions of the Grotius Society* 6 (1920), 59–79.

97 Congreso Sud-americano de Derecho Internacional Privado, *Actas y Trabados celebrados por el Congreso Internacional Sud-Americano de Montevideo* (Montevideo: Tiro-Litografía, 1889).

national systems were influenced by Mancini's systemic emphasis on nationality to determine capacity, succession and family relations.

One further attempt to unify private international law occurred during the Second and Third Pan-American Conferences (1901 and 1906). The Pan-American Conferences included delegates from the Western hemisphere, specifically the Unites States, Mexico and Latin American nations. The United States Secretary of State, James G. Blaine (1830–1893), had established the International Union of American Republics (later called the Pan-American Union), and set in motion the organisation of the first conference (1889–1890) and founding of the headquarters in Washington. During the third conference, an international agreement of 23 August 1906 appointed a commission of five jurists to elaborate public and private international law codes.[98] The driving force behind the codification project was José Hygino Duarte Pereia (1847–1901), the Brazilian delegate who died long before the report was finally presented during the twentieth session of the third conference (20 December 1906). The Montevideo Congress was at the forefront of the discussion, used as the shining example that international codification could be achieved. The committee suggested that codifications should cover topics outside national sovereign interests, such as private international law, international unions, and public international law, particularly the laws of war. During the twenty-third session of 30 December 1906, the Haitian delegate Jacques Nicolas Léger (1859–1918) proposed amendments to the first three articles of the project since they limited the scope of the international codification to the Western hemisphere only; he also wished for the project to include Europe.[99] The Mexican delegate Francisco de la Barra (1863–1939) disagreed, stating that too much time would be lost in trying to come to a legal consensus if Europe was included in this project. Much like with the Montevideo treaties, legal convergence was understood to be the underpinnings of codification. In the end, only the Haitian delegate voted in favour of the amendments. The first session of this commission occurred in Rio de Janiero and began on 16 June 1912.[100] The commission, comprised of delegates from fourteen states, scheduled the commission dedicated to private international law to meet in Montevideo and Lima in 1914. The session of 1914 would never take place because of the outbreak of the war. The codification project was only achieved in 1928 with the Bustamante Code.

98 Ernest G. Lorenzen, 'Pan-American Code of Private International Law', *Tulane Law Review* 4:4 (1930), 499–528, 499–501.

99 John Vavasour Noel, *History of the Second Pan-American Congress* (Baltimore: Guggenheimer Weil & Co., 1902), 207–213.

100 James Brown Scott, 'Congress of Jurists at Rio de Janiero', *American Journal of International Law* 6 (1912), 931–935.

11 The First Private International Law and the Comparative Law Journal (1860s)

The Dutch Tobias Michel Karel Asser (1838–1913) incorporated a more scientific approach to comparative private international law as he would explore differences and not only convergences. Asser's approach was first developed when he was involved in the creation of the first academic journal treating matters of comparative and international law: the *Revue de Droit International et de Législation Comparé* (1869). It reflected a venture begun by three young ambitious lawyers: Asser, the Belgian Gustave Rolin-Jaequemyns (1835–1902) and, to a lesser extent, Westlake.[101] In 1867, Asser had sent Rolin-Jaequemyns a prospectus detailing their new project. In a letter from 16 August, 1867, Rolin-Jaequemyns' response to the prospectus was overall positive. It was not at all a cacography as the overly modest Asser had described it. However, Rolin-Jaequemyns was surprised by the fact that unlike what was discussed previously during a leisurely stroll through the woods in Harlem, Asser had taken the liberty to enlarge the scope from a journal specialised in private international law to a journal also dealing with public international law and comparative law.[102] Rolin-Jaequemyns generally had no objections to Asser's approach, particularly the inclusion of public international law, yet he cautioned against promising more than they could deliver. An overly ambitious direction could result in them being embroiled in questions of a political nature. In a letter to Asser from 2 September 1867, Rolin-Jaequemyns was now convinced by Westlake of the importance of including comparative law. He deemed that comparative law was the principle element of their success. In this same letter, he named the journal.[103]

It is quite a historic inconvenience that Westlake and Rolin-Jaequemyns had a conversation about this matter in person since there is no way of telling what Westlake's arguments were in favour of combining comparative law and private international law. Subsequent letters between Asser and Rolin-Jaequemyns demonstrated a slow widening of the scope of the journal. In the end they decided to explore the legal systems of England, the Netherlands, France, Belgium, Italy, the cantons of Switzerland and the states of Germany. In order to deal with all these different legal systems, the strategy first suggested by Asser was to include editors of all the different nations. Naturally, their list of editors

101 Letter from Rolin-Jaequemyns to Asser, 16 August 1867, Amsterdam, Jewish Historical Museum, inv.nr. D015930. Hereafter JHM.

102 Letter from Rolin-Jaequemyns to Asser, 16 August 1867, JHM, inv.nr. D015930.

103 Letter from Rolin-Jaequemyns to Asser, 2 September 1867, Ibid.

began with themselves: Asser would be editor for the Netherlands, Westlake for England, and Rolin-Jaequemyns for Belgium.

The French proved the peskiest group to integrate into their general plan. Firstly, they could not think of a suitable editor and then in 1869 a rival organisation, *La Société de Legislation Comparé*, was founded in Paris by Édouard Laboulaye (1811–1883).[104] The first article of the statute of this organisation reflected its aim to comparatively study laws from different countries and research the best ways to improve the diverse branches of legislation.[105] This organisation made it clear to Rolin-Jaequemyns that they were not interested in any cooperation, but Rolin-Jaequemyns decided that this was for the best since overly political Frenchmen would surely compromise the independence of their scientific approach. Rolin-Jaequemyns struggled with the question of how to organise the comparative materials, asking Asser if it would be ordered according to country.[106] Through examining the journals from 1869 onwards one can note that is not the case. The different rapporteurs from different national jurisdictions would write articles on topics of comparative law and private international law but there was no clear delineation of national affiliation apart from the title and subject of the articles.

12 The Hague Conventions as the Result of Asser's Comparative Study of Positive Legal Systems (1870s–1910s)

Asser's first political call for action in terms of the harmonisation of private international law occurred in 1873 when he was asked by the Dutch government to give advice on a bilateral treaty on the execution of foreign judgements with Italy.[107] Asser argued against the treaty since there were no mutually binding rules concerning judicial competence *ratione personae* (Italian Code of Civil Procedure, Article 105). In July 1873, negotiations with Italy were suspended and Asser persuaded the Minister of Justice and the Minister of Foreign Affairs to have the Netherlands initiate an international conference precisely with the view to define the criteria of judicial powers in matters of the execution of foreign judgements. A memorandum was distributed amongst France, Germany,

104 Bénédicte Fauvraque-Cosson, 'Deux Siècles d'évolution du droit comparé', *Revue de Droit Comparé* 3 (2011), 527–540, 534.

105 Ibid.

106 Tobias M.C. Asser, 'Souvenirs Personnels Gustave de Rolin-Jaequemyns, Fondation de la Revue', *Revue de Droit International et de Législation Comparée* 4 (1902), 109–119, 118–120.

107 Inventaris van het archief van het geslacht Asser, (1610) 1797–1940, The Hague, Nationaal Archief, inv.nr 2.21.014.114. Hereafter NA.

the United States, Austria-Hungary, Italy and Belgium. In the memorandum, Asser stressed that a comparative study of private international law was needed since the current perspectives were not developed to the extent that the Dutch government could suggest rules. Asser's project did not gain traction with the governments of the nations he reached out to.

The idea of having a rapporteur for all the different jurisdictions reporting in the *Revue de Droit International et Comparée* was recycled by Asser when he set about creating the first international institution for the creation of multilateral conventions of private international law: The Hague Conference on Private International Law (first session in 1893). The first correspondence with the delegates of European and common law nations was a 'Mémoire' in which Asser presented the need for precise and uniform rules to solve conflict of laws and in which he introduced a questionnaire covering general principles and family law.[108] Asser's questionnaire zeroed in on the areas where national legal systems diverged. An analysis of the questionnaire reveals five general trends of legal divergences. Firstly, there was the conflict between nationality, domicile or territoriality to govern the form of the marriage contract and its effects, capacity – e.g. to marry, to contract –, personal laws, divorce and formal validity of testaments. Also, Asser questioned which law was applicable if there was a change of nationality or domicile. Secondly, the question of what law governed the form of the legal act was unclear although the forum law was dominant. Thirdly, for international contract law, it was uncertain if territoriality or party autonomy applied. Fourthly, public policy, public order or morality as applied in various national jurisdictions was a murky field. Lastly, for successions, would the national or domicile law of the deceased apply or would the *lex situs* (location of property) of the immovable or even movable property apply? Another aspect of the preliminary materials was the 'Disposition des Lois des Conventions qui concernant des matières de droit international privé dans les États qui ont pris part à la Conférence', a complete delineation of all the positive law in the nations participating in the first Conference: Germany, Austria, Hungary, Belgium, Denmark, Spain, France, Italy, Luxemburg, the Netherlands, Portugal, Romania, Russia and Switzerland.[109] This comparative study included both national law and international bilateral treaties signed by the nations.

108 Conférence de la Haye, *Actes de la Conférence la Haye chargée de réglemanter diverses matières Droit International Privée (12–27 Septembre)* (The Hague: Imprimerie National, 1893), 2.

109 Ibid.

The general principles of private international law having to do with contract law, public policy and succession were taken off the negotiation table during the first few sessions. Unanimity amongst European nations was reached only on matters of family law (e.g. marriage, paternity, adoption, paternal authority, guardianship and succession). Commissions were led by various delegates who drafted conventions. The commissions allowed for various individuals from the different jurisdictions to have their hand at drafting various provisions. Mancini's idea about convergences leading to easy international harmonisation was evidenced by the fact that there was a good deal of bilateral treaties already in place pertaining to private international law governing family law and that, in comparison to other fields, the national laws did not differ too much from one another. The law of Russia was the exception at the first conferences. Russian family law was deeply embedded in religious law as discussed by the Estonian-born delegate Frédéric de Martens (1845–1909).

The Marriage Convention (1902), Divorce Convention (1902), the Guardianship Convention (1902) and the Convention of the Effects of Marriage Convention (1905) bear witness to Asser's positive legal comparative approach. The main conflict in conflict of laws rules related to family law matters was whether nationality or domicile governed marriage, divorce, guardianship and effects of marriage. In order to achieve ratification, the conventions stipulated that national law governed unless the national law of the spouses or guardians pointed to another law, thereby opening the possibility for the application of domicile. Finally, the Deprivation of Civil Rights Convention (1905) highlighted that signatory states would do their outmost to ensure equal rights to foreigners. This was a reflection of Mancini's insistence on equal civil rights between nationals and foreigners. The early Hague conventions were ratified by a significant number of European nations in the first decade of the twentieth century.[110]

13 Conclusion

Comparative law was both foundational and accessorial to the development of modern private international law. Firstly, Kahn was right: comparative law was foundational for the development of modern private international law.

110 The Marriage, Divorce and Guardianship Conventions were signed and ratified by fourteen European nations. The Deprivation of Civil Rights Convention was signed and ratified by ten European nations.

Referencing the continental European conflict of laws tradition, especially Huber, was foundational in the establishment of English and American conflict of laws precedent despite Beale's outcries against European contamination. Another foundational element was German comparative legal science, which highlighted how the interplay between European national legal systems was evocative of a shared Roman and Christian legal spirit. Savigny would use the idea of a religiously Christian, racially European and historically Roman legal community as the underlying basis enabling private international law to involve the neutral selection of a real seat of the private legal relation. In the modern age, Savigny's theory of harmonised law among a European community and his system of private international law deeply influenced national legal systems (France, Germany, and even to a certain extent England) and the birth of multilateral conventions (Montevideo Treaties and the first Hague Conventions).

Secondly, Lainé was also correct: comparative law was an accessory aide to legislators, lawyers and judges. Treatises outlining comparative private international law served as food for thought for academics, legislators and legal practitioners. Particularly for the legislation of multilateral treaties, comparative private international theory (Montevideo Treaties) or comparative private international positive law (the early Hague Conventions) served to illustrate the convergences in order to lessen the difficulty of codification. The Hague Conventions with their dualistic incorporation of both Mancini's insistence on nationality and Savigny's emphasis on domicile illustrate the comparative legal study of the participating national legal systems led by Asser during the preparatory phases. The compromised incorporation of both approaches was done in order to achieve harmonised legal instruments. Furthermore, comparative private law became an important accessory for lawyers and judges in the administering of foreign or colonial law. Burge's and Levi's English treatises and on the continent, the *Revue de Droit International et de Législation Comparé* epitomised a dualistic comparative scope, serving as guides for both private international law and private law.

CHAPTER 10

The Institute of International Law's Crisis in the Wake of the Franco-Prussian War (1873–1899)

Vincent Genin

1 Founding and Early Years of the Institute of International Law

There is a lack of fundamental studies regarding the Institute of International Law, founded in 1873, as an institution within the history of nineteenth-century international law and as an association of individuals. Until now, the institute has merely been studied as a social receptacle of individualities who shared a sense of institutional belonging.[1] This chapter attempts to assess the extent to which the Institute played a role in a transnational institutionalisation of international law, since it was an intellectual hub where unclear, if not at times contradictory aspirations met and merged into a formalised, transnational ambition.

There existed constant tensions between the national, international and transnational dimensions of nationalism as a political current in the international scientific milieus in the period between 1880 and 1914, as Elisabeth Crawford has argued.[2] This complex, if not paradoxical, cohabitation between 'national' and the 'international' is reminiscent of a similar paradox within the personality of the Belgian lawyer, Gustave Rolin-Jaequemyns, who was the co-founder of the Institute, namely that between 'progressive' and 'conservative' factors. He was opposed to any reform of the tax-based voting system, to the rise of a proper labour law or to the introduction of a law instituting the 'eight hours' of daily work. He nevertheless declared himself a jurist who carried a form of 'civilisation' characterised by an eminently Eurocentric, if not

1 Vincent Genin, 'L'institutionnalisation du droit international (1869–1873). Les réseaux internationaux de Gustave Rolin-Jaequemyns', *Journal of the History of International Law* 18 (2016), 181–196; idem, *Le laboratoire belge du droit international. Une communauté épistémique et internationale de juristes (1869–1914)* (Brussels, Académie royale de Belgique, 2018) ; idem, *Incarner le droit international. Du mythe juridique au déclassement international de la Belgique 1914–1940* (Brussels-Paris-Berne: P.I.E.-Peter Lang, 2018).

2 Elisabeth Crawford, 'First the Nation: National and International Science, 1880–1914', in Elisabeth Crawford (ed.), *Nationalism and Internationalism in Science 1880–1939: Four Studies of the Nobel Population* (Cambridge: Cambridge University Press, 2002), 28–48.

 | DOI:10.1163/9789004412088_011

paternalistic 'progress'. While he was a liberal 'doctrinaire' minister in the Belgian government from 1878 to 1884, he was not very passionate about politics and belonged to a family that had accumulated disillusions about the business world. He was above all a scholar, who felt deprived of his means of acting under the Catholic government that came to power after 1884. Pushed by these various bankruptcies and forced to rebuild his financial health, seizing the opportunity to live in the East, he became the father of the Siamese legal system. There, he found a legal laboratory to match his ambitions.

A further examination of the internal mechanisms of the Institute, its recruitment process, the degree of representation of the different nations, or the evolution of the initial status of the Institute, therefore, seems relevant. The *Annuaire de l'Institut se Droit International* allows access to data that are vital in this respect. Moreover, most of the originals of the annual minutes of meetings, which were brief notes rather than complete reports, were included without further details in the *Annuaire*. This dearth of documents does not, however, account for the difference between the content of these original minutes and their published version. Private correspondence as well as printed documents have allowed to compensate for some of these shortcomings.

The *Annuaire* was published following a decision of the General Assembly on 31 August 1875. This periodical, which followed the foundation of the Institute by two years, was produced and distributed from the cities of Ghent (*Revue de Droit International et de Législation Comparée* Bureau), Berlin (Puttkamer & Mühlbrecht) and Paris (Durant, Pedone-Lauriel). The purpose of this periodical was not self-apologetic. According to its co-founder, Gustave Rolin-Jaequemyns (1835–1902),[3] its spirit was supposed to be 'impersonal'. Its aim was rather to affect public opinion and free international law from the narrow circle of specialists. A major question arose in Belgium at the time, which symbolised the largest stumbling block which the field of international law faced in the following decades, namely the, at times stormy, relationship between international jurists and diplomats:

> [The] Institute does not seek to contest or to diminish the great and legitimate influence of the two main factors of international law, namely diplomacy and individual science. On the contrary: we acknowledge that these two factors embody practicality (or historicity), and theory, which are both vital to the full development of any legal science. The Institute nonetheless wishes to develop, aside from these two forces, a new one,

3 Gustave Rolin-Jaequemyns (avec l'aide d'Alphonse Rivier et d'Albéric Rolin), 'Avant-propos de novembre 1876', *Annuaire de l'Institut de droit international* 1 (1877), v [hereinafter AIDI].

> which would arise from the collective work of a group of individuals who, in isolation and thanks to their personal work, already enjoy a degree of authority in the field of international law. Such is the spirit that the *Annuaire* must embody/reflect.[4]

This – somewhat flexible – dissociation of 'practical' and 'theoretical' elements, which points towards a necessary collaboration between diplomats and jurists was in keeping with the spirit of the end of the nineteenth century. However, it only truly took place on an institutional plane from 1919 onwards, through the presence of the jurisconsults in the Foreign Affairs Offices. Rolin-Jaequemyns supported this complementarity between jurists and historians[5] on several occasions, which went against the commonplace conception of the legal milieu at the time. That is to say, a milieu that was more sensitive to 'scientific expertise', and in which diplomats were considered to be corrupting the intentions of the jurists. The willingness of international lawyers to include international law in the diplomats' more 'practical' approach, however, was not new and dated back from the eighteenth century. The First World War led to a world where the 'practical' diplomatic aspect, out of necessity or force of circumstance, merged with a 'theoretical' aspect, which resulted in a confusion between these two aspects on the part of the internationalists.

2 Towards a Reform of the Institute?

The *Annuaire* was divided into five parts: two of them were dedicated to the Institute, two others to international political issues and the last one to international legal documents from the past year. Moreover, Rolin-Jaequemyns was aware that the *Annuaire* had the potential of preserving the history of the Institute and of the discipline within itself, in other words that it could aid in a 'historicisation' of international law:

> The reader will then find all the information related to the history of international law in a recent period in a condensed volume. In order to become aware of the usefulness of such a piece of work, one only has to wonder about the necessity of a publication condensing 25 preceding years. Yet, what has not been done in the past, we begin it for the future.[6]

---

4 Ibid, vi.
5 Ibid.
6 Ibid., vi–vii.

Gustave Rolin-Jaequemyns also highlighted the importance of the 'memorial' aspect, reckoning that the deceased members of the Institute should be paid homage to by means of an obituary: 'This custom, which is already justified in a feeling of piety towards a friendly soul, is of undisputable global usefulness.[7] With the *Conférence juridique internationale de Gand,* the first gathering of the Institute took place which voted for its first institutional make-up during the meeting of 10 September 1873. Four key men, one president, two vice-presidents and a secretary-general, were assigned to govern the association.[8] The association claimed to be scientific and 'non-official' and sought – 'within the limits of its competences' – to ensure 'either to maintain the peace or to ensure the observance of the laws of war'.[9] It was therefore out of the question to rule war out but rather to humanise it if necessary. The Institute could voice legal opinions about 'controversies' – however vague this term – and did not have to clarify the target audience of these opinions. The Italian jurist Pasquale S. Mancini (1817–1888) displayed reluctance as to whether or not all national governments would reject these suggestions. The Institute was supposed to choose its members 'freely', that is to say through co-optation. Article 6 of the 1873 statutes foresaw that 'Diplomats in active service cannot nominate members. While in the active diplomatic service of a state, his right to vote in the heart of the institute is suspended during the enture time that he is in service'.[10] Article 9, which has largely escaped attention from scholars, nevertheless merits attention as it foresaw the creation of 'Comités nationaux' within the Institute.[11]

There is no knowledge of any fulfilment of such initiative, which seemed to have been quickly abandoned by its promoters. This probably resulted from a 'democratic' agenda in which the Institute sought to reach a large audience rather than limit itself to that of international jurists. It is therefore legitimate to raise the following question. From the middle of the 1920s, the League of Nations developed an important network of national and even local committees, whose activities would continue until the eve of the Second World War.[12] After 1873, twenty-six members were added to the eleven founders of the Institute. Among these thirty-seven protagonists were six Germans and seven French nationals, as well as a considerable number of Italians, whose presence noticeably began to decrease prior to 1914. During the first years of the Institute's activity, effective members were called 'members', along with 'honorary

7 Ibid., vii.

8 Ibid., 1.

9 Ibid.

10 Ibid., 1.

11 Ibid.

12 Geneviève Duchenne, *Esquisses d'une Europe nouvelle. L'européisme dans la Belgique de l'entre-deux-guerres (1919–1939)* (Brussels: P.I.E.-Peter Lang, 2008), 63–76.

members'. The 'associates' – that is to say, the first members – formed the third category of adherents. The members' contributions were named as 'undetermined' until 1877, when they were eventually defined more clearly during a session in Zürich.[13] Honorary members contributed up to (minimum) of 3,000 Belgian Francs per year (Article 8 of the statutes), while the effective members contributed up to twenty-five symbolical Francs. The associates did not pay any contributions. During the abovementioned Zurich session, it was decided that votes would be carried out in secret. It is therefore valid to wonder under what conditions the 1873 to 1878 votes were carried out.

A further question concerns the generative causes of a series of reforms of the Institute during the 1870s and 1880s. In that context, the reworking of the statutes during the 1880 Oxford session is particularly interesting. This 1880 modification, which was often mentioned by international lawyers throughout the twentieth century, lacks details and specifications.[14] As shown by this example, the Institute's statutes remained rather vague as to the organisation's internal working. Could the reinforcement of the regulation of membership contributions, which was already foreseen by the 1873 statutes, be considered an important step towards dealing with the institutional elusiveness of the organisation? Could we speak of controlled democratisation of the Institute, which had, nonetheless, no impact on the number of members? It had in fact increased from thirty-seven to fifty-three in seven years. These data, however, should be read critically. It appears that the majority of these alleged members – as they were members in theory rather than in practice – rarely took part in annual sessions. The random nature of participations is even more important to point out because the meeting places changed from one year to the other and were sometimes quite far from where some jurists lived. The 1880 reform is nonetheless important, to the extent that it affected the Institute's mission itself. For example, it was only after the Oxford session that the Institute involved itself with what it called the 'Conscience publique du monde civilisé'; prior to that session, it was rather a matter of 'conscience juridique', as Article 1 of the 1873 Ghent statutes indicated.[15]

In 1880, Articles 1 and 2 were merged into one. The resulting article stated: '1. [...] En travaillant à formuler les principes généraux de la science, de manière à répondre à la conscience juridique du monde civilisé'.[16] Although

13 AIDI 2 (1878), 6, n.1.

14 AIDI 6 (1882), 17.

15 [...] favoriser le progrès du droit international, en s'efforçant de devenir l'organe de la conscience juridique du monde civilisé. 2. [...] formuler les principes généraux de la science [...]; Ibid.

16 Ibid.

it appears that the word 'publique' would suit a civilising mission better than 'juridique', the Institute still remained confined and was unknown by the general public. As for the word 'conscience', it appeared prior to 1880, in an essay written by Gustave Rolin-Jaequemyns dating back to 1869.[17] Specialists such as Charles Dejace (professor at the university of Liège, in charge of the *droit des gens* ou d'*économie politique* class in 1886) did not fail to notice that aspect. Dejace specialised in social issues and employment law – a field that was given recognition by Ernest Mahaim a few years later –,[18] and was not considered an 'internationalist'.[19] He nonetheless quoted Rolin-Jaequemyns' 1869 article, dwelling further upon this notion of 'conscience'.[20] Emmanuelle Jouannet pointed out that the term 'conscience' related to the status the jurists gave themselves in society, as well as in the field of law and history: 'these new scientists of international law represent an infinitesimal category people who are all male, white, European or American, and who have the same liberal and humanist project for the world'.[21]

The 1880 reform also concerned aspects that were not related to the statement of principles, such as, for instance, the membership contributions. The honorary members were still requested to pay 3,000 francs per year, which henceforth became a 'minimum'. The effective members should now pay thirty-five francs – instead of twenty-five –, while the associates were now compelled to pay twenty-five francs. The Institute lacked sufficient financial means and was fully aware of this. Although the Institute did not possess an account book, it appears that the Institute's income was irregular and its provenance largely unknown. This remained the case to until at least 1909, when the Carnegie Endowment for International Peace was founded, and started to fund the institution regularly. Although the 1873 statutes foresaw that the Institute would be sponsored by means of membership contributions and 'par des fondations ou autres libéralités',[22] the Carnegie Endowment remains to this

17 Gustave Rolin-Jaequemyns, 'De l'étude du droit international et de la législation comparée – II', *Revue de droit international et de législation comparée* 1 (1869), 226.

18 Vincent Genin, 'J'ai été longtemps minoritaire. Le processus de légitimation du droit international du travail (1888–1938). Légitimité, vécus et mémoires du belge Ernest Mahaim', Legal History Review 85 (2017), 272–324.

19 Charles Dejace', in Léon Halkin, Paul Harsin (eds.), *L'Université de Liège de 1867 à 1836. Liber Memorialis*, vol. 1 (Liège: Rectorat, 1936), 733–737.

20 *Cours de droit international, professé par Charles Dejace – 1886–1887 et 1887–1888, à l'Université de Liège*, Bibliothèque de l'Université de Liège-Salle des Manuscrits, Mss 4836, 7.

21 Emmanuelle Jouannet, *Le droit international libéral-providence. Une histoire du droit international* (Brussels: Bruylant, 2011), 129.

22 Rolin-Jaequemyns, 'Avant-propos', 5.

day one of the Institute's main patrons, as well as that of other institutions promoting international law. The 1878 and 1880 reforms seemed to have merely been an indication that the regulation of the Institute gradually became more practical.[23]

The idealism that held sway over the 1873 proceedings had to, without a doubt, give way for increased administrative efficiency. Another obvious example is related to the nationalities of the members. It was decided in 1880 (Article 6), to limit the amount of members from the same country to 16%, while the 1873 statutes allowed the number to be 20%. Was the objective of this change to allow access of people from newly created states such as the Kingdom of Romania – which succeeded 'Little Romania' when its vassalage to the Ottoman Porte ended in consequence of the 1878 treaty that put an end to the Balkan War? This hypothesis does not appear quite as far-fetched, given that the (amongst other) Belgian internationalists, such as Emile de Laveleye ou Gustave de Molinari,[24] were highly interested in the Balkans, and, more generally, the East. In September 1878, a Romanian jurist was chosen to be an Institute associate.[25]

3 The Wake of the Franco-Prussian War: An Impediment to International Law

Maintaining multiple contacts and developing an international network with Gustave Rolin-Jaequemyns – a man who enjoyed undeniable prestige and respect among his peers – as honest broker did not guarantee the durability of the Institute. After its rise between 1869 and 1874, the reputation of the Institute quickly and noticeably waned. Is it possible to talk about a 'crisis' within the Institute? In 1877, one year after Rolin-Jaequemyns deplored the lack 'd'articles actuels[26]' in the *Recueil de Droit International et de Législation Comparеé*, he further evinced his disappointment in 'notre pauvre Institut':

23 Albéric Rolin to Gustave Rolin-Jaequemyns, 3 May 1891, Archives Gustave Rolin-Jaequemyns [hereinafter AGRJ].

24 Émile de Laveleye, *La péninsule de Balkans. Vienne, Croatie, Bosnie, Serbie, Bulgarie, Roumélie, Turquie, Roumanie*, 2 vols. (Paris: Félix Alcan, 1888); Gustave de Molinari, *Lettres sur la Russie* (Paris: Dentu, 1877).

25 Romanian jurist to Gustave Rolin-Jaequemyns, Bucarest, 26 September 1878, AGRJ.

26 Gustave Rolin-Jaequemyns to Alphonse Rivier, 14 November 1877, Bibliothèque Cantonale et Universitaire de Lausanne, IS 1977 [hereinafter BCUL].

> I now tend to believe that one day I too will ditch the institute. I feel the need to rest, to seek entertainment, to study on my own, and to be independent. Moreover, I am disgusted to argue periodically, like *muezzin* do [...]. I am seriously wondering whether I will wait until the Institute looks like a bad joke, and I like a fool, to resign.[27]

In a September 1878 letter from Alphonse Rivier to Rolin-Jaequemyns, some unease was also obvious. The letter was written with the next session of the Institute in mind, which was meant to take place in Paris. The French capital stood out regarding its balanced adherence to international law. Rivier, anticipating the onerous administrative preparations for the meeting, awaited the 'orders' of his Belgian colleague as he stayed at the Bordeaux Hotel, 15 rue Jacob in the Quartier Latin. He confided:

> As a pessimist and morose philosopher, I was expecting the room to be empty, the service gone, and furniture to rent, and usurious conditions. I expect Clère[28] to be gone, Clunet[29] vanished, and M. de Parieu[30] sulking. I will do my best in order to prevent these calamities from damaging the IDI.[31]

His words reflected a mental distance from the other French jurists, whose participation in the Institute's sessions was rather sporadic, despite the fact that the gathering took place in their country, as well as unease with the Institute. Rolin-Jaequemyns, who was elected as member of the Belgian House of Representatives in 1878 and who became Minister of the Interior of the Liberal Cabinet until 1884, now dedicated himself to political life, and claimed that he

27 Gustave Rolin-Jaequemyns to Alphonse Rivier, 2 September 1877, Ibid.

28 Peter Macalister-Smith, 'Bio-bibliographical key to the membership of the Institut de Droit International, 1873–2001', *Journal of the History of International Law* 5 (2003), 77–159, 91.

29 Jacques Dehaussy, 'La part du droit international public dans le *Clunet*: brève rétrospective', in Jacques Béguin, Jacques Dehaussy, Jean-Michel Jacquet and Françoise Monéger (eds.), *Un siècle d'étude du droit international* (Paris: Lexisnexis, 2006), 3–7; Louis Renault and Thomas Erskine Holland, 'Maître Édouard Clunet', *Journal of the Society of Comparative Legislation*, New Series 16 (1916), 97–101.

30 Jean-Jacques Clère, 'Félix de Parieu', in Patrick Arabeyre, Jean-Louis Halpérin and Jacques Krynen (eds.), *Dictionnaire historique des juristes français XII–XXe siècle* (Paris: PUF, 2007), 610; Albéric Rolin, *Les origines de l'Institut de droit international 1873–1923. Souvenirs d'un témoin* (s.l., s.n., s.d), 37.

31 Rivier to Rolin-Jaequemyns, September 1878 (?), AGRJ.

was ready to drop the 'paisibles travaux scientifiques'.[32] A few years later, the doubts surrounding a possible crisis within the Institute were cleared up, when French sensitivities were disregarded. Swiss jurist Gustave Moynier (1826–1910) confided to Rolin-Jaequemyns – who had just suffered an electoral defeat – on 12 June 1886 that he wanted him to take control of the Institute, which had been passed to Rivier.[33] He feared the ensuing dispersion of the Institute:

> I wrote to Rivier that I had heard here and there our colleagues' strong regrets about the Institute's inactivity during three quarters of the year, the lack of impetus given to the study commissions, the excessive delay of the *Annuaire*'s publication, etc. There seems to be no remedy to all of this. The Institute has known better days, and it may be so again if you intervene. Maybe we should slightly change our organisation, hiring a paid secretary, for instance, as I told Rivier. In any case, I wish that you could organise a session this year, because if you do not, it will, without a doubt, be negative.[34]

The passage above is interesting and is verified by other documents: the Institute was going through a crisis from 1878 until the first decade of the twentieth century. What were the symptoms of this 'crisis'?

Belgium's mistrust of France was still alive. At the time, France became a republic that had abandoned any prospect of the Orléans returning to power, and leaving behind the fall-out of Napoleon III's annexationist projects. Concerns about this were passed down by some Belgian professors, including the anti-clerical lawyer François Laurent (1810–1887).[35] Although it had been Rivier who has been chiefly responsible for the introduction of another Belgian,

32 Association Libérale et Constitutionnelle de Gand, *Discours prononcé par M. Rolin-Jaequemyns à l'assemblée du 31 mai 1878* (Ghent: Van Dosselaere, 1878).

33 Christophe Charle, *Discordance des temps. Une brève histoire de la modernité* (Paris: Armand Colin, 2011), 175–178.

34 Gustave Moynier to Gustave Rolin-Jaequemyns, 12 June 1886, AGRJ.

35 René Warlomont, *François Laurent. Juriste, homme d'action et publiciste (1810–1887)* (Brussels: Office de Publicité, 1948), 66–80; *Hommage à François Laurent* (Ghent: Association de la Presse libérale gantoise, 1909); Frederik Dhondt, '*L'Histoire, parole vivante du droit?*' François Laurent en Ernest Nys als historiografen van het volkenrecht', in Bruno Debaenst (ed.), *De 'Belle Époque' van het Belgisch Recht (1870–1914)* (Brugge: Die Keure 2016), 91–115; Dirk Heirbaut, 'Een hopeloze zaak: François Laurents nieuw burgerlijk wetboek voor België', *Pro Memorie. Bijdragen tot François Louis Ganshof* (2012), 261–283; Frank Simon and Dirk Van Damme, 'François Laurent en de sociale kwestie: een offensief beschavingsdefensief', in Johan Erauw and François Laurent (eds.), *Liber Memorialis François Laurent* (Brussels: Storia-Scientia, 1989), 109–164.

Ernest Nys (1851–1920), in the isolated milieu of the internationalists, Nys' first master was Laurent, who was guided by two ideas: Germanophilia and Masonic ideals.[36] The first would gradually be put into perspective by Nys, who replaced Laurent's Germanophilia by a strong and appealing Anglophilia.

Laurent's Germanophilia, which was shared by the Swiss jurist Johann Kaspar Bluntschli (1808–1881), was notorious. As a graduate of the *Université Libre de Bruxelles* in 1874, Nys welcomed the German open-mindedness, while the Belgian university course programs around 1870 were very old-fashioned.[37] In his notes to the economic law course by Paul Hinschius in Leipzig, he wrote: 'I repeat that, of all this, the Belgian student does not have a clue'.[38] In the eyes of Laurent, Nys' stay in Germany, Leipzig or Heidelberg, was not only a scientific trip but also a Promethean mission: 'Should one go to Berlin? It is not to hear professors that you have gone to Germany, but to study a nation that is at the head of civilisation and that merits our recognition as such. You therefore have to make sure that you know enough of Germany [...]'.[39] François Laurent's mistrust of France manifested itself again towards January 1875, at a time when the constitutional laws of the Third Republic were being examined and defended, according to him, the 'so-called enlightened socialists (...) in the manner of Laboulaye'.[40] This liberty implied the establishment of the freedom of education which, for him, represented a scourge, and the same evil that had caused Flanders to become 'a convent [...] to retard the population!'.[41]

The consequences of the Franco-Prussian War of 1870–1871 were still felt. Alphonse Rivier, who as an 'intermediary' person succeeded Rolin-Jaequemyns at the head of the Institute,[42] entrusted him again with presidency of the

36 This curious connivance between Nys and Rivier was noticed by Paul Errera: 'What a curious antithesis between these two men, when it came to manners and habits! Rivier was refined, elevated, a smooth talker, a conservator, an aristocrat, we know already that Nys was not. And while the work, the love of science, the mutual regard and a common ideal united these two men to the point where the were made to forget their contrasting natures and their opinions', *in Annuaire de l'Académie royale de Belgique* 88 (1922), 80.

37 Ernest Nys, 'Souvenirs', *Revue de l'Université de Bruxelles* 8–9 (mai-juin 1921), 595–609, 595.

38 Ibid., 609.

39 François Laurent to Ernest Nys, 10 January 1875, AGRJ.

40 Ernest Nys, 'Souvenirs', 606.

41 Ibid.

42 Rivier became the intermediary of European internationalists in the second half of the 1880s. Rolin-Jaequemyns was now devoted to politics and then to the codification of the laws of Siam, Alphonse Rivier to Gustave Rolin-Jaequemyns, Bruxelles, 10 October 1884, AGRJ. Ernest Nys dated the beginning of his introduction in the world of internationalists by Rivier in 1878: 'Through him I created relationships with the majority of lawyers that occupied themselves with international law; I saw them when they devoted their collaboration to the *Revue de droit international*; they showed themselves sensitive of my

Institute in June 1883, and told him that the next session of the Institute would be held in Munich under the favourable auspices of their Berlin colleague, the reformist Franz Von Holtzendorff (1829–1889).[43] The meeting was scheduled for September. Very quickly, Rivier feared a 'diplomatic incident'. As he told his colleague: 'We must begin on Tuesday 4th and not Monday 3rd, and here is why: we celebrate Sedan on Sunday and Monday, and all public buildings will be decorated. We cannot offer such a spectacle to our French colleagues. It is the city that observes this customs and she is surely right'.[44] In August 1884, Rivier returned from a Bern meeting where the Institute was represented by Frédéric de Martens (1845–1909), Albert Teichmann (1844–1912) – professor of criminal law in Basel from 1877 to 1906 – and himself: 'The arbitration conference and the peace were a fiasco. I was not there, but from what they have told me, it was pitiable. They ended by quarrelling over Alsace-Lorraine. Mancini sent an accompanying letter, which he could have omitted without inconvenience'.[45] At the same time, Rivier no longer wished to be an editor of the *Revue de Droit International et de Législation Comparée* and proposed, at the suggestion of James Lorimer, to bail the journal out by becoming its own editor and, above all, by publishing advertisements. He wished to pass his duties within the secretariat of the journal[46] onto his pupil Ernest Nys.[47]

In June 1887, Ernest Lehr (1835–1919), a native of Vosges – an important element in the context of Franco-German tensions – a lawyer, historian, numismatist, and above all a professor of civil law, legal history and comparative legislation at the University of Lausanne from 1874 to 1888, wrote from

service, took notice of my publications and cited them with respect in their own works', Nys, 'Souvenirs (suite)', 706.

43 Rivier also has a certain notoriety in Italy where he had good contacts with the Milan lawyer, and member of Institute, Cesare Norsa. Another example of a link: in 1885, the *Circolo Giuridico* in Palermo asked Rivier to represent him at a legal event held in Antwerp, Alphonse Rivier to Gustave Rolin-Jaequemyns, 18 September 1885, AGRJ.

44 Ibid., 13 June 1883, Ibid.

45 Ibid., 11 August 1884, Ibid.

46 Ibid.

47 Rivier introduced Nys as a member of the Institute in 1885. However, this candidature could not be made without the approval of Émile de Laveleye and François Laurent. This is an interesting point. Indeed, it is not usual to classify these last two names, though with considerable notoriety, among the internationalists, but rather among those who have allowed this international law to find a favourable welcome in Belgium. It is confirmed that the co-option is indeed the use of recruitment to the Institute and, *a fortiori*, between Belgians, Alphonse Rivier to Gustave Rolin-Jaequemyns, 12 June 1885, AGRJ. Another example is that the *Revue* published Laurent's works, even if they were not considered as original but 'nous ne pouvons les refuser', Gustave Rolin-Jaequemyns to Alphonse Rivier, 9 October 1878, BCUL, IS 1977.

Lausanne to Rivier, whose grand-niece later married the son of Lehr in 1890.[48] He told him about an interview he had with a jurisconsult of the *Académie des Sciences Morales et Politiques* of Paris, with a view to the session of the Institute organised at Heidelberg. Lehr wondered whether 'the French members should risk going to this town. They seem to believe there are measures of expulsion and hindrance'.[49] A few months later, the Swiss Gustave Moynier mobilised his Parisian networks – he unfortunately did not mention any names – in order to somewhat remedy this situation:

> Friends of mine have gathered to put an end – peacefully that is – to the Franco-German antagonism. It is not easy, but their goal is, without a doubt, praiseworthy, and deserves our support. They are currently asking me to help them find, among what the jurisconsults from various countries have written, texts that would 'defend theories hostile to the annexation of civilised people' […]'.[50]

In January 1889, after reading an article by Rolin-Jaequemyns devoted to the thorny question of passports in Alsace-Lorraine, Lehr again welcomed his Belgian colleague.[51] The latter's opinion was in keeping with the recent positions taken by Clunet and Von Holtzendorff concerning the rescripts promulgated by the German Empire on 22 and 23 May 1888, which stipulated the conditions of access to the 'Lost Provinces' for French citizens. In the eyes of Édouard Clunet (1846–1922), the restrictions implied by these rescripts were a violation of Article 11 (2) of the Treaty of Frankfurt of 10 May 1871, relating the signatory nations' right to access and exit each other's territory.[52] Von Holtzendorff, a member of the Institute like Clunet, cordially replied and agreed to the publishing

---

48 He is the author of the *Tableau général de l'organisation, des travaux et du personnel de l'Institut de droit international: pendant les deux premières périodes décennales de son existence (1873–1892)* (Paris, Pedone-Lauriel: 1893); Alphonse Rivier to Gustave Rolin-Jaequemyns, s.d., 1890 (?), AGRJ.

49 These words, written on 8 June 1887, should be read in the context of the well-known espionage affair between France and Germany called 'Schnaebelé' (named after the double agent Guillaume Schnaebelé, an Alsatian police commissioner), which broke out on 20 April of the same year, on the occasion of his arrest by the German police forces. General Boulanger – considered as the incarnation of the 'Revanche' – French minister of war, then envisaged the general mobilisation. See Jean Garrigues, *Le boulangisme* (Paris: PUF, 1992).

50 Gustave Moynier to Gustave Rolin-Jaequemyns, 24 May 1888, AGRJ.

51 Gustave Rolin-Jaequemyns, 'La question des passeports d'Alsace-Lorraine', *Revue de Droit International et de Législation Comparée* 20 (1888), 615–623.

52 Treaty of Frankfurt, 10 May 1871: http://mjp.univ-perp.fr/traites/1871francfort.htm.

of his reply, but defended the rescripts. In his view, if France considered the loss of the two provinces to be temporary, Germany, therefore, could not treat its natives in the same fashion as those of other countries. He skilfully pointed out that the United States did the same with regard to the Chinese nationals accessing and exiting from their territories, without however altering the treaties concluded between the two countries.[53]

Rolin-Jaequemyns took a stance as a jurist of a 'neutral country' and not as a member of a transnational society. Somewhat breaking with his 1870–1871 position, the Belgian supported Clunet. The 'suspicion' displayed by the Berlin lawyer and the reference to Chinese coolies was not, according to him, 'probative'. With a magnanimous and almost seigniorial tone, he concluded:

> How can we explain that the great power that made the law [Frankfurt Treaty] is the first one to disregard it? The precedent is maybe even more annoying that the measure itself. Let us hope that the German empire will not carry on with this behavior, and that it will feel grand and powerful enough to be fair.[54]

Once again, Rolin-Jaequemyns was the honest broker, but did not sacrifice his opinion on the altar of mediation. He took a stand. Ernest Lehr was very pleased with what he heard. He hailed the words of a man whose authority was that of a 'jurisconsult and a statesman'.[55] He added:

> You made things perfectly clear, and I will make sure that not one reasonable Frenchman asks more or anything else in the best interest of the essential and legitimate relationships. The measure taken by the German government is, from a legal perspective, questionable'.[56]

Ernest Lehr was not the only Frenchman to maintain a good relationship with Rolin-Jaequemyns, although their number was limited. The lawyer Paul Pradier-Fodéré (1827–1904) shared an old friendship with him and directed his attention towards what was happening on the other side of the Atlantic. Pradier-Fodéré intended to send him an article destined for the *Revue* reiterating the proposals of the Argentinean and Brazilian delegates, which were submitted to the American International Conference on the Development of

53 Rolin-Jaequemyns, 'La question des passeports d'Alsace-Lorraine', 617.
54 Ibid., 623.
55 Ernest Lehr to Gustave Rolin-Jaequemyns, 28 January 1889, AGRJ.
56 Ibid.

Arbitration in Washington in 1889. So what was this article about?[57] One element that could easily be overlooked was the weight and intensity of the Pan-American cooperation, from which the United States had always remained at bay. Since 1826 – forty-seven years before the founding of the Institute – the project of inter-American cooperation had entailed the advocacy for compulsory arbitration as an alternative to force. Pradier-Fodéré considered that the *Revue* would benefit significantly from the publication of articles about the activities of Americans.[58] The ambition was also commercial: at a time when the United States did not yet have a journal worthy of the name – the *American Journal of International Law* was created in 1907 –, would it not be appropriate to broadcast the *Revue* across the Atlantic? To study the dialectic relation between Europe and America through the lens of Pan-Americanism was a path that could explored to great benefits.[59] This movement has long been ignored by European researchers.

The French attended more sessions of the Institute in the 1890s, at the suggestion of the Institute's administrators and thanks to the Institute's openness towards other nationalities. In 1908, Louis Renault suggested that the Institute should acquire a logo, but this remained without follow-up although it was be discussed again in 1911 and 1912.[60] In 1913, Antoine Pillet (1857–1926) highlighted a gap between the growing popularity of international law and the limited number of members.[61] Upon seeing that most of the Institute memberships were held by the French, the English and Italians, he suggested whether the geographical make-up of the Institute should be expanded?[62] His suggestion remained unanswered.

4 Meeting Places

Another factor of tension within the Institute which, *a priori*, appears superfluous, was the choice of location of the annual sessions. It seemed that these sessions, if not a great success, were not as disastrous as announced as the Madrid sessions of 1886 and those of Lausanne in 1888 illustrate. Concerns about

57 Paul Pradier-Fodéré to Gustave Rolin-Jaequemyns, 9 December 1890, AGRJ.

58 James Brown Scott, 'La Sixième Conférence panaméricaine', *L'Esprit international* 7 (July 1928), 324–325.

59 Paul Pradier-Fodéré to Gustave Rolin-Jaequemyns, 14 December 1889, AGRJ; Eugène Pépin, *Le Panaméricanisme* (Paris: Armand Colin, 1938).

60 AIDI 22 (1908), 309.

61 Ibid. 26 (1913), 645.

62 Ibid., 466.

these sessions emanated almost systematically from Gustave Moynier, which also puts into perspective the idea that the Institute was going through a 'crisis'. Between December 1885 and January 1886, Rolin-Jaequemyns no longer possessed ministerial responsibility in Belgium, but still held a seat in Parliament for a few months. During this period of relative calm, he gradually returned to academia and visited Madrid for a few days in order to find a location for the next session. Moynier was not in favour of Spain as a meeting location, which was, according to him, as 'eccentric' as Sweden. Few members would go there according to him. Perhaps he already considered a fixed seat for the Institute in Switzerland, as briefly mentioned by Rolin-Jaequemyns in 1892?[63] He considered that '[w]e should not sacrifice the survival of the sessions to satisfy the Platonique satisfaction of planting our flags everywhere. This is why I will always vote preferably for a more or less central meeting place'.[64] The acute debate around the location's choice should be put into perspective, in particular in light of Gustave Moynier's own ambitions. He implicitly pleaded for a meeting in Luzern under the favourable auspices of the Conseil Fédéral Suisse, 'because Switzeland has everything to gain by the progress of international law, of which it has to some extent already become the administrative centre'.[65]

It is true that gradually, Moynier – a very religious Protestant[66] – gained importance within the Institute. Abandoning private international law, he totally devoted himself to the law of nations. In 1877, he published an 'Appel aux Belligérants', with Bluntschli and Rolin-Jaequemyns, 'to effectually be a reminder *that there exists* a right to war that is without a doubt still imperfect but which obliges belligerents to observe certain clearly defined rules and to indicate those rules that should already be considered as forming part of the European public law'.[67] It should be emphasised that this will to affirm that there was a *jus ad bellum* was part of a promising debate, of which Alberic Rolin (1843–1937) would be at the heart in 1920, two years after the end of the First World War.[68] The first part of the 1930s saw the resurgence of this controversy in Belgium and France in a context of growing international tension. Moynier's Swiss patriotism, which somewhat reminds us of Martens' Russian

63 AIDI 12 (1893), 23–25.

64 Gustave Moynier to Gustave Rolin-Jaequemyns, 4 January 1886, AGRJ.

65 Ibid.

66 Alberic Rolin, 'Nécrologie de Gustave Moynier', AIDI 24 (1911), 447–448.

67 Ibid., 448.

68 Vincent Genin, 'Les juristes belges et la réhabilitation du droit à la guerre du Traité de Versailles au "Mouvement de Monaco" de 1933–1938', *Revue de la Faculté de droit de l'Université de Liège* (2016/1), 155–188.

imperialism,[69] manifested itself more clearly at the prospect of the Lausanne session of 1888, which should have taken place in Geneva:

> I hope that this session will be as successful as the previous ones, and that this place, which is well located, will attract numerous assistants. I am convinced that Rivier will not neglect anything in order to ensure that it will be a success: I offered to help as much as I can, but Lausanne is unfortunately not Geneva. I believe that it goes without saying that Rivier will preside over the session. He deserves that role thanks to his long and quality career as secretary-general and his name is thought highly of in Switzerland. Until now, all countries, except Switzerland, had qualified presidents at the IDI; now, thanks to Rivier, this opprobrium will cease. Did I mention that my son will offer his service as secretary; do you think he will be needed?[70]

The geographical centrality of Lausanne was certainly appreciated by all lawyers, but did not necessarily represent a short-range destination for everyone, starting with the Russians. Nevertheless, they were particularly assiduous. Frédéric de Martens, held back by the affairs of his country and assigned to attend four commissions by the Institute's Bureau, would not be able to go there, not without specifying that 'it will be the first time since I am a member of the Institute that I will be missing from the annual meeting'[71] and that Lausanne benefited, according to him, from a 'central situation'. In addition to the centrality of the place, some people, like Ernest Lehr, deemed Lausanne of the right size for a session to be held there, in comparison to Graz or Innsbruck, which were considered too large[72] for such a purpose.

It is true that Switzerland was, in the last quarter of the nineteenth century, an important gathering place for congresses. The Belgian Minister at Berne described this situation with derision in September 1877:

> While politicians are out of work [the works of the federal Council have not restarted yet], Congresses come one after the other, almost without interruption. After the Lausanne congress on the phylloxera, comes the Geneva medical congress, which is accompanied (if not preceded) by an

69 Frédéric de Martens to Gustave Rolin-Jaequemyns, 11–23 January 1889, AGRJ.

70 Gustave Moynier to Gustave Rolin-Jaequemyns, 24 May 1888, AGRJ.

71 Ibid.

72 Ernest Lehr to Gustave Rolin-Jaequemyns, 2 January 1888, AGRJ; Ernest Lehr to Alphonse Rivier, 'Les Toises', 8 November 1887, AGRJ.

> international law congress in Zurich, which opened on 10 September under the presidency of famous professor Bluntschli. Former representatives of the 1874 Brussels congress will also be there, among which Mr. Martens, professor at the University of Saint-Petersburg.[73]

In 2016, Anne Rasmussen recalled the crucial importance of choosing the venue for a congress. She nuanced the commonly accepted image of an 'international science' as fully transnational. The 'national' factor did not lose anything of its importance:

> The rivalry between the different poles who want to be recognised as the main scientific centre shows an intense atmosphere of concurrence. Becoming the site of grand congresses and scientific associations is the ambition of big capital cities. The decision must be the subject of a consensus at the end of a session for the next one. This consensus is a result of the scientific, diplomatic and symbolic considerations and shows the weight of the national delegations and the influence of men who managed to convert their national fame into an international one. […] It is noteworthy that [aside from Paris], the fact that Brussels holds the second place influences many 'smaller nations' (Belgium, Switzerland, the Netherlands, Sweden) and make strive towards achieving more weight internationally.[74]

In 1890, the choice of location caused intense debate, in anticipation of the 1891 session, which reveals various symptoms of the emerging tensions within the Institute. Alphonse Rivier, from the German seaside town of Bad-Ems – an informal meeting place of European diplomats and politicians – entrusted Rolin-Jaequemyns, who by then had withdrawn from political and academic affairs, with his concerns about this session after meeting his French colleague Louis Renault (1843–1918)[75] and Carl-Ludwig Von Bar (1836–1913), a professor of international law at the University of Göttingen and a member of the

73 M. Jooris to Guillaume d'Aspremont-Lynden, 10 September 1877 (n°168/64), Archives du Service Public Fédéral Affaires étrangères, Correspondances politiques, Légations, Suisse, vol. 9 (1876–1878) [hereinafter SPFAE].

74 Anne Rasmussen, 'L'arène internationale de la science (1860–1914)', in Christophe Charle and Laurent Jeanpierre (eds.), *La vie intellectuelle en France* (Paris: Seuil, 2016), vol. 1, 602.

75 Paul Fauchille, 'Louis Renault', *Revue générale de droit international public* 25 (1918), 1–253; Louis Renault, *L'œuvre internationale de 1843–1918* (Paris: Les éditions internationales, 1933); Jean-Louis Halpérin, 'Louis Renault', 660.

Permanent Court of Arbitration at The Hague.[76] Rivier, after experiencing two bad sessions in Paris and Cambridge, about which little information is known, no longer wanted to go to these cities, unlike Rolin-Jaequemyns. He thought of Madrid, which was already considered, and of Hamburg, which was suggested by Von Bar. Rivier was particularly irritated by the pressure exerted by Louis Renault, who wanted the meeting to be held in Bern, for both 'French' and 'Swiss' reasons:

> You are well aware that I pay a limited attention to the French due to the trick they played on us; I refuse to admit that, unable to welcome us in their country, they would bring their veto on other projects. Bern celebrates, if I am not mistaken, the seventh centenary of its founding; this could be detrimental to our meeting, although I am not quite sure. Anyway, I reckon that we are not yet allowed to mention Bern in our memorandum, neither are we allowed to mention the federal authority, which we should leave out [...]. I do not like Renault's urging for Switzerland, and I do not believe that we should let ourselves be influenced by him and become rather *indiscreet* [his emphasis].[77]

The question arose again in 1893. Ernest Lehr and Gustave Moynier remained convinced by the necessity of a fixed seat bearing several advantages: the existence of a place of withdrawal in case of conflict; obtaining judicial personality and the installation of a library. The 'judicial personality' factor was soon abandoned by a commission, which was set up in 1893 for this purpose. It considered that obtaining this would allow the Institute to benefit from donations and bequests, but that this 'patronage' was in fact already carried out without formalisation.[78] The fixed seat, however, which was never established, raised a more fundamental problem for the Italian Pasquale Fiore (1837–1914) and the Frenchman Arthur Desjardins (1835–1901): 'The Institute must not become a mere local academy or else its resolutions will lose all of their fame and authority in the eyes of the governments'.[79]

---

76 He was one of the first in 1898 to suggest the creation of an Academy of International Law, established a few years later in The Hague. From the beginning of the Institute, he had suggested that diplomats could be members, Arthur Eyffinger, *La Cour internationale de Justice 1946–1996* (Leiden: Martinus Nijhoff, 1999), 172; Thomas Hirse, *Die Ausweichklausel im Internationalen Privatrecht* (Tübingen: Mohr Siebeck, 2006), 165.

77 Alphonse Rivier to Gustave Rolin-Jaequemyns, Ems, 25 June 1890, AGRJ.

78 AIDI 12 (1893), 23–25; AIDI 13 (1894), 194–203.

79 Ibid. 12 (1893), 24.

5 Conclusion

The influence of the 'national' factor, which remained an important reality within international institutions during the last quarter of the nineteenth century, was strongly reflected in the Institute's early history. The medium-term consequences of the Franco-Prussian War of 1870–1871 immobilised the good functioning of the Institute in many ways. While France implicitly joined this new scientific movement, the prospect of holding a session in Germany required prudence and would regularly cause tensions within the organisation.

Moreover, if Belgium, a small neutral country, seemingly joined the movement energetically, its lawyers were nevertheless tormented by certain national tropes, or nationalism, beyond their Belgian patriotism. Francois Laurent did not conceal his Francophobia, counterbalanced by a strong Germanophilia shared by his disciple Ernest Nys, who was also strongly attached to British culture. Rolin-Jaequemyns, although critical of French politics in 1870, was nonetheless sensitive to a neutral position, if not a position of arbitrator: it was precisely the role he played in the so-called 'passport' case of 1887. While nationalism was not necessarily incompatible with international law, some federalist/regionalist lawyers in the 1930s would become very attached to the internationalist values of this discipline. Was it not Fernand Dehousse who called himself a 'Walloon internationalist' in the 1930s?

The Institute's crisis from the early 1870s to the early twentieth century had various causes: the attachment of France and England to their legal internalism, the isolation of those who defended the internationalist project and who mostly came from small countries and, above all, the need to reconstitute an intellectual and transnational network in the aftermath of the Franco-Prussian War. The drive for the institutionalisation of international law, which reached a peak after the 1860s, owed much to the awareness caused by the disasters of the war, a period that was particularly rich in major conflicts. The confidentiality of the Institute was also one of the origins of these disillusions. The 'men of 1873' thought, without a doubt in good faith, that their project would arouse the enthusiasm of a well-informed public opinion. However, such was not the case. Few people actually knew that they existed and many diplomats were unaware of the meaning of the abbreviation 'IDI'. In the 1880s, the institution, which claimed to be a 'conscience publique du monde civilisé', became aware that it had to resolve key internal differences to remain the 'conscience juridique' that had been originally advocated in 1873.